Tanais

Alans

CAUCASUS MOUNTAINS

CASPIAN SEA

Sebastopolis

COLCHIS

IBERIA Darial Pass

Phasis

• Tibilisi

Derbend Pass

Apsarus

Kur

ALBANIA

apezus

• Satala   • Elegeia

ARMENIA

Araxes

IA

Lake Van

Tigris

• Nisibis   • Gaugamela

• Carrhae

• Arbela

Euphrates

• Hatra

• Ecbatana

A

0   100   200   300km

SCALE

ARRIAN OF NICOMEDIA

PHILIP A. STADTER

ARRIAN OF NICOMEDIA

THE UNIVERSITY OF NORTH CAROLINA PRESS

CHAPEL HILL

© 1980 The University of North Carolina Press
All rights reserved
Manufactured in the United States of America
ISBN 0-8078-1364-8
Library of Congress Catalog Card Number 79-938

Library of Congress Cataloging in Publication Data

Stadter, Philip A
  Arrian of Nicomedia.
  Includes index.
    1. Arrianus, Flavius. 2. Arrianus, Flavius. Anabasis. 3. Epictetus. I. Title.
DF212.A77S7   938'.09'0924 [B]   79-938
ISBN 0-8078-1364-8

CONTENTS

PREFACE

ALTHOUGH Flavius Arrianus of Nicomedia is best known as the author of a history of Alexander the Great, that book was only one facet of an extraordinarily active life. In this book I have tried to present an overall picture of Arrian and his writings, viewing from several vantage points this man who was both typical of his age and one of its most interesting representatives. Despite the presence of such noteworthy figures as Hadrian and Marcus Aurelius, Galen and Plutarch, Lucian and Caracalla, the second century has not been studied with the care given the two centuries preceding it. A series of recent works on the larger intellectual movements of the century (one thinks of G. Bowersock's *Greek Sophists in the Roman Empire* or B. Reardon's *Courants littéraires grecs des IIe et IIIe siècles après J.C.*) has reawakened our curiosity toward this age, and a number of studies (among which should be noted especially those of A. B. Bosworth, who is also preparing a historical commentary to the *Anabasis*, of A. B. Breebaart, and of G. Wirth) have begun to treat Arrian as more than a source for Alexander the Great. Finally, the discovery of several new inscriptions has forced us to reconsider his biography, placing a more proper emphasis on his activity as a Roman citizen and senator. Arrian, like Plutarch, his senior by forty years, proudly preserved his Greek heritage in a Roman world. Unlike Plutarch, however, and unlike most of the Greek authors of this period, Arrian took an active part in the administration of the empire. A Plutarch, a Dio Chrysostom, or an Aelius Aristides would carry a petition to the provincial governor, or serve as ambassador to the emperor, but Arrian was one of the few of Greek ancestry in this period who himself served as a governor of a province.

In the first chapter of this book, therefore, I have tried to set out a general outline of Arrian's life, with an emphasis on the evidence for his career in the service of the emperor. In succeeding chapters I examine his works, and where possible (chiefly in chapters 2 and 3) their relation to his experiences when he was writing them. By far the largest section of the book is devoted to an examination of the *Anabasis*. This work, certainly Arrian's masterpiece, deserves a book of its own, but I hope in these two chapters to have provided a mode of looking at the *Anabasis* which gives some indication of the manner in which Arrian as author worked with the figure of Alexander which his sources had provided him. I have purposely avoided many of the problems treated by Alexander historians when I found them not directly related to the understanding of Arrian.

Much of the work for this volume was completed in 1974–75 while I held a senior fellowship from the National Endowment for the Humanities and was an honorary research fellow at Harvard University. Publication of this book has been supported by a grant from the Research Council of the University of North Carolina at Chapel Hill. I have been aided by a computer tape of the text of Arrian provided by *Thesaurus Linguae Graecae* and the Lex program of the Ibycus system in the Department of Classics at Chapel Hill. The good humor and careful typing of Erline Nipper, Shelley Pearl, Juanita Mason, and Nancy Honeycutt have made my job easier.

I am grateful to Ernst Badian, Herbert Bloch, George Houston, and Hugh Lloyd-Jones for reading draft chapters of this book and offering their criticism, as well as to C. P. Jones for his valuable comments and queries as reader for the Press. Finally, I thank my wife for her constant support and encouragement.

Philip A. Stadter
University of North Carolina
Chapel Hill

ABBREVIATIONS

ARRIAN'S works and the abbreviations used for them are listed in Appendix 1. The extant works, except for those about Epictetus, are cited according to the edition of A. G. Roos, *Flavii Arriani quae extant omnia*: I, *Alexandri Anabasis* (Leipzig 1907) and II, *Scripta Minora et Fragmenta* (Leipzig 1928); reprinted with additions and corrections by G. Wirth (Leipzig 1968). The fragments of lost works are cited both by the number in Roos II and by the fragment in Felix Jacoby, *Fragmente der griechischen Historiker* II B (Berlin 1929–1930), no. 156. The fragments in Roos are numbered separately by work: B = *Bithyniaca*, P = *Parthica*, S = *Events after Alexander*, C = *On the Nature, Composition, and Appearances of Comets*. The fragments in Jacoby are numbered consecutively and identified by an F preceding the number. Thus the citation P1 = F30 refers to *Parthica* fragment 1 in Roos, which is the same as Arrian fragment 30 in Jacoby. Testimonia to the life of Arrian are collected by both Roos (vol. II, pp. LVIII–LXV) and Jacoby. They are cited by T followed by the number and, if necessary, the name of the editor. The Epictetian works are cited from the edition by Henricus Schenkl, *Epicteti Dissertationes ab Arriani Digestae*² (Leipzig 1916).

AAA	*Athens Annals of Archaeology*
ABSA	*Annual of the British School at Athens*
AE	*L'Année Épigraphique*
AJA	*American Journal of Archaeology*
AJP	*American Journal of Philology*
AnatSt	*Anatolian Studies*
ANRW	*Aufstieg und Niedergang der römischen Welt*, ed. Hildegard Temporini (Berlin and New York 1972–)
AntCl	*L'Antiquité classique*

ArchDelt	*Archaiologikon Deltion*
AthMitt	*Mitteilungen des deutschen archäoligischen Instituts, Athenische Abteilung*
BCH	*Bulletin de correspondance hellénique*
BEFAR	*Bibliothèque des écoles françaises d'Athènes et de Rome*
BibO	*Bibliotheca Orientalis*
CAH	*Cambridge Ancient History*
CIL	*Corpus Inscriptionum Latinarum*
ClMed	*Classica et Mediaevalia*
CP	*Classical Philology*
CQ	*Classical Quarterly*
CR	*Classical Review*
CW	*Classical World*
EHR	*English Historical Review*
FGrHist	*Fragmente der griechischen Historiker*, ed. Felix Jacoby
GRBS	*Greek, Roman and Byzantine Studies*
HSCP	*Harvard Studies in Classical Philology*
IG	*Inscriptiones Graecae*
IGRR	*Inscriptiones Graecae ad Res Romanas Pertinentes*, ed. R. Cagnat
ILS	*Inscriptiones Latinae Selectae*, ed. H. Dessau
IRT	*The Inscriptions of Roman Tripolitania*, ed. J. M. Reynolds and J. B. Ward Perkins
IstMitt	*Mitteilungen des deutschen archäologischen Instituts, Abteilung Istanbul*
JHS	*Journal of Hellenic Studies*
JRS	*Journal of Roman Studies*
MusHelv	*Museum Helveticum*
NachGöttingen	*Nachrichten der Akademie der Wissenschaften in Göttingen, phil.-hist. Klasse*
NJbb	*Neue Jahrbücher für Philologie und Pädagogik*
PIR	*Prosopographia Imperii Romani*
ProcBritAc	*Proceedings of the British Academy*
PSI	*Papiri greci e latini, pubblicazioni della società italiana per la ricerca dei papiri greci e latini in Egitto*
RE	*Real-Encyclopädie der classischen Altertumswissenschaft*, ed. A. Pauly, G. Wissowa, and W. Kroll

RE s.v. Arrianus	Eduard Schwartz, *RE* s.v. Arrianus 9, II (1896), 1230–47, repr. in Schwartz, *Griechische Geschichtschreiber* (Leipzig 1959), 130–55.
REA	*Revue des études anciennes*
REG	*Revue des études grecques*
RhM	*Rheinisches Museum für Philologie*
SBBerl	*Sitzungsberichte der deutschen Akademie der Wissenschaften zur Berlin, Klasse für Philosophie, Geschichte, Staats-, Rechts- und Wirtschaftswissenschaften*
SBHeid	*Sitzungsberichte der Heidelberger Akademie der Wissenschaften, phil.-hist. Klasse*
SBWien	*Sitzungsberichte der österreichischen Akademie der Wissenschaft in Wien, phil.-hist. Klasse*
SEG	*Supplementum Epigraphicum Graecum*
SIG	*Sylloge Inscriptionum Graecarum*, ed. G. Dittenberger
StItal	*Studi italiani de filologia classica*
VDI	*Vestnik Drevnej Istorii*
YCS	*Yale Classical Studies*
ZPE	*Zeitschrift für Papyrologie und Epigraphik*

ARRIAN OF NICOMEDIA

I

THE MAN

ARRIAN was a man of contrasts. A Bithynian and a Roman senator, a philosopher and a hunter, a general and a historian, he is our only source for the thought of the Stoic philosopher Epictetus, our best source for the history of Alexander the Great, the author of the sole surviving account of the exact dispositions of a Roman army's march and battle formation, and only the second known Greek to be made a Roman provincial governor with two legions at his command. He stands firmly astride two worlds, Greek and Roman, and must be seen as part of each.

From childhood, he tells us, he shared with his namesake Xenophon an enthusiasm for hunting, generalship, and practical wisdom (*Cyn.* 1.4). If in this passage he does not specifically mention his literary interests, it is because they encompass all these areas. Like Xenophon, Arrian wrote on hunting, on the teachings of his master, and on generalship, both in theory and in historical situations.[1] But his major works were devoted to history: the expedition of Alexander the Great and the years immediately following his death, the history of his native province, Bithynia, before its annexation by Rome, and the history of the rise of Parthia and its opposition to Rome. In these works he disassociated himself not only from Xenophon, whose *Hellenica* and *Anabasis* treat events either personally experienced or contemporaneous,[2] but also from Roman senatorial tradition. A natural pursuit of the Roman senator was the composition of the history of his city, whether memoirs of his own role in politics or the military, special studies of important episodes, or annals covering the history of the city from its foundation. To this tradition belong Fabius Pictor, Sulla, Sallust, and Tacitus.[3] Though he was a Roman senator and consul, Arrian only partially accepted this tradition. He did write on the war of Trajan against Parthia, as part of his history of Roman-Parthian relations, the *Parthica*. But when he decided to write the history of his own country, he wrote on Bithynia, not on Rome, and the work belonged to the tradition of Greek local history, not *res populi Romani domi militiaeque gestae*.[4] Who exactly was this man who combined such separate interests and drew from this double heritage with such assurance? Fortunately, inscriptions and his own writings allow us to sketch an outline of Arrian's life, which can serve as an introduction to a study of his work and help us understand his position in his age.

NICOMEDIA AND NICOPOLIS

By culture and family a Greek of Bithynia, Arrian was nevertheless a Roman citizen, no doubt from birth. His subsequent career, reaching to the Roman consulship and beyond, indicates that his father and perhaps earlier members of his family had become Roman citizens, a common honor for those forming the upper class in the Greek cities of Asia Minor. His full name, Lucius Flavius Arrianus Xenophon, provides useful evidence for his background. Before a newly discovered inscription revealed his *praenomen*,[5] it was thought that Arrian's father received his citizenship from one of the Flavian emperors (A.D. 69–96),[6] or from T. Flavius Sabinus, the father of the emperor Vespasian.[7] Since Arrian's *praenomen* is now known to be Lucius, not Titus, the family's citizenship may go back well before the second half of the first century.[8] We should probably connect the family's initial grant of citizenship with a Lucius Flavius, although no known person of that name seems connected with Bithynia or Arrian's family.[9]

The *cognomen* Arrianus shows some relation, by marriage or adoption, with the *gens Arria*, but again no person is particularly indicated.[10] The final element in Arrian's name, Xenophon, often thought to be a nickname added in later years, can be shown to be an integral part of his name.[11] Greeks regularly kept a Greek name alongside the Roman names their families had acquired with Roman citizenship and were known by one or both depending upon circumstances and their own choice. Thus Plutarch in his own writings and all other literary sources appears only as Ploutarchos, but an inscription from Delphi reveals that he also had a Roman *nomen*, Mestrius.[12] In Arrian's case we find a threefold usage: in inscriptions he is regularly Flavius Arrianus;[13] in the titles to his works he is Arrianos;[14] in the body of the works, when he speaks of himself, he is Xenophon.[15] The name Xenophon was not uncommon among Greek speakers of the first century

A.D. and need have implied no particular interest on the part of Arrian's parents in the famous author. Nevertheless, Xenophon was much read and admired throughout antiquity as a historian and especially as a philosopher,[16] and Stoics especially praised his portrait of Socrates.[17] The name may reflect the parents' interest in philosophy.

The approximate year of Arrian's birth must be established by working back from the date of his consulship, about A.D. 129.[18] The age when one reached the consulship varied; a career might be slowed by imperial disfavor or hastened by patrician or imperial blood. New men such as Arrian, whose families had never before attained the consulship, regularly received it about age forty,[19] but there were exceptions. Calculating forty years before a consulship in 129, Arrian would have been born about A.D. 89, although perhaps as early as 85,[20] or as late as 92.[21]

The city where he was born and raised, Nicomedia in Bithynia, was not old as Greek cities go, but proud and exceedingly prosperous.[22] It had been founded in 274 B.C. by King Nicomedes I of Bithynia, who made it his capital. It continued in Roman times to be chief city of the Bithynian half of the province of Bithynia-Pontus, the normal residence of the governor, meeting place of the provincial assembly, and site of the temple of Rome and Augustus. Its wealth was based on the fertile plain which spread out around it and the fact that it was at the western end of a trade route which ran along the northern part of Asia Minor and beyond, and thus was a major transfer point for east-west traffic, both commercial and military.[23] Its merchants handled as well an extensive sea trade between the Aegean and the Black Sea. Although Bithynia itself was a quiet province far from the borders of the empire, it was on the road connecting the northern frontier along the Danube with the eastern along the Euphrates and had close connections with the Bosporan kingdom in Crimea.[24] It was therefore important for the emperor to assure its prosperity and stability. Our best source on Bithynia for this period is in fact the correspondence of Pliny the younger, who had been sent out as an extraordinary governor by Trajan to straighten out the confused finances of the cities and to prevent any outbreak of social unrest.[25] The problem was not so much lack of funds as their misuse, in large part inspired by a sense of competition between cities and between individual members of the ruling aristocracies in each city.[26] Dio Chrysostom, the philosopher-orator from the Bithynian city of Prusa, furnishes an example of the problem: in his orations he speaks of the need for harmony between the cities, but he himself was brought before Pliny by two of his fellow citizens in connection with a building project.[27]

Arrian's family no doubt belonged, like Dio's, to this wealthy municipal aristocracy, a class whose members were regularly granted Roman citizenship.[28] One sign of the prestige of the family was Arrian's priesthood of the goddesses Demeter and Kore at Nicomedia. The city was dedicated to Demeter and held regular games, Demetria, in her honor. We may expect that Demeter's priest would only be selected from the most important citizens. Arrian's own pride in the office is apparent from his mention of it in the preface to his history of Bithynia.[29] His love of hunting, so evident in his treatise on the sport, was a passion only the wealthy could afford. No doubt as a youth he had spent long hours hunting on his family estates or those of his friends, or on the slopes of nearby Mount Olympus. Later, when he entered the Roman senate, he would by law have to meet a property qualification which would have placed him among the richest men in the Roman Empire.

Arrian's schooling would have begun with basic studies in grammar, then progressed to work in literature with a *grammatikos*. Then, when about eighteen or nineteen, a wealthy young man began to do advanced work in rhetoric, or less commonly, in philosophy.[30] Despite the presence of such a well-known figure as Dio Chrysostom in Bithynia, and famous schools in the neighboring province of Asia and in Athens, Arrian chose to travel to the town of Nicopolis, on the northwest coast of Greece, to study philosophy with an ex-slave exiled by Domitian, the Stoic Epictetus. In this case the pursuit of philosophy led in the direction of Rome. Nicopolis had been founded by Octavian after the battle of Actium and had become a major port for traffic between Rome and the East. The harbor and the Actian games, which Octavian had made equal to those of Olympia, insured that there would be a constant flow of visitors to the city.[31] Arrian remained long enough to gain an impression of the region. "I myself know that still today this mainland [Epirus] has excellent pasture land and nourishes beautiful cattle," he tells us à propos of a variant on the story of Heracles and the cattle of Geryon (*Anab.* 2.16.6), and he can compare the channel through the shallows at the head of the Persian Gulf to that between Leucas and Acarnania, not far south of Nicopolis: "The shallows were marked on either side by poles driven down, just as in the strait between the island Leucas and Acarnania signposts have been set up for navigators so that the ships should not run aground on the shallows. However, the shallows round Leucas are sandy and render it easy for those aground to get off; but here it is mud on both sides of the channel, both deep and tenacious" (*Ind.* 41.2–3).

The impression made by Epictetus himself was unforgettable.[32] His usual method of teaching was the diatribe, in which in direct and unpretentious language he faced both his regular pupils and prominent visitors with fundamental questions about their lives and values in a manner reminiscent of Socrates' persistent inquiries at Athens. During his stay with Epictetus, which may have lasted two or three years, Arrian conceived the idea of writing up the talks of his master as the earlier Xenophon had written the conversations of Socrates in the *Memorabilia.* His *Discourses of Epictetus,* of which four of the original eight books have survived, established him as a philosopher and the new Xenophon. Unfortunately, we do not know the year of their publication, if there was any formal publication, but we may doubt that he finished them as a student. The way in which he speaks of Epictetus in the letter to Gellius which now prefaces the *Discourses* indicates that the letter at least was written after the death of the master.[33]

Although the exact period of Arrian's studies in Nicopolis is uncertain, it is probable that he began his studies when about eighteen, that is, about A.D. 107. The *Discourses* themselves give no firm dates, but the Dacian wars apparently had ended, and the Parthian war is not mentioned, so that the outside limits of his sojourn would be A.D. 105 and 113.[34] In any case, the young student of philosophy had no desire to devote more than two or three years to ethical theory, but itched to take an active part in the affairs of the empire.

IN THE SERVICE OF ROME

The earlier Xenophon, after a period spent in companionship with Socrates, went off to seek his fortune as a gentleman-soldier and friend of Cyrus, brother of the Persian king. Although documentation for much of his career is lacking, it is clear that Arrian too made an early decision to seek his fortune in a military and governmental career. The lives of other successful senators suggest that he may have been marked out from the earliest stages of his career as a military man and potentially a governor of a province like Cappadocia.

Two classes of Roman citizens, separated by their property qualifi-

cations and by various privileges and restrictions, held special positions in the administration of the empire. One, the knights, or equestrian order, usually had long careers at relatively low levels in the
military, although a select few were given prominent positions in the
financial administration and a limited number of special military or
provincial posts as prefects and procurators.[35] The other class, more
illustrious but not always more powerful, was the senatorial order,
from which were chosen the commanders of the legions, the magistrates of the *cursus honorum*, and the proconsuls and imperial legates
who governed most of the provinces. Arrian's career, at least in its
later stages, followed the senatorial *cursus*, including the offices of
proconsul, consul, and imperial legate. As long as it was assumed that
Arrian's family had received its citizenship from the Flavian emperors,
the presumption was that the family was of no more than equestrian
status and that Arrian had begun his career as an equestrian, then had
been raised to the senatorial order (*adlectus in amplissimum ordinem*)
by Trajan or Hadrian.[36] Now, with the hypothesis of a Flavian dona-
tion of citizenship rendered improbable by his newly discovered fore-
name,[37] we may postulate another alternative, that Arrian's father had
already achieved senatorial rank, and that therefore Arrian could follow from the beginning the normal senatorial career with no need for
the grant of the *latus clavus* or adlection.[38] However, for either a
knight or a senator, it was useful, indeed necessary, to attract the attention of some prominent senator who might recommend and support him,[39] and as we shall see, Arrian was no exception.

Arrian's career culminated in his legateship in Cappadocia. Now the
legateship of a vital frontier province involving the command of two
legions and a large force of auxiliaries and native troops marked the
end of a special kind of career, carefully differentiated by Trajan and
Hadrian from the normal administrative posts in interior provinces
entrusted to senators with a minimal experience in military affairs.[40]
The evidence of other careers shows that at this period only those who
had served several years as officers in the legions gaining experience
with the military were permitted to end their career, as Arrian did, as
governors of legionary provinces. If Arrian began his career as an
equestrian, he would have served several years in his early twenties
in the equestrian military career (the *militiae equestres*),[41] first as the
commander of a troop of five hundred noncitizen auxiliaries (*praefectus cohortis*) and perhaps later as *tribunus militum angusticlavius*,
one of the six major officers of a legion. These posts gave opportunity

for a young man's mettle to be tested, so that this was the normal point in a career where a man was brought to the attention of the emperor and admitted to the senatorial order.[42] After the grant of the *latus clavus*, Arrian could have gone on as *vigintivir*, one of twenty minor administrative officials at Rome, then as *tribunus militum laticlavius* with a legion. If, on the other hand, he were already of senatorial rank, he could begin his career as *vigintivir*. There is some indication that already in the vigintivirate young men were marked out as potential legionary commanders. At this stage, therefore, Arrian would already have revealed his aptitude for the military life and for holding positions of responsibility.[43]

One point stands firm in this shadowy area of speculative reconstruction of Arrian's early service: the young Nicomedian was known to and probably the protégé of one of the most prominent senators under Trajan, C. Avidius Nigrinus. Nigrinus came from a family long interested in Greek affairs and philosophy.[44] His father, uncle, and cousin had all been proconsuls of Achaea, and he himself was sent out to Greece as imperial *corrector* to straighten out the problems of the free Greek cities of the province, probably within a few years after his consulship in A.D. 110. The two brothers to whom Plutarch addressed his treatise on brotherly love were apparently Nigrinus' father and uncle. This uncle, Avidius Quietus, was a friend of the famous Stoic senator Thrasea Paetus, his wife Arria, and his daughter Fannia, and defended the latter two in the senate.[45] Nigrinus himself was consul in A.D. 110, and later governor of Dacia. In 117, when Trajan died, he was thought to be eligible for the throne. He was killed along with three other ex-consuls prominent under Trajan by some of Hadrian's supporters in 118, when Hadrian, who had just been acclaimed emperor, had not yet returned to Italy. Hadrian publicly disclaimed all responsibility; his private thoughts are unknown.[46]

Given Nigrinus' prominence and the philhellenic and philosophical bias of his family, it is significant that we discover Arrian sitting on Nigrinus' privy council when the latter as *corrector* in Achaea is judging a boundary dispute at Delphi.[47] Roman magistrates regularly sought advice from their *consilium*, a group of friends and officials formed for this purpose.[48] By this time—not long after 110—Arrian was in his early twenties, had studied philosophy with Epictetus, written down a recreation of his lectures and probably circulated them informally, and would have served Rome for two or more years, either as equestrian or future senator. Now he had come to the attention of

Nigrinus, who asked him to sit on his council, as a friend or as one of his junior staff officers. In either case, Arrian's relation with Nigrinus would have been made warmer by their common interest in philosophy.

If Nigrinus' interest helped Arrian's career under Trajan, there is no doubt that it was also a good time for a Greek to have high ambitions. The admission of provincials into the highest ranks of Roman public life was a gradual process, and for a variety of reasons those of the eastern, Greek-speaking provinces were among the last to become progressively senators, consuls, and imperial governors. The history of the accession of these "orientals," or better, Greeks, to places of power is one aspect of the Romanization of the empire and has attracted a certain attention, despite the difficulties involved in distinguishing with certainty those from the East and in excluding those who were raised in the East but descended from settlers from Italy.[49] Although some easterners had become senators before, Trajan was the first to admit them in large numbers.[50] From the point of view of wealth and culture, the Greeks of Asia Minor were eminently eligible for the senate, but it was exactly this culture which delayed their integration into the Roman system. Both Romans and Greeks were profoundly aware of the heritage of Hellenism. For the Romans, it was easier to accept into their ranks the barbarian Gauls, who when they became civilized, became Romans. The Greeks were difficult to assimilate—and reluctant to be assimilated. While Celts and Iberians eagerly embraced the civilization offered them by Rome, absorbing the language, the legal system, and the education of their conquerors and vying for the honor of having their cities made *municipia* or *coloniae*, the Greek cities remained aloof, asking only their freedom and the maximum independence.[51] Most Greeks of some pretensions in the first century A.D. preferred not to become any more involved than necessary with Rome on a governmental level: Plutarch, although a friend of highly placed Romans, urges his friend Menemachus of Sardis to settle his problems in his city among Greeks, and not take them to the proconsul.[52] Arrian is among the first to become thoroughly integrated into the Roman system. Neither from old Italic stock which had settled in the East nor from one of the dynastic families to which Rome had found it politic to grant citizenship and advancement to high position, from a province which produced no known senators in the first and only four in the second century, he nevertheless rose to one of the most important posts in the empire.

Trajan, then, would have been receptive to recommendations from someone like Nigrinus on Arrian's behalf. He may even have attached the young man to his personal staff for the war he was preparing against Parthia. In any case there is little reason to doubt that Arrian served in some capacity in these campaigns (A.D. 114–117) and that there he was able to give proof of the promise of his first years of service. As Trajan gathered the resources of the empire for the attack, he needed men like Arrian, experienced and interested in military affairs, familiar with the East, and able to communicate more easily than men from the West with the Greek speakers and native troops of Syria and western Asia Minor. Some indication of Arrian's participation is at hand: he afterwards wrote seventeen books on Parthian-Roman relations, the *Parthica*. Ten books were devoted to Trajan's campaigns of 114–117. Such detailed treatment appears to reflect personal involvement, while certain fragments suggest autopsy. Finally, a passage of Johannes Lydus affirms that Arrian held a military command under Trajan in the area of the Darial Pass over the Caucasus. Arrian could have accompanied Trajan's army as a *tribunus militum* or a higher-ranking official.[53] While on the expedition he would gain both the experience and the imperial recognition which would propel him on his future career. Hadrian, who was soon to become emperor, would also have had a chance to know his qualities as a leader.[54]

Arrian's military accomplishments were not his only recommendation to Trajan. The emperor's favorite sport was hunting,[55] and Arrian also states that this was a major interest of his from his youth and shows himself an expert in his treatise on the subject. A shared interest of this sort would hardly hinder his career. Later, when Hadrian became emperor, Arrian would have still more in common with his sovereign. Hadrian too was devoted to hunting, even naming a city Hadrianotherae, "Hadrian's hunts." Despite his avowed policy of peace, he was a military man, deeply committed to making the armies and the frontiers they protected strong, and watchful of the minutiae of legionary training and discipline. He spent many years of his reign touring camps in the farthest corners of the empire, inspecting the fortifications and ordering new ones built, such as Hadrian's wall in Britain, and encouraging the troops.[56] Arrian himself credits Hadrian with special innovations in cavalry training.[57] With Hadrian the tendency to involve the Greek East in the workings of the empire was formed into a policy not simply of philhellenism, but of integration, on peculiarly Greek terms, into the imperial system.[58] Finally, like

Arrian, Hadrian found pleasure and stimulation in philosophy and literature.[59] He was said to have known Epictetus, as well as prominent figures of the world of *belles lettres* such as Polemon and Favorinus. He himself wrote poetry, including a famous piece to his own soul, supposedly composed on his deathbed.[60]

During Hadrian's reign Arrian advanced through the *cursus honorum* to praetor and consul. A newly discovered inscription from Cordoba in what was once the province of Hispania Baetica consists of a four-line Greek poem to Artemis dedicated by "proconsul Arrian" —*Arrianos anthypatos*.[61] The identification with Flavius Arrianus is most probable: Arrianus is not a particularly common name; of those individuals named Arrian very few would have risen to the rank of proconsul; and only one is known (or likely) to have written in Greek —our Nicomedian. The epigram and the altar on which it is inscribed are dedicated to Artemis; Arrian, like the earlier Xenophon, believed it was good for a hunter to honor Artemis, and stated that he himself did so (*Cyn.* 34–35). Nor is there any reason why Arrian could not have been proconsul.[62] The poem itself reflects Arrian's backgrounds and interests, as will be shown in chapter 4. It was normal for a senator, in the period after his praetorship, to become proconsul of one of the senatorial provinces, such as Baetica. Finally, in the *Anabasis* Arrian writes as if he had been in Spain at Tartessus (modern Tartesso, at the mouth of the Guadalquivir, just north of Cadiz), which was in the province of Baetica. In discussing the temple of Heracles (Melkart) at Tyre, Arrian notes, "Likewise, I think that the Heracles honored in Tartessus by the Iberians, where one also finds the so-called 'Pillars of Heracles,' is the Tyrian Heracles, since Tartessus is a Phoenician foundation, and the temple to Heracles there has been built and the sacrifices are sacrificed in the Phoenician style" (*Anab.* 2.16.4). This statement about contemporary practices in Spain is set into a digression on Heracles which mingles standard literary references to Herodotus and Hecataeus with personal inferences (as here, introduced by "I think") and the observations on the quality of the pastureland around Ambracia and Amphilochia already quoted (introduced by "I know"). Arrian uses the same technique of combining personal observation with literary allusion in his *Periplus*.[63] He would have governed Baetica for the normal one-year term, sometime in the interval, usually about ten years, between the praetorship and consulship.[64]

In this period, between four and six pairs of consuls held office each year, each pair for an average of two months. The first pair had the greater dignity and gave their names to the whole year; Arrian shared with a certain Severus a suffect consulship later in the year. Two kinds of evidence permit us to establish a rough date for this office.[65] First, his name is found as part of the consular date on brick stamps in Ostia and in Leptis Magna in Africa.[66] The bricks at Ostia are found in buildings also containing dated bricks of 125–130 and may be assumed to belong in the same period.[67] Arrian's consulship therefore should be placed during these years. The bricks from Leptis come from the Hadrianic baths, which were finished in time to bear inscriptions of Bruttius Praesens and Valerius Priscus, proconsuls of Africa in 134/35 and 135/36 respectively, and seem consistent with the evidence from Ostia.[68] Since all the consuls for 127 and 128 are known,[69] the years can be narrowed down to 125–26, 129–30. Bloch has further shown that Arrian's suffect consulship must be placed in the brickmaking season, that is, between March and August.[70] Complementary inferences may be drawn from the second piece of evidence, Arrian's legateship in Cappadocia, a post only available to ex-consuls. Since he was already performing duties there, inspecting the Black Sea coast, in 131/32, this date is the *terminus ante quem* for the consulship.[71] Eck suggests further that Arrian would not have made this tour of inspection in his first year in Cappadocia, so that his legateship must date from 130/31, and his consulship before that.[72] The argument, however, is *a priori* and hardly certain. Nor can we presume that Arrian was made governor immediately after the consulship, so that his consulship *must* have been in 129 or 130. An ex-consul frequently held an administrative post at Rome before going out to the provinces as governor. Thus L. Burbuleius Optatus Ligarianus, Arrian's successor in Cappadocia, was *curator operum locorumque publicorum* after his consulship.[73] Syme postulates that another legate of Cappadocia, C. Bruttius Praesens L. Flavius Rusticus, also served as *curator operum publicorum* on completion of his term as consul, and Arrian may have done the same.[74] Thus Arrian's consulship may have been several years before he became legate: 125 and 126 are both possible, though 129 is more likely.[75]

The post of *legatus Augusti pro praetore Cappadociae*, which Arrian held from at least 131/32,[76] was an important one, and it appears that Arrian managed it well. Certainly Hadrian saw no need to move him, for although such posts were frequently held for only three or four years, Arrian remained for at least six, through 136/37. The responsibilities and activities of Arrian as governor have been presented

in an admirable article by Pelham.[77] Cappadocia represented the
northeastern frontier of the empire from the Caucasus mountains and
the Black Sea down the upper Euphrates River to Syria, and Arrian's
primary job was to render this frontier secure.[78] To do this he had
command of two legions, XV Apollinaris, stationed at Satala (modern
Sadak), south of Trapezus and separated by the coastal range from the
Black Sea, and XII Fulminata, stationed at Melitene (modern Malat-
ya) at an important crossing of the Euphrates, as well as auxiliaries,
native troops, and those which might be furnished by Rome's client
kings. Major roads ran from Melitene and Satala west to the Aegean,
and a military road ran along the frontier connecting the two legionary
camps. Hadrian had traversed this road only a few years before, inspecting the troops and installations as he had on the whole circuit
of the imperial frontiers.[79] Beyond the border lay the client kingdoms
of Armenia, Iberia, and Albania, and the tiny tribes of the mountains.
To the north of the Caucasus were the Alans, a Sarmatian tribe which
twice before had attacked across the mountains; to the south and east
were the Parthians, powerful despite Trajan's expedition.

One of Arrian's duties was to continue Hadrian's tour of inspection
of the frontier. He began at Trapezus where Hadrian had left off,
and sailed east and north along the coast, stopping at forts, reviewing
troops, learning about the client tribes in the mountains, and looking
at tourist attractions—such as the anchor of the *Argo* at the Phasis
River, which Arrian found to be too recent to be genuine—as far as
Dioscurias Sebastopolis (near modern Sukhum). A fragmentary inscription in honor of Hadrian that has been discovered there was set
up by Arrian, perhaps as a marker of the furthest extent of his journey.[80] Sebastopolis, Arrian tells us, was where Roman rule ended.
The new legate may have wished to explore further, but he turned
back when he heard that the Bosporan king Cotys had died (131/32).
The Bosporan kingdom, in the Crimea, was an important client of
Rome, furnishing grain to the empire and protecting it from raiding
nomads such as the Alans. Difficulties there might mean trouble in
Cappadocia as well. The journey of inspection was described in a
Latin report sent to Hadrian (*Per.* 6.2, 10.1) and also in an account
in Greek, written in a more personal tone than one would expect in
an official report, omitting details of the results of the inspection, but
adding information on the rest of the circuit of the sea, and sent in
the form of a letter to Hadrian. The Latin report is lost, but the *Periplus Ponti Euxini* (*Circumnavigation of the Black Sea*) survives.

Arrian was right to be cautious of the safety of his province. In 135 the Alans moved southward across the Caucasus, overran Albania (Azerbajdzan, in the plain of the Kur River), Gorydynene south of Armenia, and Media, and attempted to penetrate Cappadocia and Parthia.[81] They were checked by the combined action of Arrian and the Parthian king Vologases II: "The Alans were persuaded by the gifts of Vologases, and frightened by Flavius Arrianus the governor of Cappadocia," writes Dio Cassius.[82] The army with which Arrian frightened them—there is no record of a battle, though there may have been one—was described by Arrian himself, in the *Battle Formation against the Alans*. This work is or purports to be the document prescribing the order of march and battle to the army, and lists all the various troops, their position in the column, and how they are to form upon arrival at the point of confrontation with the enemy.

The Alanic invasion did not completely distract Arrian from writing: he probably composed at this time his *Alanike* (a book on the Alans now lost) and two complementary works on infantry and cavalry tactics. Of these latter two, the first is lost, but the second, the *Tactics*, has survived and can be dated by the last sentence, which speaks of the "present reign, which Hadrian rules in the twentieth year" (*Tact.* 44.3), that is, A.D. 136/37.

A dedication by the people of Sebastopolis (Suluserai) in Cappadocia witnesses that he was still legate in 137.[83] He must have left office in the course of that year or early in 138, since his successor Burbuleius is known to have governed Cappadocia under Hadrian, who died in July 138.[84] As far as we know, the governorship of Cappadocia was the end of Arrian's career. If he ever went on to the command of Syria, as did several other Cappadocian legates in the second century, or to the great honor of the proconsulship of the province of Asia or Africa, no evidence remains.[85]

Under Trajan and Hadrian Arrian had found scope for his talents and sympathy for his interests. Both emperors believed in a strong army and wished to involve the Greeks of the eastern half of the empire in imperial affairs. Both loved hunting; Hadrian had as well a continuing interest in philosophy and literature. All these features combined to propel Arrian into one of the most responsible posts in the empire. The Byzantine sources, Photius and the *Suda*, suggest that Arrian's literary ability won him the consulship.[86] No doubt his *Discourses of Epictetus*, as well as other works which he may have written in his twenties and thirties, influenced both Nigrinus and Hadrian in favoring the young Nicomedian. But Hadrian was not a romantic when the defense of the frontier was in question, and Arrian must have shown genuine military ability in his service under Trajan and Hadrian. The legates of legionary provinces like Cappadocia under Hadrian were experienced military men.[87]

ATHENS

In 137 Arrian would have been about forty-eight—an eminent figure, wealthy, traveled, an ex-consul, famous as a philosopher for his *Discourses*, no doubt famous as well for other literary efforts. He might have returned to Nicomedia, there to live in honor among his fellow citizens, hold civic office, donate some of his wealth for public buildings or games, and write his memoirs. He could have established himself in Italy (where as a senator he was required by law to hold at least one-third of his property), taken part in meetings of the senate, and felt himself at the center of the empire. Instead he seems to have determined to settle in Greece, in Athens, a center not of power but of culture. The Nicomedian who had gone so far in the Roman system had not deserted his Greek heritage, as his use of the name Xenophon in the *Periplus* and the *Battle Formation against the Alans* reminds us.

Arrian had been in Greece when in his late teens, as a student with Epictetus at Nicopolis. On his way to the western coast of Greece he had probably stopped at Athens and Corinth. Later we find him at Delphi with Nigrinus, whom he may have accompanied to Athens as well. At some time, perhaps already as a student of Epictetus, Arrian made friends with the eminent Corinthian family of the Gellii: his letter to a Lucius Gellius explaining the format of the *Discourses* precedes our texts of that work. While Arrian was legate in Cappadocia, L. Gellius Menander and his brother L. Gellius Iustus *filius* erected an honorary statue of their friend, praising him as a philosopher and benefactor.[88] At an indeterminate time after his consulship, Arrian was honored by a statue in Athens as well: its recently discovered inscription reads "Lucius Flavius Arrianus, consular, philosopher."[89] Arrian must have felt that he had friends in Greece, and in Athens in particular.

That Athens had a special meaning for Arrian before he settled there is shown by a passage in the *Periplus*. The little fleet with which he was making his inspection tour, he writes Hadrian, was caught in a storm. "Only with great difficulty did we come to—Athens. There is, as it happens, also on the Black Sea a place called by that name, and a Greek temple of Athena there, which I think has given the name to the place, a neglected fort." After describing his care for the ships, Arrian continues, "This storm kept up for two days, and we had to stay there. No doubt it was proper that we not sail by even this Black Sea Athens as if it were some desolate and anonymous harbor" (*Per.* 4–5). The passage suggests a certain respect and affection for Athens some years before he finally settled there. A few chapters later in the same work he describes the statue of the goddess of Phasis: "To judge from the posture it should be Rhea. She has the cymbal in her hands and lions under the throne, and sits like the goddess of Phidias in the Metroön at Athens" (*Per.* 9.1). Hadrian, of course, had showered attention on Athens throughout his life, and stopped there on his travels whenever he could. In the very year that Arrian was writing the *Periplus*, 131/32, the emperor made Athens the center of his newly formed Panhellenic league. Arrian could expect Hadrian to share familiarity with the major sights of Athens.

When he did choose Athens, it does not seem to have been from lack of experience of other places. We have already seen that his studies and his career took him to places such as Nicopolis, Delphi, Parthia, southern Spain, and Cappadocia. Various positions in the senatorial *cursus* would also have required sojourns in Rome, especially the posts of aedile, praetor, and consul. Arrian must besides have had a tour of duty in the northern provinces, perhaps Noricum. At *Ind.* 4.15–16 he writes, "The Danube rises small from its sources, but receives many tributaries, though not equal in number to those of the Indian rivers which flow into the Indus and the Ganges. Very few indeed are navigable, of which I myself have seen the Inn and the Save. The Inn meets the Danube in the borderland of Noricum and Raetia; the Save in Pannonia. The place where the two rivers [Save and Danube] join is called Taurunus." Alföldy has noted that Arrian is more accurate in speaking of the "borderland" (*en methoriōi*) of Noricum and Raetia than either Tacitus or the geographer Ptolemy, who give the Inn as the boundary of the two provinces. The Inn was not itself the boundary, since Noricum possessed territory west of the river. Thus Arrian must have had a more than casual acquaintance with this area. The second river which Arrian mentions, the Save, flowed for most of its length through Pannonia but ran for a short but heavily traveled course through Noricum.[90] Arrian, therefore, may have seen these two rivers, which enter the Danube so far apart, not as a traveler along the Danube (in which case we would expect him to mention other tributaries as well), but as a Roman official stationed in Noricum or a neighboring province. Arrian does not mention another navigable river which flowed through Noricum, the Dravus, perhaps because it becomes accessible to large boats only in the lower part of its course, in Pannonia. The same tour of duty would also have given him occasion to see the Celtic Alps, the height of which he compares to the Caucasus mountains as seen from Dioscurias (*Per.* 11.5).

In his book on hunting, Arrian seems to imply that he has been in both Gaul and Numidia. He describes in some detail how the Gauls hunt (*Cyn.* 3, 19–21) and the sacrifices they make afterwards (*Cyn.* 34), and is familiar with how the African nomads hunt on horseback: "The sight, it seems to me, is like nothing else" (*Cyn.* 24.5). In another passage he speaks of hunting deer on level plains, "in Mysia, among the Getae, in Scythia, and through Illyria" (*Cyn.* 23.2). All these areas were in the Roman Empire ("among the Getae" might refer to the province of Dacia, or more likely, to Lower Moesia, as does Scythia); Hadrian had hunted with especial pleasure in Mysia. It is true that if Arrian was as devoted to the hunt as he states, he would have had ample opportunity to have learned of different hunting practices, especially the popular Gallic method, without actually being in the countries where they originated. He need not have seen all he describes. It is worth noting, however, that Hadrian had been in all these areas. Finally, the fact that Arrian wrote two works on Greek generals who freed Sicily from tyrants, *Dion* and *Timoleon*, suggests that he may at some time have held a position on the island, perhaps as quaestor.

While living at Athens, Arrian participated in the ordinary life of the city, frequenting the gymnasium and discussing political affairs (*Cyn.* 5). He not only became an Athenian citizen, as he says in the *Cynegeticus*, but held the city's most prestigious office, that of eponymous archon.[91] The archon, after whom the Athenian year was named, had relatively few responsibilities—these belonged mostly to two other officials, the herald of the Areopagus and the hoplite general—but was expected to donate lavishly for certain special expenses of the city.[92] Occasionally non-Athenians were naturalized and given the post, if they consented: these include the ex-prince of Commagene, C. Julius Antiochus Epiphanes Philopappus, sometime before 88, and Hadrian in 112, before he became emperor.[93] The post bears witness to the esteem in which the Athenians held Arrian (no doubt for his literary

and philosophical interests rather than for his military accomplishments), to the good will which they thought he bore their city, and to
the wealth which they thought he could spend on it. The year was
145/46, eight years after he had left his Cappadocian command.

This is our last sure notice of Arrian. After his archonship, like all
who had held the office, he would have become a member of the Areopagus, a council which at this period had become the chief governing
body of Athens. The Romans preferred that cities be governed by a
limited aristocracy of wealth and privilege, and under their influence
the council of the Areopagus assumed more of the functions of the
Roman senate.[94] Arrian no doubt would have been one of the most influential of its approximately one hundred members. The name Flavius Arrianus recurs in Athenian documents three times in the succeeding decades, once identifying an ephebe, twice a member of the boule
or city council (A.D. 166/67 and 169/70).[95] All three may represent a
son of Arrian, or a grandson; the earlier assumption that the latter
two are Arrian himself is unwarranted, since it is most unlikely that an
eighty-year-old ex-archon and Areopagite would serve on this council, which was normally filled by much younger men.[96] Arrian and his
younger namesake may be the "two consuls named Arrian" whom a
certain Clementine claims as forebears in an inscription of the late
second century found at Eleusis.[97] These inscriptions are the only evidence that Arrian married and had children. The evocative picture of
Hadrian being entertained at Athens by Arrian and his wife drawn by
Marguerite Yourcenar in her extraordinary book, *The Memoirs of
Hadrian*, is purely imaginary.[98]

It was once assumed (e.g., by Schwartz in his fundamental article
in the *Realencyclopädie*)[99] that most if not all of Arrian's historical
works—the *Parthica*, the *Anabasis of Alexander*, the *Indike*, the
Events after Alexander, and the *Bithyniaca*—were written in the leisure of Arrian's retirement in Athens. Appealing as such a notion
might be at first sight, there is no direct evidence to connect these
works with this period, and various indications suggest that some of
the books, such as the *Parthica* and the *Anabasis*, may have been written earlier, in the lifetime of Hadrian.[100] Bosworth has pointed out
that the duties in the imperial service of even an active senator did not
necessarily prevent him from writing as well.[101] In the face of our in-
ability to pinpoint the time of composition of Arrian's major works,
it seems best to avoid inconclusive speculation, but presume that Arrian was active as a writer throughout his life, and deal with special

arguments regarding the composition of these works as they relate to the treatment of the works themselves in later chapters.

A passage from a medical treatise of Galen must give us a last glimpse of Arrian as he grew old in honored leisure in Athens. The doctor is describing how useful the outer ear is for collecting sound and making it easier to hear: "The best witness to this argument is Arrian, the Roman consul, who, since he has injured his sense of hearing, puts the hollows of his hands beside his ears and inclines them forward, so as to hear more easily." [102] Galen shared with Arrian an interest in the philosophy of Epictetus, for the doctor-philosopher wrote a book, *In defense of Epictetus, against Favorinus*.[103] He may have noted Arrian's characteristic gesture while discussing Epictetus' teachings with him. Arrian was admired by his contemporaries for his philosophical works as well as his historical writings. Aulus Gellius recalls that during his student days in Athens (in the 140s) the millionaire sophist Herodes Atticus brought out from his library Arrian's *Discourses of Epictetus* and quoted them to settle a discussion.[104] About the same time the young Marcus Aurelius discovered Arrian's *Epictetus* in the library of his teacher Rusticus.[105] As consular and writer, Arrian was known and respected by the leading figures of his generation. A phrase of Lucian might have served as his epitaph: "Arrian, the disciple of Epictetus, one of the most prominent Romans, and one who had lived with culture throughout his life." [106]

Lucian singles out from all his other achievements Arrian's discipleship of Epictetus to identify him to his readers. In the following chapter I will examine the Nicomedian's experience of Epictetus, and the writings which grew from it, before moving on to those historical works which have brought him fame in modern times.

2

THE ENCOUNTER WITH EPICTETUS

ARRIAN'S period of study with Epictetus left a lasting impression upon him. Years later, in his letter to his friend L. Gellius, which serves as preface to the *Discourses*, he described the effect of the master's teaching: "To Epictetus it would be of no concern at all if anyone should despise his words [in written form], since even when he was speaking them he clearly was aiming at nothing else but to incite the minds of his hearers to what was best. If now these words of his should produce this same effect, they would have, I think, just that success which the words of philosophers ought to have; but if not, let those who read them be assured of this, that when Epictetus spoke them, the hearer could not help but feel exactly what Epictetus wanted him to feel." So thoroughly did the force of this lame ex-slave's personality and teaching capture the admiration of the wealthy and ambitious youth, who since childhood had been exposed to the practiced skills of the orators and philosophers of Nicomedia.

Epictetus was a teacher of philosophy, but one quite unlike those to be found in the schools of Athens or Rome. His aim was not to teach theory, to argue about logic or the world-fire, but to reach out and redirect men to a new life, to preach to them a gospel of inner freedom which would liberate them from fear and false hopes—fears for their health, their wives, their money; hopes for honor, high office, the favor of those in high places. Without the concept of a savior god, he nevertheless spoke to the same need addressed by the Christian preachers, the individual's desire to be free; and like them, he depended not on logic or fine rhetoric, but upon a down-to-earth sense of the worries and longings which enslaved his fellows.

He was not a stranger to slavery. Born about A.D. 50 in the town of Hierapolis, only a few miles from Colossi, where Paul preached a few years later, he first comes to our notice as a slave to Nero's immensely wealthy freedman Epaphroditus.[1] From this position he could observe the realities of power in Rome and see the favor-seekers begging for offices, either excluded by insolent porters, or gaining entrance by lavish bribes. He could also watch the mighty fall, as Nero was driven to his death (Epaphroditus helped him commit suicide) and his own master was deprived of office. Epaphroditus eventually freed his slave, but Epictetus had already discovered how to make himself free by the teaching of the Stoic philosopher Musonius Rufus. From that time he made it his life work to share with others the truth of how to be free by having a right understanding of what was under their control and what was not.

At first he seems to have modeled himself on Socrates and attempted to accost strangers in the streets of Rome, asking them questions which would reveal their neglect of their soul. In one of his lectures he described such an encounter with a wealthy ex-consul, and the kind of result to which it might lead: a blow on the head (*Diss.* 2.12.17–25). But in the early 90s he was banished from Rome along with other philosophers by Domitian. Undaunted, he set up a school at Nicopolis across the Ionian Sea from Italy, on the route between Rome and Athens, and continued the effort which he had begun at Rome to reshape the thinking of those members of the Roman upper class willing to listen. There Arrian heard him some fifteen years later, about A.D. 107–109.

The heart of his teaching at Nicopolis, as recorded by Arrian, was a clear distinction between what is ours and what is not: "Of all that is, some things are under our control, while others are not. Under our control are conception, choice, desire, aversion, and in a word, all that is of our making; not under our control are our body, our possessions, reputation, offices, and in a word all that is not our own making. What is under our control is by nature free, unhindered, unimpeded, while what is not under our control is weak, servile, obstacled, alien" (*Ench.* 1.1). If one can maintain clearly this distinction between the two classes of things, he can come to no harm, but will live freely and naturally. This distinction lost, one must become enslaved—to one's body, one's ambition, one's superiors, one's family, one's health.[2]

The teaching of Epictetus therefore was devoted to leading the listener to understand this distinction clearly, to realize what the consequences of it were in everyday life, and to make it the basis of his day-to-day choices and actions. It was his emphasis on everyday life which made his lectures so vivid and ensured his success among the young upper-class Romans and visiting travelers who were his hearers. The Stoic school since its foundation had called for the correct understanding of the world and man's place in it, so that one could be free to live according to nature rather than in opposition to it. However, traditional Stoic thought had divided philosophy into the three fields of logic, physics, and ethics, treating respectively (1) the rational tools that man has at his disposal to understand his universe; (2) the principles of nature's action, the comprehension of which will free him from fear or irrational behavior in the face of earthquakes, storms, and other natural phenomena; and (3) the principles of right action. Epictetus ignored physical phenomena, subordinated logic firmly to ethics, and focused the great burden of his teaching on those factors in his hearers' lives which most inhibited them from living according to that fundamental distinction between "ours" and "not ours," *hēmetera* and *allotria*.

Epictetus recognized three basic goals of ethical teaching: to control our desires, to prepare us for correct exterior actions and the fulfillment of our responsibilities, and finally, to develop a full understanding of the logical principles which permit a correct ethical evaluation even in difficult cases. In Epictetus' eyes, full understanding of the theoretical base of ethics was only for the advanced student/philosopher, after he had already begun to live a good life. The beginning of the philosophic life is instead open to everyone because the principles are so simple.

Our mind constantly receives outside impressions (*phantasia*) and reacts to them, in terms of desire, impulse to action, and consent. These external impressions are a given which cannot be changed, but God has granted man the power to choose, using his reason, how he will react to them. This choice gives man the freedom he longs for in the face of all external troubles. If he can by means of his reason (*logos*) use his impressions correctly, he will be free; if not, he will be a slave to what is outside himself. A man must therefore clearly understand the fundamental distinction (*diairesis*) of all that exists between that which is under our control and that which is not, stated so succinctly in the opening sentence of the *Manual* (quoted above). Our desires and actions must be directed toward what is under our sole control, for if not we must necessarily meet with failure, even disaster. Our body is not under our control, and thus if we desire health, we may be disappointed; our property is not under our control, for it may be stolen, or destroyed by storm or flood. What makes us unhappy however, is not sickness, or theft, but the wrong opinion (*dogma*) in our own minds, which has said that we could hold our body or property securely. On the other hand the man who distinguishes correctly will not accept any impression which presents what is not his as a good, will be able to fulfill his responsibilities toward others, with no desire to treat them unfairly for the sake of externals, and in his activity will not expect outward success, which does not depend on him alone. In sum, his reaction toward every external impression will be first to test whether it has to do with things under his control or not, and if it does not, immediately to say, "This means nothing to me."

Within the mind of the ethical person, therefore, Epictetus sees a set disposition, a fundamental moral stance, which recognizes this distinction of what is good and evil, based on the understanding of what is under our control and what is not. The decision to take this stance represents a kind of conversion from the normal life, for it represents a rejection of many popular values,[3] but it is exactly this disposition (*proairesis*) which sets us free. Epictetus' first task as a teacher was to bring his hearers to assert this choice by revealing the falseness of their present self-satisfaction and the inadequacy of popular ideas on the good and the necessary.

Once the listener had established a firm *proairesis*, then he could begin a process of moral growth through self-training and self-examination. This gradual strengthening of one's capacity to recognize what is his and what is not in everyday life was in fact the most difficult stage. In this development, Epictetus was not impressed by outward ascetical practices or a show of philosophical learning. Philosophy meant learning one's particular weaknesses and working on them, establishing a habit of correct use of external impressions.

The ethics of Epictetus were thus built on the interior judgment of the mind, but as with other Stoics, there was also a strong sense of how our mental impulses lead to action in fulfillment of our responsibilities. Each man had a responsibility toward himself: toward his body, which despite its deficiencies should be fed and clothed with not excessive but sufficient care, and toward his own individual personality, which is different from every other, and which therefore will consider different things important or trivial, evil, neutral, or good. But the proper area of our responsibility is toward our fellow man: "Zeus has so constituted the nature of the rational animal that he can attain none of his proper goods unless he contributes something to the common benefit" (*Diss.* 1.19.13). For Epictetus, the philosophic man is not completely isolated and without feeling: "I should not be un-feeling like a statue, but should preserve my relations, natural and acquired, as a pious man [toward the gods], as a son, as a brother, as a father, and as a citizen" (*Diss.* 3.2.4). These obligations exist even though the other party is not a good father, brother, or whatever, for their deficiency has no bearing on our conduct, but is for them to correct. A man's duty is to do what is right himself (*Ench.* 30).

In various passages Epictetus speaks of responsibilities toward fam-ily. Adultery especially is an evil, because it debases a man and hurts society; child-raising is seen as a civic as well as a family responsibility. In the larger community, our duties are many: to supervise the educa-tion of young men, run the gymnasium, or hold other offices (*Diss.* 3.7.19–21). We should recognize the authority of civil rulers over external matters, and the philosophic man himself may accept offices, although he will not grovel for them, for they are not worth it (*Diss.* 4.7.19–24, *Ench.* 24). Epictetus saw himself as another Socrates, edu-cating men to be good citizens, not by making them docile to every whim of authority but by making them free men, since only one free of external pressure can in fact fulfill his responsibilities effectively. He frequently cited Socrates as a model for behavior, and in the area of general benefits to mankind, Heracles. The latter hero, a familiar example in the teaching of the earlier Stoics as well, is praised by Epic-tetus for his willingness to face danger and death in doing good works. "Since you must die in any case while doing something—farming, dig-ging, selling, holding a consulship, suffering from dyspepsia or dysen-tery . . . I for my part would choose to die doing something human, beneficient, of use to the common good, noble" (*Diss.* 4.10.12).

For most men of Arrian's day, the incentives to public service were the fame, wealth, and power which came with high office. In challeng-ing the value of these common incentives, while urging his students to public service, Epictetus introduced a deep-seated tension into his teaching which only the most philosophical would overcome. He him-self had become famous by doing his duty preaching philosophy, but he constantly challenged his own role as professional philosopher. Likewise, he urged his students to duty and service but challenged their bondage to the values normally associated with it. Arrian, an ambitious and intelligent youth, must surely have felt this tension more than most. Some indications of it appear, as we shall see, in the *Anabasis*, when Arrian tries to evaluate the achievements of Alexander, whose chief incentive to action was a desire for fame.[4]

Finally, behind all these responsibilities, is our duty to God, who has put his divine fire within us, who knows our innermost thoughts, who is with us even when we are alone. To him we owe our existence and all that we have, especially our reason, which is our only true good because it frees us from evil. God cares for the world, and for every person, and so the wise man will follow the directives of his divine master. Of course, God's care does not extend to externals, but only to what is in our control.[5] The philosophic man knows that he owes to God his true good. Although we may offer sacrifices and even consult oracles (*Ench.* 31–32), the chief act of piety is to have the right opinions about the gods and to seek to obey them, because they administer the world well and justly. Recognizing this divine care, the philosopher praises the god who watches over him. In Epictetus' words, "I am gifted with reason, and therefore I must sing hymns to God. This is my task, and I will not desert this post" (*Diss.* 1.16.21).

For Epictetus, his teaching was his service to God, and he followed this profession as a divine calling. His fundamental teaching technique, as far as we can learn from Arrian's record in the *Discourses*, was the lecture, chiefly for students but open to the public.[6] Since they did not strictly concern dogma or theory, they were not rigidly organized, but it is possible to see a pattern in the general distribution and in the connections of various lectures one with another.[7] The lectures themselves were not scholarly discourses, but formed on the model of the Cynic diatribe, a form which filled out a fundamentally popular philosophical topic with examples, both literary and contemporary, questions directed at the audience, and short snatches of dialogue between two imaginary figures or the speaker and an interlocutor.[8] These informal performances were intended both to awaken the hearer's interest and to allow him to understand how the principles which underlay Epictetus' philosophy could be applied to his life. The richness of Epictetus' imagination, the vividness of his insight into the common pitfalls and foibles of human life, and the spontaneity of the dialogue scenes he conjures up before his audience involve the listener in the world of the philosopher, and as Arrian says, "the hearer could not help but feel what Epictetus wanted him to feel."

Undoubtedly Epictetus was gifted with an extraordinary ability to find the right tone with his hearers, whether young students or worldly-wise Roman officials. With a young person who appeared before him elaborately clothed and coiffured, he could be gentle yet firm in showing the youth the error of boasting of the beauty of his hair rather than of his mind (*Diss.* 3.1). But with the prominent Romans who would drop in on his lectures, frequently from simple curiosity, he used a more direct attack.[9]

Thus when an imperial *corrector*, known to be an Epicurean, called at the school, Epictetus did not kowtow to him as a representative of the emperor, but following his divine mission to call men to the philosophic life, immediately entered into a dialogue with the visitor (*Diss.* 3.7).[10] By insistent questioning and vivid examples he exposed to the *corrector* the weakness of the Epicurean position. His words show a Cynic directness:

—Do you know how to act as a judge? How have you learned?
—Caesar has written a credential for me.
—Let him write for you to be a judge of music: will that do you any good? In any case, how did you become a judge? Whose hand did you kiss, Symphorus' or Numenius' [the names of imperial freedmen]? Outside whose door did you sleep? After all, don't you see that the position of judge is worth no more than Numenius is?
—But I can throw whomever I wish into prison!
—You can do that to a stone.[11]

(*Diss.* 3.7.30–31)

Harsh words were necessary to break through the crust of self-satisfaction of a successful senator, and necessary also to warn Epictetus' young students, many of whom would have ambitions for high imperial or local office. The philosopher knew well that the corrupting effect of money and power would readily draw the most idealistic youth toward a life of flattery and fear. Epictetus tells the story of a Roman who had been exiled and later recalled. On his way back to Rome, he stopped at Nicopolis to meet with the philosopher. There he denounced his former life but rejected Epictetus' sage comment, "Once you just get a whiff of Rome, you will forget all else," swearing that he would now live quietly. In fact, even before he arrived, he was greeted with letters from the emperor, "and as soon as he received them, he at once forgot everything, and ever since has piled one post on another," until he became *praefectus annonae*, responsible for the grain supply at Rome (*Diss.* 1.10.2–6). Epictetus wished to liberate his hearers from this kind of slavery. He therefore insisted that they must make a decision as to how they would like to live: whether they wish to seek those things over which they have no control, or whether they wish to value that which is theirs. To talk philosophically is nothing; one must live the philosopher's life. Logic and theory could help a man understand what really was in his control, but if he spent his life merely interpreting the works of philosophers, he became a grammarian, not a philosopher (*Ench*. 49). Rather, we must live our principles: "At a banquet, do not say how one ought to eat, but eat as one ought" (*Ench*. 46.1).

Epictetus' lively diatribes had an immeasurable effect on the young Arrian, which led him to record the master's words for his own use. The result was at least eight books of *Diatribes* or *Discourses*, of which four are still preserved.[12] Arrian describes his work in a letter to Lucius Gellius which is prefixed to the *Discourses* in our manuscripts: "I have not composed these talks of Epictetus as one would normally compose such works, nor have I published them, inasmuch as I do not even admit to composing them. But I have tried, by writing down whatever I used to hear him say, as far as possible word for word, to preserve a record for myself of his thought and frank speech" (*Epist. Gell.* 1–2). These words seem clear enough, but in fact scholarly opinion has varied widely on their interpretation. Hartmann argued that Arrian used shorthand to take down the master's words and that our present text of the *Discourses* therefore represents a quite accurate account of Epictetus' exact words in the lecture hall and reproduces as well the chronological order of his talks.[13] As evidence he cites not only Arrian's words in the letter to Gellius, but the use in this work of the contemporary Greek popular language (*koinē*) rather than the standard literary dialect used by Arrian in his other writings. On the other extreme, Theo Wirth argues that the letter to Gellius must be read as a literary preface, intentionally composed to give an idea of lack of form and care.[14] After analyzing several chapters of the *Discourses* (especially 1.11), Wirth concludes that Arrian has united bits of Epictetus' talks which had been delivered separately and most importantly that he has reconstructed private conversations between Epictetus and those who came to him for advice, reporting them as if he had heard them in the lecture hall. Thus we must talk not of Epictetus' *Discourses* but of Arrian's *Discourses of Epictetus*.

The truth may lie somewhere between these positions.[15] The letter to Gellius seems to be an apology and explanation of the unusual style of the *Discourses*. Fascinated by the directness and freedom of Epictetus' speech, Arrian had tried to capture these qualities in his record by using as often as possible the exact words of the speaker. By this decision Arrian sacrificed literary diction to Epictetus' vivid vernacular but preserved the impact of Epictetus' teaching. It is unnecessary to think that Arrian made a stenographic record—stenography existed in his day, but was the work of a professional, not of a young man of wealth and culture—nor does he state that he recorded every word of his teacher. The *Discourses* are selective, for many of the talks as found in Arrian are too short for regular diatribes, and as Wirth points out, several (*Diss.* 3.6, 11, 14) combine short statements apparently made on different occasions. We must assume, therefore, that the work as it stands reflects Arrian's own interests, as he took notes or recalled the talks afterwards, selecting what seemed to him especially important or striking. We cannot be sure whether the thoughtful disposition of the talks noted by Wirth and De Lacy is due to Epictetus or to Arrian. However, Wirth seems to go too far in arguing that Arrian invented conversations of which he had no direct knowledge. Wirth's assumption in this portion of his article is that eminent men who came to consult Epictetus must usually have done so privately and that Epictetus would never have been so tactless as to reveal these conversations to his students.[16] On the contrary, the fascination of Epictetus' method apparently lay exactly in his correcting wrong thinking publicly, as part of his diatribe. In this Epictetus imitated Socrates and insisted on questioning people on their principles in the marketplace, before a crowd of curious listeners. It was Epictetus' gift, like Socrates', to penetrate rapidly beneath the outer defenses of these visitors and lay bare the inner inconsistencies which lay beneath their fears, their ambitions, their desires.

We know that Epictetus' pupils exercised themselves by writing philosophical dialogues in the style of Plato, Antisthenes, or Xenophon (*Diss.* 2.17.35–36). We can imagine the young Arrian deciding instead to attempt, on the basis of notes and memory, to capture the exact flavor of Epictetus' teaching for his own use, and incidentally to imitate the writers of Socrates' dialogues much more genuinely than by a scholastic dialogue in the Attic dialect. As Wirth has pointed out,[17] Arrian's *Discourses* in both conception and execution are strongly influenced by Xenophon's Socratic works, especially the *Memorabilia*, but Arrian even as a student did not imitate slavishly.

In this case he responded to the particular impression of Epictetus with a variation on the *Memorabilia* format which would allow him to capture the flavor of the master's inimitable diatribes.

The letter to Gellius raises a second question: how exactly were the *Discourses* published? Wirth sees in the letter to Gellius an elaborate literary device concealing the fact that Arrian had carefully prepared the discourses for publication. To me the letter seems a simple explanation and justification of Arrian's manuscript, which had been written in a style so distant from the usual literary language. The letter implies a history of Arrian's text quite different from Wirth's theory. Arrian as a student, and perhaps in the years immediately subsequent, wrote up this account of Epictetus' teaching. Various friends and fellow students borrowed his work, copied it, and in turn distributed it to their friends, until without Arrian's active support or knowledge, it had become effectively "published." At this time, apparently after the death of Epictetus, Arrian wrote to his friend Lucius Gellius (one of the family of Corinthian philanthropists who also erected a statue honoring Arrian as a philosopher)[18] that these discourses, which had now become widely known, were indeed his work, but that he could not be said to have "composed" them in the normal fashion. Following the precepts of Epictetus, he is not disturbed that they have now become public, but only hopes that they might convey some of the force of his master's teaching.

Even this letter does not mean that Arrian is "publishing" the *Discourses*; it only shows that he admits that they are now in the public domain, and explains why they have the form they do. Perhaps, then, Gellius affixed this letter to his own copy and saw to a wider distribution of the work, so that our medieval archetype would be descended from the copy of Lucius Gellius.

Unfortunately we have no evidence of the date when the *Discourses* became generally accessible. Accepting the theory propounded above, Arrian would have written the *Discourses* while a student of Epictetus (ca. 107–109) or shortly after. His philosophically inclined friends, such as Nigrinus, on whose council he served at Delphi, may have asked to make copies not much later, although we may suppose the work became known only gradually. The statue erected by L. Gellius Menander honoring Arrian as philosopher was not erected until he was proconsul of Cappadocia, that is in A.D. 131 or later. This seems to fit with the impression we receive from the letter to Gellius that Epictetus was already dead, since he probably died somewhere about

125–130. Aulus Gellius would have seen the copy in Herodes Atticus' house when he was a student at Athens in the 140s.

The importance of Arrian's record of Epictetus' lectures for his contemporaries, as indicated by their interest in copying his text, in large part explains the title "philosopher" which he was frequently given. The influence of the book was felt at once, and prominent figures such as Herodes Atticus and Aruleius Rusticus, both of whom had copies of the book, were probably his friends.

A second work on Epictetus by Arrian provides additional evidence that his interest in the philosopher's teaching was more than passing. At the request of a certain Messalinus, his friend and an admirer of Epictetus, Arrian prepared a *Manual* (in Greek, *Encheiridion*), picking out the most important and striking precepts of the master. However, rather than merely accumulate excerpts from the *Discourses* in their original order, Arrian rearranged them according to a simple scheme that reflects Epictetus' threefold division of philosophy (*Diss.* 3.2.1):

1. On desires and aversions (*Ench.* 1–29)
2. On impulses and refusals, and in general on duty (*Ench.* 30–51)
3. On accuracy in judgment (*Ench.* 52).

Chapter 53 gives concluding thoughts and quotations from Cleanthes, Euripides, and Plato. The various principles in the *Manual* have been drawn together from both the lost and the extant parts of the *Discourses* and combined in topic paragraphs under these general headings. Although short (some 33 pages in Schenkl's edition, against the 452 pages of the four extant books of *Discourses*), the *Manual* encapsulates the essentials of Epictetus' teaching, and despite the aridity natural in a compendium and the absence of those vivid touches of Epictetus' personality which abound in the *Discourses*, it has remained popular throughout the ages, becoming the chief vehicle of Epictetus' influence in later centuries. The Neoplatonist Simplicius wrote a bulky commentary to the *Manual* in the fourth century, and two Christian paraphrases were prepared in antiquity. The *Manual* was rediscovered early in the Renaissance and translations were prepared by Niccolò Perotti and Angelo Poliziano. Since then it has gone through numerous editions and translations.

A few fragments of a third work, chiefly quoted by the anthologist Stobaeus, indicate that Arrian's philosophical studies extended more widely than the ethical problems treated by Epictetus in his talks.

Drawing either from traditional Stoic studies which Epictetus may have required at his school in addition to his talks, or from informal reading in Stoic writings, Arrian composed a treatise on meteorological phenomena.[19]

According to Photius[20] "Arrian in writing his pamphlet (*biblidarion*) on the nature, composition, and appearances of comets, tries to show that this kind of prodigy portends nothing either for good or evil." The notice supplies a title, *On the Nature, Composition, and Appearances of Comets*, and indicates that the purpose of the work is philosophical and ethical. To maintain the kind of spiritual autonomy urged by Epictetus in the moral sphere, it was necessary to have a proper attitude toward occurrences in the natural world. Despite Epictetus' apparent avoidance of the subject, physics and the study of natural phenomena had always been a fundamental feature of Stoicism, forming a triad with logic and ethics.[21] In the first century B.C. Posidonius had written widely on numerous questions dealing with physical phenomena,[22] and a century later Seneca wrote our best presentation of later Stoic physical thought in the eight books of his *Quaestiones naturales*. These fragments reveal that Arrian as well took time to address such problems. We have no means of establishing the date of the work, which could have been written at any time in Arrian's career. However, it is possible to suggest, in a purely speculative manner, an occasion, not long after Arrian left Epictetus' school. The ancients were notoriously superstitious about comets, and soldiers especially considered them ominous. A comet appeared in November 115,[23] and might have discouraged Roman troops fighting the Parthians, and even given pause to their commanders. Arrian probably took part in this Parthian expedition and may have written at this time a work reviewing the rational explanations for the startling phenomenon.

To Arrian, as to many of the ancients, comets were atmospheric phenomena, appearing in the upper air.[24] He describes the various types, which the Greeks knew by different names—long-haired stars, torches, bearded ones, kegs, and sticks—and how each is formed by the accumulation of fire in a particular way (C6). In other fragments of this work we find Arrian treating a variety of common natural questions: the cause of thunder and lightning (C3),[25] the nature of mist, dew, frost, and snow (C4), and the interrelation of winds, tides, and the moon (C2). Despite the range of topics covered, which led Roos to suggest that these fragments derive from two distinct books, one on atmospheric phenomena and one on comets alone,[26] there is an under-lying unity. Lightning, mist, winds, and comets for Arrian were all manifestations of the changing atmosphere, and our fragments would easily cohere in a single work, as Brinkmann has shown.[27]

Arrian's studies with Epictetus, his books of *Discourses*, and per-haps his way of life won him the title of philosopher from his con-temporaries. Well-wishers dedicated honorary statues at Corinth and Athens to Arrian the philosopher.[28] In this, as in so much else of his life and work, Arrian imitated Xenophon, for despite his historical works, Xenophon's Socratic dialogues and especially the *Memorabilia* won him the appellation "philosopher" in antiquity.[29] In making Epictetus a new Socrates, Arrian had fulfilled the promise of his name, and become a new Xenophon.[30]

3

THE GOVERNOR OF CAPPADOCIA

AFTER these years with Epictetus, so skillfully evoked in the *Discourses*, the influences and impulses of Arrian's life become obscure to us, until once more his own works written while he was imperial legate in Cappadocia reveal his thinking. Undoubtedly, his account of Trajan's wars in the *Parthica*, if preserved, would have helped us understand his relation to that emperor; the little we can deduce from the fragments remaining is presented in chapter 8. What we can reconstruct of his career in the years between his schooling at Nicopolis and the governorship of Cappadocia has already been outlined. Perhaps some of his writings also belong to this period, but not until the three works datable to his governorship are we again able securely to relate his interests and thinking in his own writings to a particular time in his life.

THE *PERIPLUS OF THE BLACK SEA*

"We arrived at Trapezus, 'a Greek city,' as the other Xenophon says, 'settled on the sea, a colony of Sinope,' and we welcomed the sight of the sea from the same place that Xenophon and you did." With these words addressed to Hadrian, Arrian begins his *Periplus of the Black Sea*,[1] displaying in one sentence that singular combination of personal experience, literary allusion, and empathy with Hadrian his friend and emperor, that characterizes the whole work.

Although the title would appear to place this short work in a traditional genre of coastal guide or mariner's aid, Arrian in fact has interwoven his own travels, material from earlier guides, myths, and items of interest to Hadrian into an original treatise, which although quite varied in structure and content, succeeds in creating an intriguing whole.

A *periplus*, or description of a coastline as seen from the sea, with notices of rivers, harbors, and tribes friendly or unfriendly, was one of the most ancient of Greek prose genres.[2] Often bare lists of names and distances, with no attempt at artful presentation, they nevertheless were valuable to seamen and travelers. Over the years they were copied or rewritten again and again, with only minor changes. Arrian's work on the Black Sea owes much to this genre, and to earlier *peripli* describing the same coasts, yet it is remarkably different from other specimens known to us.

It is, first of all, cast in the form of a letter, a letter to the emperor Hadrian. This is apparent both from the superscription, "Arrian, to Emperor Caesar Trajan Hadrian Augustus, greetings," and the regular use of the second person in referring to Hadrian. The epistolary format in which Arrian couched his work permitted an informality not possible in the usual *periplus* and encouraged an intimacy between reader and the author which allows notices and comments on a variety of subjects to be introduced easily into the rather rigid outline of the *periplus*.

A second notable feature of Arrian's works is the first-person narrative used in the chapters 1–11.[3] Journey narratives in the first person usually appear as a genre quite distinct from the objectively presented topographical description found in other *peripli* and indeed in the later chapters of Arrian's essay. Xenophon's *Anabasis*, with which our author was quite familiar, may have influenced the presentation, but is not really parallel. An autobiographical travel narrative, it was nevertheless neither a *periplus* nor written in the first person. A closer model may be found in Nearchus' first-person narrative of his voyage from the mouth of the Indus to the Persian Gulf, preserved by Arrian himself in his *Indike*. But whatever the source of his inspiration, Arrian's markedly personal description of his own voyage along the short segment of the coast from Trapezus to Sebastopolis revitalizes the traditional *periplus* and blends perfectly with the epistolary format he adopted.

Finally, in keeping with the emphasis on his own experience and his relationship with Hadrian, Arrian has broken with the natural and traditional structure of the coastal gazetteer, which was a continuous itinerary tracing the features of the coast from one end to the other. On a closed body of water such as the Black Sea one would naturally begin at the Bosporus, circle the sea, and return to one's starting point. Arrian, by a striking dislocation, treats the sections of his *periplus* discontinuously, beginning with the part he had personally toured.

The effect again is to emphasize his own experiences and to encourage us to look with a fresh eye on his entire account.

The *Periplus of the Black Sea* is divided into three parts: (a) the coastline from Trapezus to Sebastopolis (1–11); (b) from the Thracian Bosporus to Trapezus (12–16), with a transitional paragraph (17); and (c) from Sebastopolis to Byzantium (18–25). Although it describes only a small fraction of the coast, the first part is both the longest and the most interesting. It undoubtedly was the first part of the work conceived, a natural product, for a literary man, of one of the duties of the governor of Cappadocia. Shortly before Arrian took office, Hadrian had inspected that part of the Cappadocian frontier where the river Euphrates formed a defensive line against Parthia, visiting the legionary camps of Melitene and Satala and proceeding north to Trapezus on the Black Sea before turning his attention to other areas.[4] Arrian therefore found it his first duty—probably on the direct instructions of the emperor—to inspect the northeastern frontier of the province and of the empire. The voyage of inspection which Arrian undertook sailing around the southeast corner of the Black Sea from Trapezus (Trebizond) to Sebastopolis (Sukhum) proved the inspiration for the present work.[5]

The purpose of the voyage would have been both military and diplomatic: to check on the Roman garrisons and fortifications in the towns and to strengthen the influence of Rome over the tribes and kingdoms of the interior.[6] The region south of the Caucasus had been recognized as important to Roman interests since Pompey first pursued Mithridates into Colchis in the second quarter of the first century B.C. Never prone to lose interest in an area once contacted, the Romans continued to maintain a network of alliances with the petty kings of the region, as well as with the major states of Iberia and Albania. Garrisons were stationed at strategic points, to help or threaten the native rulers. Roman ships patrolled the Black Sea, and at one time Nero thought of forming a transcaucasian province. When Arrian arrived in Cappadocia, about A.D. 131, the northward extension of his province was limited to the coastal cities as far north as Sebastopolis, but his responsibilities extended inland to the various semiindependent native tribes whose kings had been established or recognized by the emperor.[7]

Arrian's voyage, therefore, represented official business, and he presents us with interesting glimpses of the activities of a governor on inspection.[8] At Hyssou Limen, he put an infantry cohort through its paces (3.1); at Apsaros he paid the five cohorts and inspected their weapons, the fort, the sick, and the supply of grain (6.2); at Phasis he examined the natural and artificial defenses of the place and constructed a ditch to protect the anchorage and the town that had grown up around the fort (9.3–5). At Sebastopolis he paid the soldiers and made a general inspection reviewing horses and arms, watching the cavalry leaping onto horses, visiting the sick and examining the grain supply, the wall, and the ditch (10.3). The amount of detail is sufficient to satisfy the reader and to teach a lesson, undoubtedly intended by Arrian, concerning the proper performance of the duties of a commanding officer.

These activities, of course, would have been reported in the regular dispatches in Latin which Arrian mentions were sent back to Hadrian (6.2, 10.1).[9] Not only would the Latin dispatches have gone into more detail on the dispositions and recommendations of the governor, they would have contained material which Arrian did not see fit to publish in the *Periplus*. Both citations of the Latin dispatches show that Arrian thought they would have a more limited audience than his *Periplus*, despite the fact that the latter was formally a letter to Hadrian. After describing his inspection of the five cohorts at Apsaros, he states (6.2) that his opinion or decision (*gnōmē*) on what should be done with them can be found in his dispatch; on a second occasion (10.1) he alludes to a special mission in Chobos: "Why we stopped there, and what we did there, the Latin documents will explain." There is no question of avoiding repetition between the dispatches and the *Periplus*; such facts as the reviews of the various garrisons and the payment of troops were surely reported in the dispatches as well as the *Periplus*. Rather, Arrian intended the *Periplus* for the general public, as well as for Hadrian, and therefore found it desirable to suppress certain kinds of information, such as his recommendations on (reducing or enlarging or transferring?) the garrison at Apsaros. As has been seen, this area was sensitive and involved judicious use of military strength and diplomacy. Only a few years after this trip the Alans crossed the Caucasus and threatened Cappadocia, "having been stirred up by Pharasmanes," the king of Iberia, the state which guarded the Caucasian passes.[10] Arrian wished to keep his recommendations for Apsaros secret, and the same is true of his dealings, presumably of a diplomatic nature, at Chobos. The latter town was in the country of the Apsiliai, whose king, Julianus, had received his crown from Hadrian, as had his neighbor Rhesmagas, king of the Abasci (*Per.* 11.3).

Arrian may well have met with Julianus or his representatives, or other natives of the area, but not wished to mention the encounter or its results in the *Periplus*.

Arrian conceived of the *Periplus* as a literary exercise as well as a letter to Hadrian. In fact, the two ideas are wedded, for the author allows his intimacy with the emperor to establish a particular personal tone for the work, an informal report of what he has seen and done. In the first section especially, Arrian's personal observations suffuse with special charm the scheme of an itinerary which underlies his work. The governor visits the temple with the statue of Hadrian on the height of Trapezus, overlooking the sea: "Your statue stands there, in a quite suitable posture—it points to the sea—but as to workmanship it is neither a good likeness nor otherwise handsome. Please send a statue worthy to be called yours in the same pose" (1.3–4). He also comments on the inscription which had been on the altars ("the letters are not clear, and the Greek epigram is also incorrect, as you might expect, since it was written by barbarians"),[11] on the statue of Hermes there, and on the sacrifice he himself offered for Hadrian. Thereafter, Arrian describes a storm which forced them to land at the little port of Athens: the scene is developed in the best rhetorical manner, with references to Homer and a citation from tragedy. Again, the governor visits the garrison on the Phasis, but the gentleman tourist discourses on the sweetness of the river water (with another citation from Homer), the statue of the goddess of Phasis, and even the anchor of the *Argo* the natives pointed out: "But since it was iron it did not seem to me old—although the size is not that of modern anchors, and the shape is somehow altered" (9.2). Finally, "as we turned from Astelphos toward Dioscurias, we saw the Caucasus range, about equal to the Celtic Alps in height. One peak of the Caucasus was pointed out—the name of the peak was Strobilos—where according to the story Prometheus was hung by Hephaestus on Zeus' order" (11.5).[12] The author in these chapters continually reminds us of his presence, his experiences, his thoughts. Even when this personal account is interrupted by the two chapters listing rivers and tribes passed on the journey (7 and 11.1–3), the first person is preserved in the phrase "we sailed by" at 7.1, 3, 4, 5 and 11.1. Moreover, when speaking of the Sanni, Arrian intrudes forcefully, identifying them with the tribe called by Xenophon Drillai and declaring that although they had been recalcitrant in the past, "now they will pay tribute, God willing, or we will destroy them."[13]

The second part of the *Periplus of the Black Sea*, describing the south shore of the sea, represents a middle ground between the journey narrative of the first section and the impersonal account of the third.[14] The first-person directness found in the first section is for the most part absent, yet one still finds a knowledge and interest in the area not common in the traditional *periplus*. Several causes would appear to contribute to Arrian's attention to this part of coastline. As a native of Bithynia, he would have had opportunities from his youth to become acquainted with people and towns along the coast. About a third of this coastline belonged to Bithynia, and one of the most important cities, Heraclea, was Bithynian. Not long before, Hadrian had stopped at inland points on his journey from Trapezus westward, although he had probably not touched the coast.[15] Arrian himself may have sailed along this coast as far as Trapezus when taking up his post in Cappadocia, although he does not mention such a trip.

The greatest influence on the Nicomedian in this section, however, was undoubtedly Xenophon. The Athenian soldier-author had returned with the Ten Thousand from Trapezus to Byzantium along this coast, and described his adventures in Books V and VII of his *Anabasis*. Xenophon was in many ways Arrian's favorite author; as we have seen, his own Greek name was Xenophon. He alludes to the famous narrative of his namesake in the first sentence of the *Periplus* and quotes his description of Trapezus, "a Greek city, settled on the sea, a colony of Sinope."[16] He cites Xenophon twice more in the first section, comparing his own rich sacrifice at Trapezus with the poor one with which Xenophon had had to make do at Kalpes Limen,[17] and equating the Sanni and Drillai,[18] and once in the third section, with respect to Salmydessus.[19] But the whole second part of the *Periplus* recalls the march of Xenophon. Although there are only four direct citations of Xenophon in this section, Arrian has in fact included every notice of a city given by the earlier author.[20] Even in a bare mention such as that of Heraclea Pontica (13.3: "from the Lycus to Heraclea, a Greek city, Doric, a colony of Megara, twenty stades"), the words "Heraclea, a Greek city, a colony of Megara" are quoted from Xenophon. In this case as in other works, Arrian composes independently, but pays homage to his classical namesake.

While personal comments are relatively sparse compared to the first section, they are not wholly absent. Fittingly in a letter to Hadrian, the section begins and ends with words addressed to the emperor. After describing the strait from the Black Sea into the Propontis, he adds, "I speak to you as one who knows" (12.2). When he finally reaches Trapezus, he notes, "At this place you are constructing a harbor" (16.6). In between, although the notices generally follow the spare *periplus* formula, "whence, whither, and distance" (e.g., 16.1, "from the Thermodon to the Beris River, ninety stades. From there to the Thoaris River, sixty"), he occasionally allows himself to describe a post in some detail.[21] The most notable case is suggested by the river Halys, made famous by Herodotus as the boundary of Croesus' kingdom. The Roman senator and consular recalls Herodotus, but adds that "now [the river] flows under Roman sovereignty" (15.1).

A transitional paragraph (17) explains the author's reasons for including the third section of the coastline. The first section held a special interest because of Arrian's own observation; the second because of the echo of Xenophon and Arrian's long contacts with the area. The third and by far the longest stretch of Black Sea littoral held neither of these attractions, but Arrian suggests that Hadrian might wish to visit the area, especially since Cotys, king of Bosporus, had just died, and therefore he will give an account also of the northern and western coasts. In fact, however, he has very little to say, and this section is overall the least original of the three and closest to the other extant descriptions. To enliven the ancient *periplus* scheme, Arrian inserts four brief digressions and one major excursus into the monotonous flow of names and distances.[22] The first digression concerns the Tanais (Don) and the old question of the division between Europe and Asia,[23] and gives occasion to recall the passage from Aeschylus' *Prometheus Unbound* in which not the Tanais but the Phasis is called the boundary of Asia (19.1–2). In other digressions he mentions Herodotus on the Scythians (18.1–2), Xenophon's activities at Salmydessus (25.1–2), and the Argonauts' passage of the Cyanean Rocks (25.3). But by far the longest digression, one third of the whole section, is devoted to an account of an island sacred to Achilles and the special cult observed there.[24] The narrative of the excursus smoothly progresses from the island itself (Leuke, opposite the mouth of the Danube), to the dedications and epigrams in both Greek and Latin found there, to how the hero himself selects those who may offer sacrifice. The climax of the digression is an encomium of Achilles, who was truly deserving of the special honors paid him on the island: "For I believe that Achilles was a hero if anybody was, considering his high birth, his beauty, his strength of character, the fact that he left the world of men when still young, the poem of Homer about him, and the fact that he was a lover and attached to his comrade, even choosing to die for his favorite" (*Per.* 23.4). The immediate relevance to Hadrian is unmistakable. In October 130 the emperor's favorite, Antinous, had drowned in the Nile. Some said that he had died so that Hadrian could continue to live. At once a cult was founded in his honor and statues of him erected by cities and individuals throughout the Greek world. Arrian, writing about two years after Antinous' death, in this digression on the isle of Achilles discreetly alludes to the sacredness of the relationship between the emperor and his beloved.

Here, apparently, is a major, if unexpressed, reason why Arrian decided to include an account of this third section of the Black Sea coast. In chapter 17 he had suggested that Hadrian, who so much enjoyed travel to every part of his empire, might wish to undertake a trip to the Black Sea. The isle of Achilles would certainly tempt the emperor to make the journey, for there he could find feelings such as he held for Antinous remembered and honored. But Hadrian's travels regularly combined business and pleasure, and if Arrian suggested that he should visit the Black Sea, it was not just for sightseeing. The death of Tiberius Julius Cotys, king of Rome's most important client on the Black Sea, the Bosporan Kingdom,[25] noted in the same transitional paragraph, would undoubtedly mean a reevaluation of Rome's role in the area, and Hadrian might well wish to inspect the situation personally. In this last section Arrian adroitly combines practical knowledge and the appeal of the cult of Achilles on Leuke to match the emperor's varied interests.

Arrian makes no claim to having seen this coast and expressly states that he has heard the tales of Achilles' island from others.[26] What in fact was the source of his information? The roots of the problem lie in the dual nature of the work itself—a *periplus* written with knowledge of the tradition, but by a Roman governor on active service, who in the first section at least shows a lively interest in contemporary facts. Is this third section, on an area which Arrian did not visit, a rehash of older guides, reporting information long obsolete, or does it incorporate up-to-date information furnished by Roman patrols, merchants, and diplomatic contacts? In this century archaeological finds along the northern and western shores of the Black Sea have challenged the accuracy of Arrian's account. The focus of the problem is his treatment of two cities, Theodosia in the Crimea and Tyras (modern Belgorad) on the estuary of the Dnestr. Theodosia, according to Arrian, was deserted (19.3–4), and the entire coast from Isiakon

Limen, just south of Odessa, to the Danube—in which would be included the region of Tyras—was deserted and without names (20.3). However, inscriptions and artifacts found on the site demonstrate that both these cities were active long after Arrian's day.[27] At the turn of the century, scholars concluded that this contradiction proved that the third part of the *Periplus* was not in fact by Arrian, but was composed some centuries later.[28] This extreme view was rightly rejected by Reuss, Patsch, and Roos, who demonstrated that Arrian was indeed the author.[29] Roos, however, found it necessary to argue that Arrian's account did not represent the contemporary situation, but rather that described by an earlier writer, datable in the period between 50 B.C. and A.D. 50. The most satisfactory suggestion has been advanced by Rostovtzeff,[30] who pointed out that the cities of the Black Sea coast beyond the Roman frontiers suffered frequent and unpredictable raids by the highly mobile Sarmatians, who controlled the steppes. Although the Roman presence on the northern and western shore of the Black Sea was strong in the time of Nero and Vespasian, under Domitian and Trajan—perhaps as a result of the new attacks by the Dacians— the Romans withdrew, not to reappear again until Hadrian and the Antonines. Given this situation, Rostovtzeff argued, it is possible that, deprived of Roman protection, cities such as Theodosia and Tyras were overwhelmed by the Sarmatians and temporarily abandoned. Thus Arrian's report could be valid for the time he was writing, although the cities had flourished not long before, and would again. In support of his position, Rostovtzeff adduced the strong "Scythian" presence in the Crimea attested by Arrian's work, in which several cities normally considered Greek are called Scythian or Scythotaurian.[31]

If Rostovtzeff's hypothesis is valid, Arrian's account emerges not only as accurate and contemporary, but as the first indication of a renewed interest in this area on the part of the Romans. By calling the emperor's attention to the cities left deserted by the nomad raiders, Arrian would have encouraged Hadrian to act to strengthen the Bosporan kingdom and the Greek cities of the north. Two years after Arrian wrote his *Periplus*, the new Bosporan king, Rhoemetalces, dedicated a statue of Hadrian as his benefactor and donor of his kingdom (*ktistēs*).[32] Hadrian had begun a policy of active involvement in South Russia, which was continued in the second half of the century with numerous Roman garrisons in the Crimea, and the corollary, a new life for the Greek cities of the area. Arrian's interest in the area, as a native of a Pontic land and as governor of Cappadocia, would have been one of the factors alerting the emperor to the defense of the Black Sea settlements.

The *Periplus* of Arrian, while uneven in content and interest, remains a highly unusual and ultimately successful treatise, revealing the author's literary skill, confidence in managing ancient traditions, and ability to achieve a variety of purposes in a single work. In this case he has combined discreet praise of the emperor, thoughts on the proper duties of a governor on a tour of inspection, a travelogue, and a general view of the lands beyond the frontier, all in the framework, and frequently in the style, of the ancient *periplus*. We can be thankful that Arrian decided to supplement his Latin dispatches to Hadrian with this multiform booklet.

THE TACTICS

The same capacity to combine contemporary interests with references back to the classical past is discoverable in different ways in two other short works, the *Ars Tactica* or *Tactics* and the *Ectaxis* or *Battle Formation against the Alans*, both of which can be securely dated to the period while Arrian was governor of Cappadocia, and reflect Arrian's knowledge of military matters and his ability as a commander. The *Tactics* was only partially relevant to the military procedure of Arrian's day, since the first half of the work described the practices of Macedonian and Hellenistic armies.[33] The military organization of these armies was passed down from generation to generation by a series of manuals, of which three have survived, by Asclepiodotus (first century B.C.), Aelian (ca. A.D. 110), and Arrian himself in the first portion of the *Tactics*. It is the nature of manuals, especially those on technical subjects, to repeat themselves, and these are no exception. All three seem to derive independently from a common source, for although there are various differences they frequently repeat each other verbatim. Arrian and Aelian are especially close in certain sections.[34]

Arrian's essay, however, while carefully preserving traditional material, is distinguished from the other manuals on military affairs. As governor of Cappadocia, with two legions under his control, he would have been familiar with the problems of organizing and maneuvering an army, and this knowledge reveals itself in his book. Although we have lost the first page of the treatise, which might have explained his decision to write, the book itself shows that he had a double purpose.

The first portion, describing Hellenistic tactics (1–32), since it is derived from the standard manuals through the source used also by Aelian and Asclepiodotus, represents simply a better presentation of standard material. Arrian's innovation is the second part, an account of contemporary Roman cavalry exercises, which demonstrates his recognition that the earlier manuals were not enough but needed to be supplemented by a section on present-day practice. This second part indicates a dissatisfaction with standard works and implies an attitude toward the purpose of such manuals different from that of his predecessors.

The *Tactics* was not in fact Arrian's first work on the subject, for at *Tact*. 32.3 he writes, "I have already explained the infantry exercises [used by the Romans] in a treatise I wrote for the emperor himself." This earlier work on contemporary Roman infantry exercises has been lost, but evidently it formed a unit with the *Tactics*, which complemented it both by giving a version of the standard historical material on Hellenistic infantry and cavalry practice and by describing contemporary Roman cavalry training. This earlier work on the infantry, Arrian tells us, was dedicated to the emperor Hadrian, who was very much occupied with military reform and visited frontier camps throughout his empire, including those in Cappadocia. The *Tactics* was written for an unknown third party, but we may presume that Hadrian would have read with interest both works, composed by a trusted friend in a responsible position.

The first part of the *Tactics* follows the exact scheme of the earlier manuals, with their standard pattern of subdivision and explanation: types of combatants by equipment (3–4); organization of infantry and cavalry units, from the *lochos* of 16 men to the full army of 16,384 (5–10); formations and use of troops in battle, including the phalanx, cavalry, and chariots (11–19); the movements of the army (20–27); march formation (28–30); and the proper form of commands (31–32). Although very similar to Aelian's manual, Arrian's shows significant minor changes, generally in the use of examples drawn from history or contemporary Roman practice to clarify the abstract definitions and categories of the traditional handbook. Arrian's experience along the Danube and in Cappadocia led him to supplement the standard account of cavalry weapons by mentioning the lances used by the Alans and Sarmatians, the missiles of the Armenian and Parthian cavalry, and the special weapons of contemporary Roman cavalrymen. The traditional but no longer relevant section on the names of the various chariot and elephant formations was replaced by a brief account of the use of chariots in warfare, influenced both by Xenophon's fictional *Education of Cyrus the Great* and Roman experience against chariots in Britain. The general effect of the numerous small changes in Arrian's version of the traditional manual is to weed out unnecessary repetition and present the Hellenistic practices as being at least potentially useful to a contemporary military commander.[35]

In the second half of the *Tactics*, the change of contents, as Arrian describes cavalry exercises in which he has been directly involved, is reflected in a new tone, lively and enthusiastic. No longer summarizing a manual, Arrian now recounts from his own experience a typical sequence of cavalry maneuvers before observers. Such demonstrations were a regular feature of military camps. A speech of Hadrian, partially preserved in an inscription, commends the various companies of cavalry and their commanders after a performance at the legionary camp of Lambaesis in Africa in A.D. 128,[36] and Arrian himself mentions one he had observed at Sebastopolis in his own province (*Per.* 10.3). No longer content with a drab recital of long-forgotten formations, Arrian makes the troops of horsemen rush and swirl before our eyes, executing the complicated maneuvers required of them.[37]

All was specially prepared: the field carefully spaded up to loosen the earth, the troops in special uniform, more elegant and impressive than battle dress. Especially striking were the helmets, which covered not only the head but the whole face behind the metal mask and had long golden hair which would flare out as the riders rushed onto the field. The tunics of the riders, worn over trousers of the Parthian type, dazzled the eye with their scarlet, yellow, or other bright color. The exercise began when the whole troop suddenly entered and swirled across the field, each company following the striking standard flowing behind its leader. The standards, in the form of snakes, had been borrowed from the Scythians and "are made of dyed cloth sewn together, shaped like snakes from the head and the body all the way to the tail, as terrible as possible. When the horses are still, these devices seem no more than colored cloths hanging down, but when they run, they are filled with air and become impressive, coming to resemble the animals quite closely, and they whistle somewhat from the strong movement caused by the violent rush of wind" (35.3–5). The high visibility of these distinctive standards also aided in executing complicated maneuvers, as each man simply followed his dragon standard.

After this dramatic entrance, the troops performed several exercises in which the men could demonstrate their ability throwing their spears at a target while riding past, either in a company or single. The mass maneuver, when group after group rode by hurling their spears at the target, was especially impressive, Arrian assures us. After these exercises, the best men were selected for a special contest—a ride at full gallop across the field, launching as many spears as possible. A good man could throw fifteen, and an expert twenty.

Finally the troops put on regular battle armor to shoot at targets, first in companies and then individually, as each man's name was called, following special figures ordered by the emperor. This last individual exercise was especially difficult, and Arrian states, "Whichever squadron furnished the largest number of men outstanding in this drill I praised more than any other, as being truly practiced in deeds of war" (42.5).

Arrian alludes to but does not describe in detail many other drills, including the use of other missiles, such as stones, and of the thrusting lance.

Throughout this half of the work Arrian stresses the excellence of the Roman system, especially its readiness to incorporate foreign ideas into its own practice. Initially he noted that many of the names of the exercises were foreign because they had been imported from other nations, and he recalled Roman willingness to assimilate foreign ways: clothing from the Etruscans, the Great Mother from Phrygia, and laws from Athens (*Tact.* 33). Among the maneuvers described are several foreign exercises—the Petrinus and the Toloutegon (Celtic), and the Cantabrika (Iberian). The last chapter praises Hadrian for incorporating still other exercises, not described, which were borrowed from the Parthians, Armenians, Sarmatians, and Celts, and for encouraging the barbarian troops in the cavalry to use their native war cries. Hadrian also insisted that the cavalry learn to jump ditches and walls and revived old exercises, some of which had been abandoned, and encouraged others, some for show, some for battle. Arrian enthusiastically concludes, "So that in this present reign of Hadrian, now in its twentieth year, those famous verses seem to me to be much more appropriate now than to ancient Sparta: Here the spear-point of youth blooms, and the smooth-voiced Muse, / And broad-wayed justice, the support of fine deeds" (44.2–3).

Although not written for Hadrian, as was the book on infantry maneuvers, the *Tactics* was written with him very much in mind. Hadrian had taken a personal interest in the army and especially in the cavalry, as his addresses to the troops at Lambaesis attest. In the *Tactics* we see how warmly Arrian supported this care of the emperor's and how he shared his interest in the improvement of the army. Several times in the second half Arrian injects his own comments, either to remark on the impressiveness of the sight or to praise participants (37.1, 39.1–2, 42.5). Arrian has participated in these exercises and has stood on the platform as a commanding officer watching proudly but critically as his men went through their paces. He is excited by this army, and the role he has had in training it. The first section of the *Tactics* might seem irrelevant, simply pinned on to the second, more personal half. However, there is a connecting link in the paragraph already mentioned recalling the many customs which the Romans have borrowed from other peoples (*Tact.* 33). There were many good features in Hellenistic military practice, and the implication is that the Romans might find here also features which they could with profit incorporate into their own training. There are indications of such an attempt in Arrian's third work on tactics, the *Battle Formation against the Alans*.

THE *BATTLE FORMATION AGAINST THE ALANS* (*ECTAXIS*)

This work is short, truncated at the end,[38] and most unusual in form. The booklet is a detailed statement of the troops which Arrian led against the Alans when they threatened the Roman province in A.D. 135, his plan of march, his dispositions before the battle, and his instructions to his forces for the battle itself.[39] But rather than use a standard narrative presentation, such as one would find in a historian, Arrian uses throughout third-person imperatives and infinitives with imperative force, following the usage of an actual military order. The affinity with a genuine document is increased by reference to identifiable military contingents, such as the *Cohors III Ulpia Petraeorum miliaria equitata sagittariorum*, somewhat more simply named by Arrian as "the Petraean horse-archers." There are no direct parallels to Arrian's use of imperative forms, since we have no other copies of a battle order, but a military regulation from several centuries earlier preserved on stone uses the same forms.[40] The extended use of these forms also seems to indicate that this work was not a part of Arrian's lost account of the Alans, the *Alanike*, or of another historical work, for there is no precedent for such an insertion into a historical composition.[41] Arrian frequently describes marches and battle dispositions in the *Anabasis*, but never in this form. Bosworth seems right in concluding that it represents a separate essay, written as a sidepiece to another work. He suggests that it complemented a report to Hadrian on the Alan campaign, as the *Periplus* did Arrian's formal report on his expedition along the Black Sea coast. More likely, however, it belongs in the context where we find it in our unique manuscript, that is, immediately following the *Tactics*. We might then imagine this work as united in conception with Arrian's other tactical works: the first, now lost, on Roman infantry maneuvers; the second, the *Tactics*, on Hellenistic practice and Roman cavalry maneuvers; and the third, the *Ectaxis*, giving a practical example of the use of the formations and exercises described in the previous books. Arrian would have rewritten his dispositions as commander of the expedition for readability and comprehension, while preserving the format of a series of orders.

There is no doubt that the style of the *Ectaxis* has been polished to make it accessible to a larger audience than the officers of the army in Cappadocia. This is especially evident in vocabulary, where he uses an archaizing terminology, echoing in some cases that used in the first part of the *Tactics*. Most notable is his use of *phalanx* for *legio*, rather than any of the several regular Greek equivalents.[42] The Alans are regularly given the general classical name for the Northern nomads, Scythians, although by this time the term was no longer accurate. The same affectation is found in the *Periplus* and the *Tactics*. We have already noted that Arrian does not use the precise technical names for the components of his army, but a less cumbersome but sufficiently precise form, such as was in general use. He has also included explanatory phrases which would hardly have been necessary in an actual order of battle, such as the description of the lance bearers at *Ect.* 16: "That is, those who have lances with long, thin points." Despite these modifications, the *Ectaxis* has its basis in the actual dispositions made against the Alans and provides us with a unique document on the activity of the Roman army. The marching order (*Ect.* 1–10) is similar to that described by other writers,[43] but Arrian shows unusual caution in protecting both flanks with his cavalry, using the horsemen attached to the individual contingents and two special squadrons detailed to ride in a single file on either side of the column. Archers and javelin-men positioned before each contingent provided a further safeguard.[44] In his dispositions for the battle (*Ect.* 11–24) Arrian's posture is defensive: to resist the anticipated onslaught of the Alan armored cavalry he established a mass of infantry eight deep, similar to the Hellenistic phalanx in appearance but not in purpose. Rather than charge the enemy, Arrian's phalanx was to meet the horsemen with thrusting pikes and spears aimed at horses and riders. However, Arrian places his greatest confidence not in this massed formation but in the large number of missiles his force could launch— in modern terms, in his firepower. On his flanks, in fact, and behind the legions he has stationed archers, horse-archers, javelin-men, and catapults, and from these he expects to lay down a devastating barrage: "At the moment the enemy approaches all should shout the war cry 'Enyalios' as loudly and terribly as they can, and shoot missiles and stones from the catapults and arrows from the bows, and the light-armed javelin-men should throw their javelins. The allied troops on high ground should throw stones onto the enemy, and the whole barrage should be from every direction as thick as possible, to bewilder the horses and kill the enemy. The hope is that because of the indescribable quantity of missiles the Scythians in their rush will not draw nearer to the infantry phalanx" (*Ect.* 25–26).

Apparently Arrian's army was completely successful at halting the Alan attack—it is unlikely that Arrian would have written up his battle order if this were not the case, and the historian Dio tells us that the Alans were frightened away by Arrian. It is possible that there never was any confrontation, but rather that on hearing that the Romans had marched against them, the Alans decided to withdraw north of the Caucasus.

Bosworth has collected evidence indicating that after Arrian opposed the Alans, he went on into Iberia, the country which controlled the Darial Pass through the Caucasus.[45] Pharasmanes, the king of that country, had rejected an invitation to meet Hadrian when the emperor was in Cappadocia and called a congress of the client kings of the area. We have noted in discussing the *Periplus* that Arrian visited an unusually large Roman garrison at the mouth of the river Apsaros, watching the route to Iberia, and at Chobos was busy about some business which he chose not to discuss.[46] Pharasmanes clearly was troubling the Romans, and his decision to invite the Alans across the Caucasus, even though their ostensible goals were his neighbor Albania and the Parthian vassal state of Media Atropatene, was considered dangerous to Roman interests. After repulsing the Alans Arrian therefore seems to have proceeded to Iberia and reasserted the Roman presence there, regulating as well the boundary between Iberia and Albania. In any case we find at this time that a high official of the Iberian court has a Roman name (Publicius Agrippa, the *pitiax*),[47] that toward the end of Hadrian's reign Pharasmanes made a royal present to Hadrian, and was given a Roman cohort in return, and finally that early in the reign of Hadrian's successor, Antoninus Pius, the king made a personal visit to Rome and was confirmed in his kingdom by the emperor. Arrian's march against the Alans therefore not only drove that horde from the frontiers but furnished an occasion for Roman influence to be reasserted in this important client kingdom.

One of the striking features of the *Ectaxis* is the similarity of the tactics described to those we find in the *Anabasis*. One such feature is the use of massed infantry, which Arrian goes so far as to call a phalanx, although in fact he intended to use these troops defensively rather than as an attack force. The fact that many of Arrian's troops were armed with long pikes which they were to hold firmly before them increased their resemblance to Alexander's soldiers with their long sarissas. Arrian also drafted for himself a special guard of two hundred legionaries who were to be called bodyguards, imitating the elite corps which Alexander kept as bodyguards to himself.[48] Finally, both the *Ectaxis* and the *Anabasis* stress the effectiveness of missiles in difficult situations. The *Anabasis* presents innumerable occasions in which Alexander used his javelin-men and archers to good purpose, such as against the Thracians in the mountains (*Anab.* 1.1.11–12), against Darius' scythe-chariots (*Anab.* 3.12, 3.13.5), and against Scythian horsemen (*Anab.* 4.4.4–5), and Nearchus used them to cover his amphibious landing against the natives at the river Tomeros (*Ind.* 24.4–8). On one occasion after Alexander's death, recorded by Arrian, a Macedonian phalanx opposed a cavalry charge by drawing up in close ranks and stationing their own cavalry in the rear, who "began to fire javelins where the opportunity offered, in order to throw back the cavalry charge by the continuity of their barrage."[49] Arrian used archers to protect his march, and especially to break the charge of the Alans. These and other similarities are surely more than fortuitous. Many of the techniques used by Arrian on this occasion would have evolved over the years as the Romans fought with nomad horsemen, most recently against the Getae in Dacia and the Parthians during Trajan's Parthian adventure. But a wise general learns also from earlier campaigns, and Arrian seems to have learned not only from Trajan but from Alexander. Although we cannot assert with any confidence that he had written the *Anabasis* by this time, there is no doubt that he had read the campaigns of Alexander carefully and attempted to draw upon them for his own use.

In this respect we should note especially a technique of narrative found in the *Ectaxis* which is found also in the *Anabasis* and *Indike*, by which Arrian interprets his presentation of troop dispositions, adding explanations and statements of purpose. The method is clear in the following passage: "Before these should be stationed the two hundred Apulians and the one hundred Cyrenians, so that the heavy infantry can serve as a defensive wall in front of the missilemen, and the latter can throw over them from the high ground" (*Ect.* 14). The *Ectaxis*, like the historical works, was written for an audience interested in tactics, and therefore Arrian not only reports his orders but explains to his readers the intention behind them.

The written works which can be securely dated to Arrian's term as governor of Cappadocia, the *Periplus*, the *Tactics*, and the *Ectaxis*, reveal the dual citizenship of this unusual man, between the world of the past and that of the present, between literature and military arts, between Greek curiosity and Roman competence. Xenophon is set side by side with Arrian's own experience on the Black Sea coast, a Hellenistic military manual is linked with the exercises he has marshalled and witnessed in his own camp, and Alexander's tactics are made to serve in his own campaign against the Alans. Arrian neither retreats into his Greek heritage nor flees from it; proudly and consciously he incorporates it into his active life as a Roman imperial official. In Hadrian, moreover, he found a kindred soul, under whom he could serve proudly. The philhellenist emperor shared the same interest in innovation, in the past, in learning from others, and in renewing oneself. In addition to the interest in philosophy and the military, they shared a passion for hunting, another subject on which Arrian wrote a treatise.

4

THE JOY OF HUNTING

IN no work does Arrian reveal himself more directly and personally than in his little treatise on hunting, the *Cynegeticus*.[1] Hunting was one of the major delights of Arrian's life,[2] and his pleasure in his dogs and in the chase suffuses every page of this essay. The influence of the classical age on the life of cultured Greeks of the second century A.D. was such, however, that this booklet also gives us the best evidence of Arrian's devotion to this past and especially to his namesake Xenophon, who had written a handbook on the same subject.

Hunting—of every sort of animal, from hares to lions—was the favorite sport of the emperors and their friends in the first half of the second century.[3] Both Trajan and Hadrian were passionate hunters, though in different ways. Trajan seems to have pursued animals as he did enemies, finding in those few periods when he was not leading armies a similar satisfaction in attacking boars or bears. Hadrian in this as in everything else appears the connoisseur of experience, tempting every part of the world for the swiftest, bravest quarry, the greatest challenge.[4] The *Life of Hadrian* in the *Historia Augusta* comments on his constant hunts, which even resulted in his injuring his neck and leg. After the chase he would banquet with his hunting companions, among whom we may expect Arrian on occasion to have been numbered. As Hadrian moved restlessly from province to province of the empire inspecting the camps and frontiers, he relaxed with vigorous hunts. A description in his own words of his pursuits in Italy is found in a poem inscribed on a monument to his horse Borysthenes, one of the Scythian breed which Arrian tells us had improved the sport: "Alan Borysthenes, imperial steed. He used to fly after Pannonian boars over plains and marshes and Etruscan hills. No boar dared harm him with foaming tooth as he pursued, nor spray the tip of his tail with the spit from his mouth, as usually happens. Whole, young with untouched limbs, he was cut off by his day. In this field he lies."[5] Although written in praise of the hunter's horse, the poem gives a vivid picture of the ruler of the world racing across the fields of Tuscany, chasing boars imported from Pannonia, astride a stallion bred on the steppes of Russia, exulting in the strength and bravery of the animal he rode. Hadrian had particularly successful hunts in Mysia in Asia Minor, and founded a city on the spot, aptly named Hadrianotherae, "Hadrian's Hunts." We possess as well an inscribed poem dedicated at Thespiae in Greece to the god Eros, himself a hunter with a bow, recalling the kill of a bear and asking the god to be temperate. In Egypt he and his favorite, Antinous, killed a lion, a deed which was celebrated by the Greek poet Pancrates in a flattering poem.

The sport appealed to the Roman upper class, and especially to the emperors, for a variety of reasons. It was, of course, enjoyable and exciting, and had been a traditional sport for centuries, especially among the wealthy at Rome—the younger Scipio praised hunting as being the ideal activity for a gentleman of leisure. But the rationale went much deeper, as Aymard has shown, drawing upon the references in literature, on coins, and in art. First of all the chase was seen as parallel to war and thus good both to train the young in the martial arts and to exercise the warrior in time of peace. As in a battle, one could learn the use of weapons, display courage, and win a glorious triumph over a dangerous enemy. The equation of manly strength in battle and in the hunt is found in the coins of Hadrian, where the sovereign appears galloping with a javelin raised to strike a lion, with the caption *Virtuti Augusti*, "the bravery of the emperor." Character was also formed by hunting, because it taught one to endure labors and dangers. Pliny the Younger in his panegyric addressed to Trajan stressed the emperor's constant devotion to the duties of his office and argued that his time spent hunting was not a cessation, but a change of work, necessary for recreation: "What relaxation do you have but riding through woods, prodding beasts from their dens?" he states approvingly.

Both Trajan and Hadrian on their coins present their hunting as a sign of their own courage and vitality and of that of the empire. Both Trajan and Hadrian especially honored Heracles, who in this period was seen as a hero who had roamed the world killing monstrous beasts and freeing men from the evils which oppressed them. The image of the emperor slaying lions and boars is similar, and it gave a political justification and meaning to this sport. The tondos on the arch of Constantine, which were originally made for a monument of Hadrian, are perhaps the best expression of this role of the emperor. In the eight finely carved reliefs the emperor is seen alternately sacrificing to the gods of the chase and hunting, either spearing a bear and a boar, or standing proudly over a fallen lion.[6]

Not only the emperors and their friends, but other upper-class Romans, especially those stationed as governors or officials in the provinces, shared the mystique of hunting. In the time of Hadrian, we might mention the African Tullius Maximus, commander of the *Legio VII Gemina* stationed in northern Spain, who celebrated in a dedication to Artemis his prowess against goats, deer, boars, and wild horses.[7] The newly discovered inscribed altar dedicated by Arrian at Cordoba provides further evidence, if it were needed, that Arrian was one of this group, not only when at ease in Athens, where the *Cynegeticus* was written, but when in Spain as proconsul of Baetica. The altar is inscribed with an epigram which reveals something of his attitude toward the sport: "I offer to you, Artemis, immortal gifts of the Muses, better than gold or silver and much better than the catch; it is not right for those who feast on others' property to bring as gifts the horns of their enemies to a goddess."[8] The altar and epigram are dedicated to Artemis, traditional goddess of the hunt. The epigram explains Arrian's dedication; using a common conceit, the poem notes that poetry, the Muses' gift, is immortal, and better than precious metals or the catch itself. In fact, Arrian goes on, it is not suitable for those who eat what belongs to others—presumably referring to the hunters who eat the animals who belong to Artemis—to bring the horns of their enemies (the animals) as gifts to Artemis.

The epigram confirms that Arrian hunted and that he believed that the goddess of the hunt should not be neglected.[9] The unusual thought lies in the second half, which suggests that it is in some way wrong for the hunter to offer a part of the prey to the goddess, as Tullius Maximus, for example, had dedicated deer's horns and boars' tusks. Giangrande argues that Arrian is being something of a skinflint in holding back from the goddess even the customary offering of horns, tusks, or head. However, even if we think of this as a humorous epigram, the idea of being cheap toward the gods is not what one would expect of Arrian. Rather we must look to Epictetus' teaching, with its insistence upon the difference between what is one's own and what is foreign and belongs to another. One could reasonably only be proud of one's own things, not of what one owed to another. Arrian elegantly plays on this theme in this epigram—not only is the poem immortal, and therefore better than silver, gold, or the catch, but also it is something created by Arrian, and therefore properly his to offer. Over money or a good catch he has no control, but he can proudly dedicate his epigram to the goddess. The altar and its inscription reveal that Arrian was one of those Romans who took advantage of their duties in the provinces to try the hunting there, but they equally demonstrate that—at least in writing this epigram—he brought an independent mind to his sport.

A similar independence is apparent in his treatise on the chase. The classic work on hunting in Greek has come down to us under the name of Xenophon, and it was treated by Arrian as a genuine work by that author.[10] After an elaborate introduction recalling how the Greek heroes learned to hunt from Chiron, the centaur, and praising the effect of hunting on the individual and the body politic, Xenophon turns to practical instructions, advising in turn on nets, stakes, and net-keeper, the good and bad qualities of hounds, the scent and behavior of the hare, general hunting procedures, breeding of dogs, tracking hares in snow, and hunting other animals, such as deer, boar, and more exotic game. After these chapters of practical wisdom Xenophon concludes with a discourse on the advantages gained from hunting, citing first the various ways in which it prepares one as a soldier and citizen, then contrasting the honest hunter with the sophists and politicians who neither practice nor teach what is necessary for the state. Despite his concentration on the tracking of hares on foot, and avoidance for the most part of other sorts of hunting, Xenophon presents a useful handbook, which is still our chief source of information on this kind of hunting in the ancient world.

But hunting as practiced by Arrian and his contemporaries had changed beyond recognition from the simpler days of Xenophon. Hadrian's poem is an indication: the emperor's wealth permitted him to enjoy the best in mount and quarry, even in Italy—a horse from the steppes, boars from Pannonia. However, the most far-reaching innovation was the introduction of fast Celtic dogs, *vertragi*, akin to our greyhounds.[11] Xenophon's Laconian hounds were slow and hunted by scent, so that a hunt for a hare was time-consuming and not infrequently unsuccessful, as the hare's speed would allow it to escape if it could confuse its trail. For this reason Xenophon found it necessary to describe subsidiary equipment such as nets, snares, and caltrops, which could increase the chance of bagging the quarry. On the contrary, the Celtic hounds used by Arrian and his friends hunted by sight and could overtake the fastest hare—Arrian in fact complains that if a hare is started too close to the dogs, they will catch it before it has a chance to run at all. The hunters followed the chase on horseback, not on foot, as described by Xenophon, and the pleasure of the hunt was in the excitement of the chase itself and in watching the performance of the dogs and prey.

When he decided to supplement Xenophon's work by describing the techniques of hunting used by his contemporaries, Arrian did not reject his namesake outright but chose to use him as a model and interweave his own presentation with that of Xenophon.[12] From the very beginning he recognizes his debt to his predecessor, opening with the words "Xenophon the son of Gryllus has said" and summarizing Xenophon's work in his preface. This introductory précis permits Arrian to note the omissions which make the present work necessary— ignorance of the Celtic hounds and of Scythian and Libyan horses. Since he already shares so much with Xenophon, the author tells us —name, city, and common interests in hunting, generalship, and philosophy (*Cyn.* 1.4)—it is proper that he undertake the work, which moreover is justified by its usefulness.

After a brief demonstration that Xenophon could not have known the kind of hunting practiced by the Romans, Arrian sets out in straightforward fashion to describe modern hunting. The Celtic hounds, *vertragi*, are described in chapters 4 and 5.7–7.7, the care of the hounds in 8–14, the chase in 15–18, hunting with Scythian, Illyrian, and Libyan horses in 23–24, the particular rules for training and breeding *vertragi* in 25–32, and the honors to be paid the gods in 33–36. Other uses of Celtic hounds than those favored by Arrian are more briefly described in 19–22. The treatise is neatly organized, with a more rational scheme than that of Xenophon, but does not convey the air of a technical manual in the manner of, for example, the first half of Arrian's *Tactics*.

On the contrary, the *Cynegeticus* is distinguished by the human warmth and feeling of Arrian's personality as dog-lover. Arrian loves his hounds, and his sensitivity to their qualities comes alive in his treatise. At one point, when discussing the proper eye-color for these hounds, he bursts spontaneously into an encomium of his own favorite, which is worth quoting in full:

Gray eyes are not at all bad, and they are not a sign of inferior hounds, if they also happen to be clear and bright. In fact I myself have raised a hound, gray-eyed as can be, which was fast, eager for work, stout-hearted, and stout-footed, so that in his day he once held out against four hares. Moreover he is quite even-tempered (he is here with me now as I write this) and friendly, and never has another dog missed me or my comrade and hunting-companion Megillus as he does. For since he has abandoned the chase, he never leaves the side of one or the other of us. If I am inside, he waits for me, and he accompanies me wherever I go, and he follows with me when I go to the gymnasium, sits beside me while I am exercising, and goes ahead as I leave, turning every once in a while to make sure that I haven't turned from the road. Then when he sees me he smiles and goes on once more. If I go about some political activity, he stays with my comrade and does the same thing to him. If one of us is tired, he does not leave him. And if he sees one of us even after a short absence, he jumps up gently, as if giving a greeting, and with the greeting speaks as if showing affection. When he is with me when I am eating, he places himself on one or the other of my feet, quietly reminding me that he should be given a share of some of the food too. Moreover, he has a variety of barks, such as I don't think I have noted in any other dog: whatever he needs he signals with his voice. Because when he was a puppy he was punished with a whip, if anybody even now says "whip," he goes up to the person who has said it, and cowering down entreats him, and places his mouth against his as if he were kissing, and jumping up clings to his neck, and does not give up until the one who is angry stops threatening him. Therefore, I have no hesitation to set down his name, so that something of him may survive: Xenophon of Athens had a dog, Horme by name, very fast, very intelligent, and very special. (*Cyn.* 5.1−6)[13]

Here Arrian reveals himself more perhaps than in any other passage in his works. We are permitted a brief glimpse into his life at Athens with his friend Megillus and his daily routine visiting the gymnasium or doing public business. Most evident, however, is his feeling for his hound, his pride in its hunting skill, its little tricks and habits. The passage implies a reciprocity of friendship between man and dog, seen in the walk from the gymnasium or the awareness of the dog at dinner. Such faithfulness and devotion prompt Arrian finally to immortalize his dog by including its name in his work.[14]

His feeling for his animals is revealed in other passages as well.

He delights in their appearance: "The noblest of them are a thing of beauty in eyes, in body, in coat and color; the pied color stands out so well in the pied hounds, and the solid color in those which are solid-colored—it is the sweetest sight to a hunter!" (*Cyn.* 3.7). The adjectives with which Arrian describes the *vertragus* are tactile, sensual: the neck is long and supple, and "if you pull the dog backwards by its collar, the neck will appear to bend double"; tails are "thin, long, shaggy, flexible, curved, shaggier at the tip." Moreover, to Arrian the animal's temperament is as important as its appearance. In particular, hounds should be friendly. Those which dislike humans should be avoided, and even those which respond well to their handlers are not as desirable as those which are friendly to all. Again, the relation of hound to hunter is reciprocal. The hunter must be concerned for his animals and watch how they eat; in fact it is best if a man sleep with them, so he can notice whether they are sick, need water, or need to be let out.

Interestingly enough, Arrian's feeling for his hounds extends to his quarry. Unlike Xenophon, Arrian finds it crude to hunt hares for meat and insists that for true hunters the pleasure is in the chase itself, when there is real competition between hare and hounds. They rejoice when a hare can escape, and try to rescue a hare which has run well. He himself tried to do this, Arrian writes, "and if I arrived too late to save the hare, I struck my head, because the hounds had destroyed a brave antagonist." Unlike Xenophon, Arrian does not enjoy the sight of the hare as it is caught, which he finds rather disgusting. The goal of hunting for him is not the quarry, but the chase.

Yet another aspect of the author's personality is apparent in Arrian's insistence that good hunting, like anything else, is a gift of the gods and that due acknowledgment to Artemis and the other gods of the hunt is necessary. He imitates the eclecticism he elsewhere praised in Hadrian and the Romans in general in recommending that hunters honor Artemis in a manner borrowed from the barbarians: "I myself and my hunting companions follow the Celtic custom." Rather than dedicate a piece of the slain animal to Artemis as the Romans did, the Celts would set up a kitty, into which they would put a certain sum for each animal—two obols for a hare, six for a fox, etc. Then at the end of the year an offering would be bought with the money and sacrificed to the goddess. Arrian followed this practice and considered his honors to the goddess essential to his activity as hunter. Not only success in the chase, but every good thing depends on the favor of the gods. Just as those traveling on board ship sacrifice to Poseidon, farmers to Demeter, artisans to Hephaestus, and lovers to Aphrodite, Eros, Persuasion, and the Graces, hunters also should sacrifice to the proper gods. If not, their efforts will remain incomplete, their hounds will be injured, their horses lamed, the men disappointed.

Perhaps the most interesting feature of the *Cynegeticus*, however, is that Arrian writes this very personal statement of his joy in hounds and hunting in a continuous counterpoint with the earlier treatise by Xenophon which he is supplementing. He hints at this relationship by frequent citation of his namesake, quoting or paraphrasing phrases or sentences. But the relationship is much deeper, amounting in places to an unspoken dialogue with Xenophon. Perhaps most noteworthy is the case of Arrian's description of the qualities to look for in a *vertragus* (*Cyn.* 4–6). This dog, as we have seen, was rather like a greyhound, tall, very fast, and a sight hunter, markedly different from the scenthounds used by Xenophon. Yet Arrian, in listing the physical features of this hound, moving from head to tail to feet, chooses to follow Xenophon's description point by point, feature by feature. The only hint that he is using Xenophon appears in his introductory phrase, "I too will describe [the ideal hound]," implying that he is following after an earlier writer. He takes pleasure in preserving whenever possible the adjectives used by Xenophon, but since the animals were so dissimilar, he must frequently contradict Xenophon's description, sometimes in quite determined opposition to his mute and anonymous interlocutor. To take but one example, Xenophon had specified that the head should be "light, snub-nosed, well-formed, sinewy in the back." The *vertragus* did not fit this description, but Arrian tries his best to use the same words: "They should have light and well-formed heads. It does not matter much whether they are long-nosed or snub-nosed; nor should much be made of whether their heads are sinewy in the back. Rather only those who are heavy-headed are bad, and those which have muzzles which are fat and cut off sharply rather than drawn to a point." Arrian's description becomes more complicated than it need be because he wishes to consider all the points raised by Xenophon regarding a quite different breed of dog. The warm description of the excellent qualities of his favorite hound, Horme, is provoked by Xenophon's stricture against gray eyes, since Horme had gray eyes.

Similar passages appear throughout the work. Arrian will echo with approval what he can accept of the earlier writer—on having the puppies suckled by their own mothers, for example, or on the proper form of names for dogs. But when the nature of the dogs requires, Xenophon is adroitly corrected, as in the manner of training the young dogs, so different in the case of hounds that hunt by sight.

In Arrian's use of Xenophon's *Cynegeticus* two features especially stand out which are important indicators toward our understanding of all his works. First, the case of the *Cynegeticus* is one of the few in ancient literature where we can trace the influence of one ancient work on another, not by hypotheses about a lost original, but by comparison of the two extant works. What becomes apparent in this instance is that Arrian has treated Xenophon's text respectfully yet freely. Although his booklet reveals that he has read and considered every word of the earlier work, his citations run the whole gamut from general reference to free paraphrase to verbatim quotation and frequently glide back and forth from one to the other in the same passage. The phrase which introduces the citation gives no indication of its nature or limits, and the use of the earlier author is not limited to those passages in which he is cited.[15] In sum, it would be impossible for us to delimit Arrian's debt to Xenophon, or his own original contribution, or to reconstruct Xenophon's book, from the text of Arrian alone. Arrian writes as if conversing with a reader familiar with Xenophon, or with Xenophon himself, carefully examining each point raised by that author and insisting on his own consideration, but the resulting composition does not lend itself to a simple source-analysis, assigning certain paragraphs or sentences to Xenophon and others to Arrian. This fact becomes particularly important when we turn to consider Arrian's use of sources in his historical works, especially the *Anabasis* and the *Indike*.

The second feature is Arrian's attitude toward the great writers of Greece's classical past, appreciative yet self-assured and independent. There is no doubt that he admires Xenophon and has studied his treatise with painstaking thoroughness, yet he suffers from no sense of inferiority or longing for that golden age. This citizen of the Roman empire and friend of Hadrian is confident that his age represents an improvement over the past, and his personal goal is emulation, not mere imitation of authors like Xenophon. By his use of Xenophon he sets himself in the classical tradition, but his belief that modern methods of hunting were preferable to those of the past indicates his pride in the accomplishments of his own age. Nowhere is this fact more manifest than in the passage where Arrian recalls a scene from Xenophon's *Anabasis*. Xenophon describes how Cyrus the Younger, a son and brother of the kings of Persia, had found it impossible to capture the wild asses of the Syrian desert with the horses he had at his disposal unless he set up relay stations to provide him with fresh mounts until he could run his prey to exhaustion. Yet in his own day, Arrian notes, eight-year-old Libyan boys riding bareback and without bridles on Libyan horses could ride down such wild asses and lead them docilely home (*Cyn.* 24.2–3). The contrast is so dramatic that it prompts Arrian to a rhetorical outburst: "This is how those hunt who have good dogs and good horses, not tricking the animals with snares, nets, nooses, cunning, or traps, but challenging them openly. How different the spectacles are! The one kind of hunter approaches his prey as a pirate stealthily sails up; the other conquers openly, as the Athenians conquered in the sea battle at Artemisium or at Salamis and Psytalleia or off Cyprus." Far from being one of those Greeks who turned wistfully back toward a greatness which they now had lost, Arrian sees himself as part of a world which in many ways had progressed with respect to the classical past, not least in the excellent animals the modern hunter has at his disposal. A Greek, he shows himself thoroughly assimilated into the ruling class of Rome and considers his own their wealth and privileges, their sports and pastimes. The use of Celtic hounds and Scythian and Libyan horses was one way in which the elite of the Roman empire enjoyed the fruit of Roman rule, and although Arrian respects and cites his classical namesake, he is proud to live in his own day and exults in practicing a form of hunting he considers immeasurably superior to that of earlier times.

5

THE *ANABASIS*: AIMS AND METHODS

DESPITE the variety and interest of his other writings which have survived, the history of Alexander the Great remains for us Arrian's major work, both in size and in quality. It is his only sizable historical work to survive, and although shorter than others now lost, one of which he apparently was quite proud. While from his other historical works we possess only fragments, and can draw only tentative conclusions about them, in the case of the *Anabasis* one can hope to come to a closer understanding of the author, the way he worked, and the way he thought, not least because in this work he expressed his own opinions frequently. On the other hand, our study of the datable works has alerted us to certain themes which we may expect to find in the *Anabasis*: the sense of ethical independence taught by Epictetus, the emphasis on proper formations and dispositions in warfare, the proud yet critical attitude toward the Greek past.

THE PREFACE AND THE OTHER PREFATORY STATEMENTS

The most obvious statement of Arrian's attitude to his own work is his preface to the *Anabasis*, which must be supplemented by two other related statements at 1.12.2−5 and 7.30. The preface or proem as a formal element of a history was a well-defined feature of ancient historiography. Best known from Herodotus (1.1−5) and Thucydides (1.1−23), it is found from the earliest historians down to Byzantine times.[1] The content was represented by a set of standard features (*topoi*) which included the name of the author, his method, an indication of the importance of the work or of its subject, and a justification for publication.[2] Thus Herodotus in his first sentence gives his name and the purpose of his work, the preservation and praise of the deeds of the Greeks and barbarians. The following chapters (Hdt. 1.1−5) explain the method of impartial inquiry he will use. The whole brings

out a strong sense of the author's individuality and his relation to the
material, particularly his manner of acquiring knowledge.[3] Internal
proems, such as Herodotus 7.20–21 and Thucydides 5.25–26, may
be recognized by the appearance of those same features. Arrian, by a
creative reworking of these *topoi*, which had been standard for centuries, established his own relation to his history.[4]

The preface proper (*Anab*. pref. 1–3) is built on three *topoi*: the
subject, the method, and the justification of the work. The subject is
presented firmly, though indirectly: Alexander the son of Philip. Each
sentence discusses Alexander historians,[5] and Alexander's name appears five times in these few lines. The method is stated straightfor-
wardly. From among the host of these historians,[6] Arrian has chosen
two, Ptolemy and Aristobulus. He will present the matters on which
they agree as true and will select from those matters on which they
conflict according to probability and interest (pref. 1). The two were
chosen because they had the double advantage of having participated
in the expedition, yet had written their histories after Alexander's
death. Occasionally other historians report matters which are interesting and not completely incredible, and these he will report as *legomena*, that is, "what is said" (pref. 3). Arrian's method of using his
sources as stated in this paragraph is also a partial justification for
writing the work, for the historian concludes his proem with a bold
statement: "Whoever is surprised that I have decided to write this
history, after so many others, should read first their works, and then
mine—then let him be surprised." Arrian had argued that Ptolemy
and Aristobulus were more reliable than other historians of Alexander, and decided a history compounded of the two would be more
reliable still and thus by its superior accuracy and credibility justify
the existence of yet another history of Alexander.

The self-assurance of such an emphatic statement shifts attention
from the method to the author himself.[7] The name of the author, one
of the most regular *topoi*, is missing from this preface, yet the presence
of the author is strongly felt as the force behind the whole and expressed through the frequent use of first-person pronouns. The depth
of the author's involvement in the work is made explicit in the so-
called second preface at 1.12.2–5. Arrian has described the activities
of Alexander's first year as king and now is narrating the beginning
of the Persian campaign.[8] After Alexander crossed the Hellespont, he
visited Troy and the tomb of Achilles, and there "Alexander called
Achilles fortunate, in that he had found Homer as herald for his fame

in time to come." [9] The long passage which follows is a new proemial statement developing some of the ideas of the first and introducing new ones. There is a clear progression of thought:

1. Achilles' deeds were made famous by Homer (12.1).
2. The deeds of Alexander have not been worthily celebrated (12.2).
3. Therefore the deeds of others who have done less are more famous, e.g., the Sicilian tyrants, Xenophon and the Ten Thousand (12.2–3).
4. But Alexander did more than any other man (12.4).
5. So I have decided to make manifest his deeds (12.4).
6. I am worthy to do this (12.5).

Or, more briefly: This history of Alexander needs to be written and I am the one to write it.

Several thoughts are combined in this passage. First of all, by the reference to Homer and Achilles, Arrian places himself in the tradition of those who celebrate the great deeds of the past, whether in prose or poetry, and recalls not only the "famous deeds of men" of Homer but the proem of Herodotus, "lest great deeds . . . become obscure." [10] As elaborated in the following sentences, the purpose of the book will be a combination of preservation and praise, as it was with Herodotus.[11] Unlike Herodotus, however, Arrian is making the point that earlier historians of his subject have not been satisfactory. Arrian is not a near contemporary of the events he celebrates, and many years and many historians have intervened, as Arrian noted in the preface: "There is no one about whom more have written more variously." Jacoby in his collection of fragments lists over thirty writers of histories, including contemporaries to Alexander such as Callisthenes and Onesicritus, and famous rhetorical historians such as Clitarchus and Hegesias, not to mention Ptolemy and Aristobulus. In Arrian's own day Plutarch had written a hundred-page biography of the conqueror, and Dio Chrysostom eight books on the virtues of Alexander. Not long before, Curtius had written his *History of Alexander the Great* in ten books.[12] The second century saw as well the origins of the Alexander romance, which influenced so strongly—and unfortunately—the later view of Alexander.[13] In stating that Alexander has not been properly "published to the world," therefore, Arrian is developing the thought expressed at the end of the preface, that his history will surpass all previous histories of Alexander. The preface had implied that the *Anabasis* would be more reliable; here Arrian suggests that it will make Alexander more famous. The comparisons adduced, the choral odes of Pindar and Bacchylides for the Sicilian tyrants and Xenophon's history of the march of the Ten Thousand (and of course, Homer's *Iliad*), show that Arrian is thinking of fame of the highest level and that in this passage the criterion of superiority is artistic excellence. His history of Alexander's deeds will make Alexander justly famous by being in a class with the works of Homer, Pindar, Xenophon.

Such excellence is demanded by the subject matter, Alexander and Alexander's deeds (12.3; cf. 12.2, 4). Alexander accomplished deeds matched by no Greek or barbarian, and he deserves to be made famous. The use in this section (12.3–4) of comparison, especially to the expedition of the Ten Thousand, and of rhetorical magnification is part of the *topos* of establishing the importance of the subject. The *topos* is the more suitable in this case because it is exactly Alexander's greatness which requires a new and better history. Alexander was hardly an obscure figure in the second century, either among the Greeks or the Romans,[14] but Arrian argues that he was not known worthily, that is, by a history which in reliability and literary merit would be on a par with Alexander's deeds.[15]

As a further indication of the purpose of the history, we should note that the subjects of the works cited for comparison, Achilles, the Sicilian tyrants, and Xenophon and the Ten Thousand, all reflect personal achievements. Herodotus and Thucydides, both of whom described movements more than personalities, are notably absent. Despite its many debts to Herodotus, the *Anabasis* was not intended to be a history of a war between East and West (or Macedonia and Persia), and still less a history of the world during the reign of Alexander. The single-minded focus in the *Anabasis* on Alexander and his deeds is the source of many of the complaints addressed against it by modern historians. Its silence on affairs in Greece, on Persian strategy, on the problems of administration—in short, on almost anything that did not involve Alexander directly—is a natural consequence of Arrian's conception of his work. Combined with the idea of praise, this restriction of subject gives a strong biographical color to the whole. The *Anabasis* is not the study of a war, or of a movement of peoples, but of a man.

Having justified in this way the necessity and importance of the history, Arrian turns to himself and his own decision to undertake the work. The sentence in which he explains himself has troubled interpreters and translators:[16]

> I who make this decision [to write about Alexander], whoever I might be, have no need to record my name—in fact it is not unknown among men—nor my native city, whatever it is, nor my family, nor whether I have held any magistracy in my country. But I do record this, that for me these writings are and have been since my youth native city, and family, and magistracies. (*Anab.* 1.12.5)

These words represent a reversal of the proem *topos*, identification of the author. Herodotus and Thucydides are the most familiar historians to include in their proems their name and native city, but the usage both preceded and followed them. One need only recall Arrian's contemporary, Appian:

> Who I am who write this, many know and I have set forth, but to say it more clearly, Appian of Alexandria, who have come into the first rank in my native city, and have pled cases in Rome before the emperors, so that they thought it suitable to entrust their property to me [i.e., as *procurator Augustorum*]. And if anyone desires to know the rest, I have written a treatise on this subject as well. (Proem 15.62)

Name, city, offices, and even a reference to his autobiography. This recording of family and offices was common in imperial writers, not so much for identification as to lend dignity and authority to the work.[17] Arrian is specifically renouncing this *topos*, refusing to give his name, city, family, or offices. This renunciation is based on two motives.

The first is philosophical, representing an attitude of mind taught by his master Epictetus. As we have seen, the Stoic ex-slave insisted that man should not glory in anything which depended on outside forces, nor should he regret or lament their loss. Among these external possessions, Epictetus repeatedly told his hearers, are magistracies, honors, friends, parents, children, and native city. None of these are solely under one's control; their possession is not a glory, nor their loss a hurt.[18] In the passage in question, then, Arrian is following the teaching of his master: he will not record his name, native city, family, or offices, because they are not really his to boast of.[19] He will record, and therefore glory in, what is his—his writings, which can be truly considered his own, over which he has control, and for which he is responsible. They are important for establishing who he is and whether he is truly worthy to write a history of Alexander.[20]

The second motive is literary, a consequence of the need for artistic excellence in a fitting history of Alexander. The only valid evidence of such excellence is Arrian's work itself, and it is on this basis that he refers to it here as a guarantee of this history's quality. In the preceding paragraph Arrian has established a series of great men and writers who made them famous: Achilles—Homer, Sicilian tyrants—Pindar, Xenophon—Xenophon. To this list he wishes to add Alexander—Arrian. Alexander won his place by skill in warfare; Arrian must win his by his writings,[21] which, he tells us, have been everything to him since his youth.[22] This passage naturally leads to the following sentence: "For this reason [the importance of my writings to me] I consider myself worthy of the first rank in the Greek language, if indeed Alexander was in arms." Like Homer and Achilles, he and Alexander will be united in excellence, each dependent on the other, each completing the excellence of the other.[23]

Most of the foregoing proemial themes reappear in the concluding chapter of the *Anabasis* (7.30). As in 1.12.2–5, the central themes are praise of Alexander and the relationship between Alexander and his historian. Following upon two chapters in which Arrian evaluated Alexander's virtues and failings and found the latter minor in comparison with the former, this last chapter begins with a challenge which echoes the challenge at the end of the preface.[24] "If someone finds fault with Alexander, let him first . . ." consider the whole man, and his greatness, and his own insignificance. The challenge at the end of the preface asserted the greatness of Arrian's history, the challenge here the greatness of Alexander. The two are related because it is exactly Arrian's history which will allow a man to consider "what Alexander became, what height of human prosperity he reached, how he became undisputed king of both continents, and spread his name throughout the world." Alexander's fame, in the sense of the opinion held of him by posterity, is assured by Arrian's history. In that an honest presentation of Alexander must reflect this greatness, Arrian's is essentially a work of praise. In rejecting the carping of insignificant men, he is clearly thinking of those philosophers and rhetoricians who took pleasure in denigrating Alexander's achievements, minimizing his

virtues, and ascribing all he accomplished to the blind goddess Fortune.[25] The scorn heaped on those struggling with insignificant things,
and not accomplishing even these, seems to recall the consideration of
name and offices at 1.12.5. Although he does not boast of them there
or here, Arrian has accomplished things of importance. Since he has
likewise considered the whole Alexander, he has also the right to
criticize (7.30.3, *ekakiza*, the same word used earlier in 30.1) certain
acts of Alexander, yet he does not hesitate to admire the man. It was
this admiration which moved him to write this history (30.3).[26]

Arrian does not believe that Alexander's success was due to Fortune, but he does recognize and affirm a supernatural involvement in
Alexander's greatness (30.2) and like Homer sees it as strengthening
his hero's claim to fame. After Alexander's death oracles and visions
urging men to honor him confirmed the favor he found with the gods.
Arrian himself is of course fulfilling this divine injunction to honor
Alexander in writing his history. This is one meaning of his final sentence, "I too with God's help undertook this history." But another
meaning certainly present is "As the greatness of Alexander's accomplishments is a sign of divine favor, so is the excellence of my history."
The self-confident assertion of superiority, found in the last sentence
of the preface, "let him read, then let him wonder," is present here as
well. Arrian and Alexander are united as Homer and Achilles. And as
Arrian wonders at Alexander, we—for thus we should conclude the
proportion—may wonder at Arrian.

ARRIAN AND HIS SOURCES

Despite the deceptively simple statement in his preface, Arrian's practice in his use of sources needs careful evaluation, especially in the
light of the self-awareness of the author which has just been considered. The statement in the preface stresses the author's intention of
presenting a true and credible account, based on reliable authors, yet
leaves a large area free to Arrian's judgment of his material, with regard not only to its credibility but also to its narrative interest.[27] Two
related problems thus are posed: why exactly did Arrian choose to use
Ptolemy and Aristobulus, and on what basis did he select material
from them and the rest of the tradition (*legomena*), i.e., what to him
was more credible and especially more worthy of narration?

Our author, when he set out to compose the *Anabasis*, was a successful and self-confident writer. Besides works in other genres, he had

probably written the seventeen books of his *Parthica* and perhaps other historical works. His control of style, ranging from an educated *koinē* in the *Discourses of Epictetus* through the Attic of his shorter works and the *Anabasis* to the Ionic of the *Indike*, is apparent in all he wrote. Thus we need not expect Arrian to have considered narrative or stylistic criteria in selecting a source: those qualities he could himself contribute.[28] The function of his sources was to be in the nature of a commentary or memoir, which he could use as the factual basis for his history. Whether in fact they were written with such an idea is of course irrelevant; Arrian's intention was not to preserve his sources but to supersede them, as his own challenge in the preface makes clear.

In choosing Ptolemy and Aristobulus, Arrian rejected more famous writers for two rather obscure authors. Ptolemy is hardly known apart from Arrian; Aristobulus, although known and even praised by Plutarch, is not in the mainstream of Alexander historians. The choice indicates a rejection also of much that Alexander history represented: flattery, gossip, the marvelous, the romantic and novelistic. Arrian notes two motives for his choice (pref. 2), the facts that both writers had accompanied Alexander and that both wrote after his death, when the most obvious reasons for bias were removed. Both features were guarantees of relative reliability long known to ancient historians.[29] Other factors also would have influenced our author, especially the presence of "documentary" material (lists of satrap assignments, detailed accounts of marches, etc.) and the basically favorable attitude shown to Alexander by both writers. However, the very fact that Arrian chose relatively obscure authors as his sources renders difficult the discussion of their use, since in large part the writers are known only through Arrian himself. We thus have no easy touchstone by which we can positively distinguish the contribution of his sources from Arrian's own artistic composition and invention.

A great deal is known about Ptolemy Lagou, later Ptolemy I of Egypt, as a historical figure, very little as historian.[30] He was said to have been a boyhood companion of Alexander (perhaps even a bastard of Philip), but he only came to prominence in the later years of Alexander's reign. After Alexander's death, he managed to build his satrapy of Egypt into a power base which allowed him to repulse all efforts to reunite the empire or be absorbed by the Seleucids. His brilliance as statesman and soldier did not blind him to cultural values, for he founded the library and *museion* at Alexandria. Yet of his history of Alexander, despite the thirty fragments listed by Jacoby (*FGrHist* 138), we know neither title, nor scope, nor size, nor purpose, nor date. Everything that we know of his life suggests that it would not have been merely an old soldier's memoirs, but just as dynamic and purposeful as his other activities. Most likely, it was conceived as one more weapon in the battle to maintain his position in Egypt, its date being more probably in the period 318–311 B.C. than in the 280s as once was believed.[31]

The fragments surviving are preserved almost exclusively by Arrian. Of the rest, three are parallel versions of citations in Arrian and two parallel unascribed paragraphs in Arrian, although with some discrepancies. The rest remain dubious, not to say incredible.[32] Needless to say, we doubt the latter precisely because they differ so strongly from the impression we gather from Arrian. With our knowledge of Ptolemy so strictly limited to what Arrian tells us, we have no indication of exactly what sort of things he described, or of what material from Ptolemy's history the later author might have omitted, an essential part of the selection process.[33] However, a few positive statements can be made about Ptolemy's history. It described military affairs, especially those in which Ptolemy himself was involved, such as the capture of the pretender Bessus.[34] It reported supernatural signs, such as the two snakes which led Alexander's way across the Libyan desert to the oracle of Ammon.[35] Ptolemy wrote about things which he had not seen (or said he had not), such as the wounding of Alexander among the Malloi (*FGrHist* 138 F26). He painted in vivid colors Alexander's gracious treatment of the Persian queen and princesses captured at the battle of Issus, but was able as well to note his politic use of bad omens as an excuse for retreating from Hyphasis after his officers had opposed him (F23). He omitted not only the fabulous (the Carmanian bacchanal, the Amazons, the Roman embassy—F27, 28, 29), but things which we might have expected to find, such as a description of the Indus bridge (F19). Ptolemy is quoted on occasion for details, but despite his close ties with Alexander, only one notice seems to show special knowledge: the queen mother's request for mercy for the Uxians (F12).

Aristobulus' case is rather different, for about his life we know next to nothing, while his history was quoted not only by Arrian but by Strabo, Plutarch, Athenaeus, and others.[36] Nevertheless, concerning the scope, purpose, title, and size of his work, we are as ignorant as with Ptolemy's history. Those who attempt to deduce something

of the character of his history from the assumption that he was an
engineer, architect, or technical officer of some kind with Alexander's
army build on sand.[37] There is no evidence for his having held such a
position. He was a Greek, and not involved in military operations, but
he may have come with Alexander as a historian, secretary, botanist,
geographer, or whatever.[38] He was curious enough to visit Cyrus'
tomb and write down a record of its contents, a sufficient explanation
for his being chosen to supervise the restoration of the tomb after its
despoliation (*FGrHist* 139 F51). His neglecting to describe the Indus
bridge (F34) argues against his being an engineer. But whatever his
reason for accompanying Alexander, the story of Cyrus' tomb does
suggest that Aristobulus was taking notes even during the expedition
(as does the anecdote of his reading to Alexander while sailing on the
Hydaspes, T4). Nevertheless, he delayed the final composition of his
history for some time, for he mentions the battle of Ipsus of 301 (F54).

From the geographer Strabo we learn that Aristobulus was a mine
of detailed geographical and ethnographical information. He is quoted
by that writer fifteen times, seven times for India.[39] Only a small part
of this material was used by Arrian and the rest was excluded—rich
sections on Hyrcania, India, the Gedrosian desert, and the customs
of the Brahmins and the inhabitants of Taxila.[40] Plutarch and Athenaeus quote Aristobulus for a number of anecdotes, odd details, and
witticisms, only a few of which found their way into the *Anabasis*.
For example, Arrian reports Aristobulus' version (together with that
of Ptolemy) of Alexander's generous care for the captured Persian
women (F10), but he suppresses the story that Alexander took Barsine
to his bed (F11). He uses an anecdote from Chares of Mytilene about
Callisthenes' being denied one of Alexander's kisses (*FGrHist* 125
F14 = 4.12.3−5), but not that told by Aristobulus, in which Callisthenes retorted that he would need Asclepius if he had been kissed
(F32). A reference to the spring of Achilles at Miletus (F6), which
might have been used in the development of the Achilles-Alexander
comparison in the *Anabasis*, was omitted, and a brilliant descriptive
passage on Tyre (F12) apparently was replaced by Arrian's own
thoughts on Heracles Melkart (2.16.1−6). These cases indicate that
Arrian had felt no compunction in deleting what he thought "un-
worthy of narration" from Aristobulus' history, and presumably from
Ptolemy's as well.[41]

A major purpose of the *Anabasis* was to present a credible account,
and these two basic sources were chosen for their reliability. Ptolemy

and Aristobulus seemed to Arrian both serious enough and, apparently, sufficiently in agreement to provide a firm basis for his narrative. In his preface Arrian makes their agreement the foundation of his narrative, and in fact he frequently cites the two authors together for a fact, usually against the vulgate. A smaller number of citations marks their disagreement on minor details.[42] In these latter cases, Arrian generally decides that exactitude is neither possible nor necessary. So at 5.20.2 he writes, "The name of the tribe [in India] was Glauganicae, as Aristobulus says, or according to Ptolemy Glaucae. I do not care which name it had." In two cases of disagreement, however, Ptolemy is preferred for special reasons, Ptolemy's own involvement (3.29–30) and Arrian's judgment of military probability (5.14–15). Once, however, Arrian reveals his exasperation with his two fundamental sources when they disagree. After writing of the condemnation of Callisthenes, he continues, "Aristobulus says that Callisthenes was bound in fetters and led about with the army, then died of an illness, but Ptolemy says that he died by hanging after being tortured. So not even those who are completely reliable for their account and accompanied Alexander at the time have written concordant accounts of what happened concerning well-known matters of which they were aware" (4.14.3). The historical method explained in the preface had held out a promise of complete accuracy based on the agreement of eyewitnesses. Arrian regretfully discovers that occasionally even trustworthy contemporary accounts will differ.

Nevertheless Arrian hopes that his narrative will correct the generally mistaken accounts current in his day, as he explains in his major statement on the subject. At 6.11.1–2 he describes the wound Alexander received among the Mallians, then comments, "Many other stories have been written about this wound by historians, and legend has picked them up from those who first lied and preserved them to our day, and will never cease passing on to others in turn these inventions, unless it is halted by this history" (6.11.2). In the following digression he corrects two mistakes, the first implicitly, the second explicitly, by the use of Ptolemy and Aristobulus. First, Alexander was wounded among the Mallians, not the Oxydracae; second, the great battle with Darius was fought not at Arbela, but at Gaugamela. He grants that Arbela was better known, but notes that it was at least five hundred stades from Gaugamela and concludes, "If we must consider that the battle was at Arbela, when it was actually at such a distance, we can say that the battle of Salamis took place at the isthmus of Corinth, and the battle of Artemisium in Euboea at Aegina or Sunium!" (6.11.6). Accounts were also confused about the number of wounds that Alexander received, but this was a small mistake compared to "the greatest error made by historians of Alexander": some put Ptolemy beside Alexander, protecting him with his shield, whereas Ptolemy himself wrote that he was off fighting some other tribes on that day. Finally, Arrian expresses the hope that historians will be careful in the future in narrating such important events (6.11.8).

Much as he criticizes others, Arrian's method of combining two sources did not preserve him from errors.[43] Every Macedonian knew that the Olympia in honor of Zeus was held at Dium; Arrian becomes confused and places it at Aegae, the capital (1.11.1). In describing Alexander's arrangements at Susa, the name he gives for the new garrison commander is really that of the Persian, Mazarus (3.16.9). As far as we can tell, Alexander did not actually delay his pursuit of Darius by stopping in Ecbatana, as Arrian seems to say (3.19.5–8). These and other similar errors seem to stem from the confusion which arose in collating Ptolemy and Aristobulus, or occasionally from Arrian's tendency to supply more specific information than his source warranted. Such would seem to be the case with the Olympia; the sources may have been silent on the location, but Arrian concluded that it was held in Aegae.

The relatively minor disagreements noted by Arrian suggest that Ptolemy and Aristobulus presented narratives which fundamentally were similar in factual content. Whether this was due to the use of one by the other, or to coincidence, cannot be established.[44] Certainly the omissions practiced by Arrian, which we have been able to document in the case of Aristobulus, served to bring the two accounts closer together. Arrian indicates no preference for Ptolemy over Aristobulus except that indicated in the preface, that he was a king, for whom lying would be more shameful.[45] This is worth remarking, since some scholars have incorrectly taken certain statements as expressing a preference for Ptolemy, misunderstanding their context.[46] Thus at 5.14.5, describing the engagement between Alexander and the son of Porus, Arrian first gives the version of Aristobulus, then of other writers, then concludes, "But Ptolemy the son of Lagus, with whom I agree, writes differently." "With whom I agree" is not a general statement but a choice of a particular variant, based on the probabilities of military action, as he explains in the following sentence ("For it is not likely that . . .").[47] Again at 6.2.4, where Arrian writes, "Ptolemy,

whom I especially follow . . ." the contrast is not so much with Aristobulus as with Onesicritus, who has been cited (and called a liar)
in the preceding sentence. When given a choice between Onesicritus
and Ptolemy, he follows the latter. This interpretation explains his use
of the same expression at 5.7.1 for both his main sources: "Neither
Aristobulus nor Ptolemy, whom I especially follow. . . ." Here, as regularly in Arrian's citations, the two writers are given equal treatment.[48]

In a similar vein it has sometimes been asserted that Arrian relied
on Ptolemy for his military information.[49] The notion is quite without
foundation, as both Aristobulus and Ptolemy reported military matters. Arrian cites Aristobulus, for example, for the Persian battle order
at Gaugamela, which the latter gave on the basis of a captured Persian
document (3.11.3−7 = FGrHist 139 F17). Arrian refers also to his accounts of the capture of Bessus (4.6.1−2 = F27) and the battle with
Porus (6.14.3 = F43). From Plutarch we know as well that Aristobulus
described the capture of Thebes (F2), the number of Alexander's
troops at the beginning of the expedition (F4), the casualties at the
Granicus (F5), and the battle among the Malloi (F46). Ptolemy of
course reported military information,[50] but Arrian found military information in Aristobulus as well as Ptolemy, and the fact that he finds
it necessary to explain on two occasions why he prefers Ptolemy to
Aristobulus indicates that the latter's general reliability was not in
doubt. Arrian nowhere states or implies that Ptolemy is his "military
historian," and we should not presume that military accounts are fundamentally Ptolemy's. Arrian's own military experience would have
aided him in combining his sources not into a patchwork affair, but
into a smooth and straightforward account of military operations.

Granted the general agreement of Ptolemy and Aristobulus, it is useful to consider those areas in which Arrian has chosen to report a story
told by one and not by the other or to supplement both accounts with
legomena, since those were the occasions, according to the methodology expressed in the preface, which Arrian found especially worthy of
narration, even when they did not have the authority of both his major
sources.[51]

A large number of these citations concern specific facts which presumably were not available in other accounts. Ptolemy is cited for the
number of casualties in the battle with the Triballi (FGrHist 138 F1),
Perdiccas' attack on the Thebans (F3), and the size of the river Acesines (F22); Aristobulus for the exact distance to the oasis of Siwah

(F13), the Persian battle order, reported from a captured document (F17), the women Alexander married (F52), and his age at his death (F61). Many of the *legomena* citations (introduced variously by "it is said," "the story has it," etc.) continue this practice of filling in details or providing exact figures. Thus we learn that it took ten days for the army to reach Mount Haemus (1.1.5), the strength of Darius' forces at Issus (2.8.8), the division of the government of Egypt (3.5.7), the number of Darius' forces at Gaugamela (3.8.6), the size of the rock of Aornus (4.28.3), the manner of catching hares in the Gedrosian desert (6.22.8), the number present at the feast in Opis (7.11.9), that the Araxes flows into the Caspian Sea (7.16.3), that Alexander considered rebuilding the temple of Bel in Babylon (7.17.2), that Alexander sent various captured statues back to Athens (7.19.2), and that he gave sacrificial victims to the army before he fell ill (7.24.4). Such notices reflect that love of precision which distinguishes the *Anabasis* from other Alexander histories. Ptolemy and Aristobulus were remarkable, it appears, for the quantity of specific information they provided, in terms of stages of the march, administrative assignments, and movements of troops, but Arrian wishes even so to supplement his narrative with details from other sources.

A particular category of citations is formed by notices of omens, in which those from Aristobulus and *legomena* predominate. A *legomena* version is frequently presented as a variation on a story by Aristobulus. Such notices are the omens seen before the fall of Thebes (1.9.8, *leg.*), the untying of the knot at Gordion (2.3.7, *leg.*, Arist.— whose version is more favorable to Alexander), the grain which marked where the walls of Alexandria would be built (3.2.1−2, *leg.*), the divinely sent guides—either crows or snakes—which led Alexander to the oracle of Ammon (3.3.5−6, Ptol., Arist., *leg.*), and the story of the Syrian woman who saved Alexander from the conspiracy of the pages (4.13.5, Arist.). The largest number appear in Book VII as intimations of the death of Alexander: the interchange between Apollodorus and Pithagoras (7.18.1−5, Arist.), Calanus' enigmatic words predicting the king's end (7.18.6, *leg.*), the sailor and the crown (7.22, *leg.*, Arist.), the man on the throne (7.24.1−3, Arist., *leg.*), and Alexander's words on his deathbed (7.26.3, *leg.*). Clearly Arrian considered such stories important for his narrative. In fact, they supplement the many notices of the interpretations of omens by Aristander and other seers[52] to present, in Arrian's account, a consistent sequence indicating the gods' involvement with Alexander, from the first predictions of his greatness to the end, when they warned him of his imminent death, although he seemed to be at the height of his power.

As with omens of the divine will, so also with many other themes and elements of his story Arrian introduces material from one or the other historian or especially from the *legomena* to reinforce his presentation of Alexander. *Legomena* tend to cluster, for instance, in the accounts of his temperance toward women, of his noble acts as king and leader, and of other anecdotes which reveal character. Likewise, important moments in Alexander's life are developed with the help of other historians, far beyond the material provided by Ptolemy and Aristobulus. One of the most noteworthy of these moments is the first crossing into Asia in 334 B.C.[53] Between 1.11.1, when Alexander returns with his army to Macedon after the Theban campaign, and 1.12.1, when he visits the tomb of Achilles, there are seven citations of *legomena*.

The first, on the occasion of sacrifices and games to Zeus, simply notes that "some say that he also held a contest in honor of the Muses" (1.11.1; cf. Diodorus 17.16.4). The underlying notion, that Alexander wished to accomplish deeds worthy to be celebrated by the Muses, is brought out by the incident immediately following, the sweating of the statue of Orpheus. This omen was interpreted by the seer Aristander as a presage of the great effort that would be required by poets and writers to sing Alexander's deeds (cf. Plutarch *Alex.* 14.8–9). This story both tells us that Alexander's destiny was already known to the gods and refers directly to Arrian's own attempt to write worthily of Alexander, to be affirmed explicitly in 1.12.2–5.

Shortly thereafter Arrian heaps four *legomena* accounts one on another (1.11.6–8): Alexander's sacrifice in the middle of the Hellespont, his leap onto Asian soil, his use of the armor dedicated after the Trojan War, and his sacrifice to Priam. Troy had overlooked the Hellespont, and the ships of Agamemnon and Achilles had been drawn up along its shore. Centuries later, Xerxes had bridged the Hellespont, bringing war to the Greeks. Alexander's crossing, then, was more than a military action; it was part of a continuing history of conflict between the continents which had been dramatized first of all by Homer, but especially by Herodotus. Arrian by his citation of *legomena* accounts gives Alexander's action this historical perspective. Alexander, like Xerxes, was said to have poured a libation from a golden *phiale* as an offering for the crossing (cf. Hdt. 7.54). He himself steered the flagship, and he was the first to leap onto the shore of Asia. A stirring picture is presented of Alexander as leader of the whole force, and Arrian suppresses any mention of the fact that Parmenio and an advance force sent by Philip had been in Asia since 336 to prepare for the expedition. The picture of Alexander leaping to the shore also recalls the story of the ill-fated Protesilaus, the first soldier to land on Asian soil in the Trojan War, who however was killed at once and buried in Europe. Arrian had mentioned only a few lines previously (1.11.5) Alexander's sacrifice at the tomb of Protesilaus, asking for a more fortunate landing; here we see that landing taking place. Protesilaus was mentioned in Homer (*Iliad* 2.701), but also by Herodotus, who ends his history with the story of a Persian who had insulted the memory of the hero and of the revenge which the Greeks took on him after they had driven the Persians from Europe and captured what was left of Xerxes' bridge (Hdt. 9.116–121). The tie with the Greek troops of the Trojan War is reinforced by the story of Alexander's dedication of his armor to Athena at Troy and his decision to take up arms dedicated after the Trojan War, "which, it is said, his bodyguard carried before him into battle." Many years and thousands of miles later, we find Peucestas carrying the shield taken from this temple and using it to protect Alexander in the battle in the Mallian town (6.9.3). The fourth *legomenon* of this group, the sacrifice to Priam, recalls Alexander's special relation to the Trojan War, as the direct descendant of Achilles and of his son Neoptolemus, the slayer of King Priam.

This relationship to Achilles is again recalled in the report that Alexander and Hephaestion laid crowns on the tombs of Achilles and Patroclus, implying that Alexander is not only a descendant of Achilles, and the hero like him of an expedition against Asia, but also a lover, as Achilles was of Patroclus. The parallel with Achilles will be brought to the fore once more in Book VII, on the occasion of Hephaestion's death (7.14.4). Finally, the story that Alexander envied Achilles for having a Homer to celebrate his deeds (1.12.1) not only provides an insight into Alexander's love of fame but introduces Arrian's justification of his own decision to write this history, the second preface. The whole series of *legomena* serves to place the beginning of the expedition and the crossing of the Hellespont in the context of heroic endeavor, on the same plane with the greatest deeds celebrated in epic or history. The deeds of Alexander emulate those of Achilles; his expedition parallels that of the Greeks against Troy and avenges that of Xerxes against the Greeks. Arrian's history therefore will be in the mold of Homer and Herodotus.

It is apparent from Arrian's use of *legomena* that this view of the heroic role of Alexander at the Hellespont was not present in Ptolemy or Aristobulus. Not content with their accounts, Arrian introduced into his narrative from other writers such elements as he thought "worthy of narration," in this case those which would enhance the heroic image of his protagonist and place his own history among the noblest representatives of Greek literature.

THE FORM OF THE *ANABASIS*

The proemial statements had established Alexander as the subject of the *Anabasis*, and in fact the center of action is always wherever Alexander happens to be at the time. In his book Arrian follows the march of his hero across Europe and Asia to his deathbed in Babylon.[54] Thus his history of Alexander, like Xenophon's *Anabasis* from which it takes its name, and much of Herodotus, is a march narrative consisting of alternating marches and halts.[55] Arrian used a similar narrative technique in the *Periplus* in reporting to Hadrian his own inspection of the Black Sea coast, and again in the *Indike* in recording the voyage of Nearchus. We may presume that something of the same format was used to report Trajan's invasion of Parthia in the *Parthica*.[56] The practice in the *Anabasis* is found reduced to bare bones at the beginning of the expedition against Persia: "Crossing the Strymon he passed Mount Pangeon on the road to Abdera and Maroneia, Greek cities built on the sea. From there he came to the Hebrus River and crossed it easily. From there he went through Paetice to the Melas River. Crossing the Melas he reached Sestus twenty days in all after he set out" (1.11.4–5). Once the expedition has crossed into Persian territory the narrative is fleshed out to a greater or lesser degree, depending on the reception accorded Alexander. The march is marked by embassies from cities or kings, administrative details, geographical facts, and especially battles or sieges necessitated by military opposition. The pattern is clear in the following scheme of 1.12–24.

March from Ilium to Hermoton (12.6)
    Scouts sent out, surrender of Priapus accepted (12.7)
    Persian war council (12.8–10)
March to the Granicus (13.1)
    The battle at the Granicus (13.2–16.7)
    Administration: assignment of satrap, taxes, etc. (17.1–2)

March to Sardis (17.3)
  Surrender of Sardis (17.3–4)
  Alexander's visit to the citadel (17.5–6)
  Administration: Sardis, other areas (17.7–8)
  News of the abandonment of Ephesus (17.9)
March to Ephesus (17.10)
  Administration (17.10–18.2)
    The affairs of Ephesus (17.10–13)
    Ambassadors, dispatch of officials, orders (18.1–2)
  Sacrifice to Artemis and parade (18.2)
March to Miletus (and capture of outer city) (18.3)
  Persian plan (18.4)
  Alexander's countermoves (18.4–5)
  Parmenio, Alexander, and the omen: decision to attack (18.6–9)
  Capture of the city (19.1–11)
  Administration: Alexander disbands the fleet (20.1)
March to Caria and Halicarnassus (20.2)
  Persian decision to defend city (20.3)
  Series of engagements during siege, until city (except citadel) falls
    (20.4–23.5)
  Administration (23.6–24.3)
    Halicarnassus (23.6)
    Satrapy of Caria, Ada (23.7–8)
    Newlyweds sent home (24.1–2)
    Parmenio sent to Sardis (24.3)

The basic pattern continues through the *Anabasis*,[57] and when Arrian breaks it he usually finds it necessary to explain himself, as with the long digression at 4.8–14, justified at 4.8.1 and 4.14.4. The pattern is extremely flexible, allowing for the insertion of any activity connected with Alexander, although the headings of administration, embassies, military operations, geographical notices, and religious observations account for most items. The whole is held together by Arrian's consistent notices of the next stage of the march; thus in 1.17–24.3 we find: "he himself went on toward Sardis" (17.3), "he encamped at the Hermus river" (17.4), "when he came to Ephesus" (17.10), "he set out for Miletus" (18.3), "he set out for Caria" (20.2), "he went on toward Lycia and Pamphylia" (24.3). The format fits the purpose of the history precisely and keeps Alexander constantly at the center of attention, since everything that is reported has a direct relation to him. Persian preparations and plans normally appear only as explanations for the steps which Alexander took.[58] Only rarely, as at 2.1–2, the war in the islands, does Arrian swerve from the march sequence to include events which produce no immediate effect on Alexander. In these cases, as at 2.3.1, he is careful to mark his return to the location where he left Alexander ("Alexander, when he came to Gordion . . ." resuming from 1.29.6).[59] Most of the material could be accommodated by insertion at the point in the narrative where some information was reported to Alexander, as for example the conspiracy of Alexander son of Aeropus (1.25.1–4). The words "While at Phaselis Alexander received news that Alexander son of Aeropus was plotting . . ." serve as introduction to a brief account of the man and what seemed to be the plot. Then Arrian returns to Alexander at the time that he is informed of the plot: "Parmenio sent this man [Sisines] under guard to Alexander, and Alexander learned from him the same story."

This continuous sequence of marches and halts does not, however, serve to organize the expedition of Alexander into manageable units, for by its nature each stop is potentially equal to every other and is only differentiated by the length of the account of Alexander's activities there. Arrian finds a larger unit of organization in the book, which allows him to mark off certain major segments of Alexander's expedition, and of Alexander's life, into recognizable parts.[60] Thus the first three books each mark a stage in the conquest of Asia: Asia Minor (I), the Syrian coast (II), and the center provinces of the empire (III). Book IV covers the difficult conquest of the Sogdian, Bactrian, and Indian mountain barons, Book V the sweep across the Punjab to the Hyphasis, Alexander's most eastward point. The return march to Persepolis occupies Book VI, and Book VII is devoted to Alexander's last year in Susa, Opis, Ecbatana, and Babylon.

There is no doubt that the division of the books as we have them is deliberate, and not just an arbitrary splitting of the narrative.[61] They differ greatly in length, from fifty-three pages in Book I to forty-three pages in Book V, adjusting to the material allotted to each book. A trace of a chronological scheme may be partially responsible for the fact that the first two books end in the winter of the year, but the books of the *Anabasis*, unlike those of Polybius, do not cover any fixed period.[62] The length of each book is controlled not by number of pages or of years, but by the content. Especially remarkable is the disparity in treatment between the first three books, the six-year march from the Danube to the Iaxartes, and the last three, the three and a half years from the Indus to Babylon. In the center is Book IV, unusual for its length and the number of years covered, as well as for other factors to be considered.

Geographical boundaries play an important part in deciding the division into books. Book II ends at Gaza, the last city before Egypt. Egypt, as Herodotus wrote, was the gift of the Nile,[63] and the whole valley of the Nile formed not a separate country, but the dividing line between Asia and Libya (cf. *Anab.* 2.26.1 and 3.30.9). Thus at Gaza Alexander had reached one corner of Asia. In Book III he advances into Egypt, and imitating his ancestors Perseus and Heracles, goes beyond the Nile deep into the Libyan desert, to the oracle of Ammon at Siwah. From Egypt Alexander marches through Asia to the Tanais or Iaxartes River, the modern Syr Darya. Arrian carefully notes in a brief geographical excursus that this Tanais is not the Tanais of Herodotus (the Don), which is regarded by some as the boundary of Asia and Europe. Clearly he wishes to have his cake and eat it too—to say that Alexander reached the boundary of Europe and Asia, and yet to admit that this statement is not really accurate. This notice on Alexander's arrival at the Tanais occurs in the last chapter of Book III: Alexander has marched from the Nile to the Tanais, from one boundary of Asia to another. In the first part of Book IV, as before in the previous book, he pushes beyond the frontier of Asia, this time into the "European" desert, pursuing the Scythians (4.4). Book IV ends with Alexander at the Indus, the great river of the East, beyond which lay the subcontinent of India. The wonder of crossing into this new country is emphasized by the series of digressions on Nysa, India, and the Indus bridge at the beginning of Book V. The fifth book, like Alexander's army, stops at the Hyphasis, although the last sentence brings Alexander back to the Hydaspes. Thus the books move Alexander from one great river to another, from one corner of Asia to another.[64]

Within this framework of geographical progress, each book marks certain stages both in the military situation, as Alexander works first to become a master of Asia and then tests himself beyond the boundaries of Asia, and in Alexander's character, as the power he has acquired works to change him. Broadly speaking, the first three books chronicle Alexander's rise to supreme power, the fourth considers internal and external challenges to that preeminence, and the last three books explore Alexander's efforts to push to the furthest limits of heroic endeavor.[65]

After the introductory section on the European campaigns, Book I is devoted to the first year of the Persian expedition. Various touches serve to place the expedition in the history of the great wars between the Greeks and the barbarians: Alexander's election as leader of the Hellenic league (1.1.1-3), the recollection of the Trojan and Persian wars at the Hellespont (1.11.5-12.1), the reference to Xenophon and the *Anabasis* (1.12.3).[66] The success of Alexander is foreshadowed by an omen, the sweating of the statue of Orpheus, intimating the efforts by poets to celebrate his deeds adequately.[67] The first great battle, the cavalry engagement at the Granicus, although less important militarily than the subsequent operations at Miletus and Halicarnassus, demonstrates the highmindedness, daring, and leadership of the conqueror. The Granicus began the myth of Alexander's invincibility, as far as the Persians were concerned, and his triumphal progress through Asia Minor to Gordion reinforced it. The last item in Book I is Alexander's response to the Athenian embassy requesting the freedom of Athenians captured fighting for the Persians at the Granicus (1.29.5-6). The king refuses, but the incident serves to relate the end of the book to the beginning, when Alexander was chosen leader of the Hellenic crusade against Persia, and to the beginning of Book II, which describes Memnon's attempt to unite the Greeks against Alexander.

The second book contains Alexander's two most important military actions, the battle at Issus and the siege of Tyre. In a certain sense the overriding question in the period treated in this book is whether the expedition will be merely a punitive sally, hardly more conclusive than the depredations of Agesilaus earlier in the century, or whether Alexander can actually conquer a substantial portion, if not all, of the Persian empire. Arrian throughout this book stresses the risk that Alexander takes, while reassuring the reader of the final outcome by various remarks and narrative devices. The book begins with the Persian naval operations in the Aegean (2.1-2), potentially so dangerous. Mytilene and Tenedos are forced to surrender and throw down the steles recording their treaty with Alexander and the Greeks. It might appear that Alexander would be cut off, yet two items are introduced which undercut the effect of the Persian victories: the death of the commander, Memnon, "which especially injured the situation of the king at the time" (2.1.3), and the capture of eight ships of a Persian squadron by Proteas (2.2.4–5). Although Persian strength is hardly touched (there were still one hundred ships at Tenedos), the victory is an omen of future success. Finally, the victories of Memnon in the Aegean war are counterbalanced in the next chapter by the story of the Gordian knot (2.3). According to Arrian's account, Midas on becoming king had dedicated his chariot to Zeus, and now whoever unloosed the yoke-knot of the chariot would "rule Asia." However Alexander resolved the problem, he went away thinking that he had fulfilled the oracle, and that night thunder and lightning confirmed the interpretation. Alexander would indeed be lord of Asia.

The first step in fulfilling the sign at Gordion was of course the battle of Issus, the importance of which is marked by two passages before and after the battle. In the first (2.6.3–7), Arrian analyzes[68] Darius' decision to abandon his strong position on favorable ground and pursue Alexander, wonders whether something supernatural may have driven him to it, and concludes, "Indeed it was necessary for the Persians to be deprived of the rule of Asia by the Macedonians, as the Medes had been by the Persians, and earlier the Assyrians by the Medes." In the second passage, the exchange of letters between Darius and his challenger, the question is again that of the sovereignty of Asia. Darius says that he fought to defend his rule (2.14.3), and Alexander writes back that he is now "Asia's master, and yours" (2.14.8), and "king of Asia" (2.14.9). Issus also had its effect on the Aegean war: discussions were broken off between the Spartan king Agis and the Persian commanders (2.13.4–6), and the son of one of the leaders of the Persian naval contingent joined Alexander (2.13.7–8).

There follows the siege of Tyre, not attempted for vain bravado, we are told by Arrian, but from strategic necessity, to end the opposition to the Macedonians in Greece and the Aegean (2.17.2). As Alexander predicted (2.17.3), the Phoenician naval contingents surrendered when their cities were threatened (2.20.1–3). Not least among those who came to aid Alexander at Tyre was the lone boat of Proteas, who first put the Persian navy to flight (2.20.2; cf. 2.2.4). After the fall of the city, the arrival of the second embassy from Darius (2.25.1–3) and Alexander's response completes the episode and reinforces Alexander's claim to be the master of Asia. The final incident of the book, the siege of Gaza (2.25.4–27.7), shows Alexander in a different role, the conqueror of the unconquerable.[69]

In the third book Alexander makes good his claim to be master of all Asia. In geographical scope it is the broadest book, ranging from the Nile across the Hindu Kush to the Scythian desert, through all the capitals of the empire—Babylon, Susa, Persepolis, Pasargadae, Ecbatana. In a host of incidents four stand out: the visit to Siwah (3.3–4), the victory at Gaugamela (3.8–15), the burning of the palace at Persepolis (3.18.11–12), and the death of Darius (3.21.6–22.5). The first, early in the book, gives Alexander the encouragement of the god, though in what exact manner Arrian cannot say. The second is the great battle for empire: "In this battle we fight not for Coele Syria or Phoenicia, or for Egypt, as before, but for all Asia, and who must rule it" (3.9.6). With the victory, Alexander gathers the spoils, the captive cities and their treasures. The burning of the royal palace illustrates the tension between the two motives of the expedition, conquest and vengeance. Alexander burns the palace in vengeance for the destruction of buildings and temples in Greece by Xerxes' army, but Parmenio advises that he spare them, since they are now his. Burning will only suggest that he is a raider, and that he will not keep the rule of Asia. (Later, Alexander comes to feel the same way: 6.30.1.) Finally, the death of Darius marks the end of legitimate opposition to Alexander. Arrian honors the Persian king with a royal obituary (3.22.2–5), giving the date of his death and his age, an evaluation of his life, and an account of the honors paid him after death. Alexander buried him with the kings who had died before him, for he himself was now Great King. The book ends with the pursuit and capture of Bessus, the pretender to Darius' throne. With Bessus in chains, Alexander was undisputed king of Persia, even if certain areas should be in revolt.

Unlike the other Alexander historians, Arrian makes little of the death of Philotas and Parmenio, which occurs in this book (3.26). His sources reported it as a real conspiracy, and he chose not to doubt them. The time for strictures of Alexander would come.

Book IV sees the ascendancy of Alexander tested, externally and internally, by the resistance of the Bactrians and Scythians and by a series of Alexander's own actions which raise questions about his self-mastery (sōphrosynē). The book begins with the visit of the Abian Scythians, "whom Homer in his poem called the 'most just of men' [cf. *Iliad* 13.6]. They live in Asia and are independent, chiefly because of their poverty and sense of justice." The notice seems to establish a moral tone which although present throughout the *Anabasis* is particularly strong in the fourth and seventh books. Alexander is not poor but rich and powerful; how does this affect his character? The moral problem becomes more apparent when we are informed that Alexander is sending ambassadors to the European Scythians not for friendship but as spies (4.1.2) and that he is founding a city on the Tanais (Alexandria Eschate, later Chodjend) where it would be in a fine position for an eventual expedition against the Scythians (4.1.3).

The revolt of the Sogdians and Bactrians, and the opposition of Spitamenes and the Scythians, marks the first effective resistance to Alexander as king. The local tribes are put down (4.1.4–3.5), but when Alexander attempts to pursue the Scythians across the river, he is halted by diarrhoea (4.4). The warning of the seer Aristander and Alexander's comparison of himself with Darius the Great[70] give this sally beyond the Tanais more than casual significance: the river is a limit beyond which he goes at his peril. Spitamenes is still at large when Alexander winters at Zariaspa, the point at which Arrian injects into the narrative a long section on Alexander's acts of *hybris* (4.7–14). This carefully presented series of incidents occurs at the midpoint of the *Anabasis* and raises those questions of character fundamental to Arrian's evaluation of Alexander. The purpose of joining to the Bessus episode, without regard to chronology, the murder of Clitus, the argument on *proskynesis*, the pages' conspiracy, and the death of Callisthenes is not military or political but biographical and moral; the problems raised are those of power and happiness, of excess and limit, of the distinction between gods and men. The central question is that of self-mastery. Will the ruler of Asia rule himself? Arrian poses the paradox after describing the mutilation of Bessus, asserting that neither a strong body nor good birth nor victory in war is of any use toward a man's happiness, unless he also learns self-control (4.7.5). Once posed, the question of Alexander's self-mastery hangs over the rest of the work, until the final summation after the king's death at 7.28–30.

Almost immediately after this series of episodes of intemperance, an omen suggests an answer to the question. A spring of oil is found near Alexander's tent; the seer interprets it to mean "toil, but after the toil, victory" (4.15.8). The rest of the book goes on to describe these toils in the mountain fastnesses of Sogdiana, Bactria, and India: Spitamenes hounded to his death, the victories of the Sogdian rock, the rock of Chorienes, Massaga, and Aornus. Each battle is won only by heroic efforts, and the last stronghold had never been conquered even by that champion of labors, Heracles: "And so Alexander held the rock which Heracles could not take" (4.30.7). By his superhuman labors, Alexander proves his right to victory and honor. At the Sogdian rock he also demonstrates his self-control. When he fell in love with Roxane, the daughter of the baron Oxyartes, "he did not treat her arrogantly, as a captive, but married her" (4.19.6). At this point Arrian chooses to recall, far out of chronological sequence, Alexander's even greater self-control toward the wife of Darius after the battle of Issus, and relates a tale which combines the motifs of self-control and rule of Asia. When informed of Alexander's generous and respectful treatment of his mother and wife and that "Alexander is the noblest and most self-controlled of men," Darius had prayed, "O Zeus, King, to whom it has been given to apportion among men the affairs of kings, do you now protect for me the sovereignty over the Persians and Medes, as you have given it to me. But if in your mind I am no longer king of Asia, do you give my power to no other but Alexander. For he does not forget his self-control even toward his enemies" (4.20.3). Self-control and toil are the internal and external factors which can render Alexander truly great and worthy of the conquests he gains. The last significant incident of the book is the fall of Aornus, by which Alexander surpasses Heracles; with the last sentence Alexander arrives at the Indus.

The Indus marked a limit: beyond it lay India, a land of wonders.[71] Alexander's push beyond this boundary is emphasized at the beginning of Book V by a series of digressions. The Nysa story (5.1.1–3.4) is not only difficult to believe, as Arrian admits several times (5.1.2, 2.7, 3.1 and 4), but out of place. Nysa, in the common account (Diodorus, Curtius, Justin), is one of the first cities Alexander encounters coming from Bactria, before the Choaspes River and before Aornus. Arrian places it much later, seemingly as Alexander is about to cross the Indus. Actually Arrian does not say where exactly the city was, or when it was reached, but locates it very generally between the Cophen and the Indus (5.1.1). The whole story is cited as a *legomenon*; we may presume that it was not to be found in either Ptolemy or Aristobulus. Arrian took it from the vulgate, no doubt Clitarchus,[72] and placed it here at the beginning of Book V, as Alexander was about to cross the Indus. The move is not really strange. In the vulgate tradition, the anecdote is located at the beginning of the Indian expedition; Arrian has moved the boundary of India, and so the story. Thematically, the Nysa episode fulfills two functions. The marvels of Mount Meros enhance the wonder of Alexander's invasion of India. The mention of Dionysus recalls that Alexander surpassed that demigod as well as Heracles.[73]

At 5.3.5 Arrian resumes the narrative from the end of Book IV. Alexander is at the bridge over the Indus, performing sacrifices and holding games before his crossing. But at once the historian interjects a second digression, on the size of the Indus, which he calls the greatest of the rivers of Asia and Europe except the Ganges (5.4.1–2). At 5.4.3 the army crosses the river "into the land of the Indians." There follows another digression on accounts of the Indian people, prefaced and concluded by cross-references to his book on India (5.4.3–5.1). At 5.5.2 intervenes a fourth digression on the geography of India, "as much as is necessary for an account of Alexander's deeds," emphasizing the great size of India (5.5.2–6.8). Finally, Arrian discusses the manner in which the Indus was bridged, providing for comparison a description of Roman pontoon bridges (5.7). Not until 5.8.1 does Alexander actually cross the Indus and move on to Taxila.[74] The whole section, 5.1–7, forms an elaborate introduction to the crossing of the Indus and the invasion of India, magnifying Alexander's achievement in going beyond the Indus and outdoing the legendary heroes.

Books V and VI in fact can be taken together as showing the young conqueror pushing the extremes both of geography and of human endurance. These two books focus on a few major episodes: the battle with Porus (5.9.4–19), the mutiny on the Hyphasis (5.25–29.3), the wounding of Alexander in the attack on the Mallian city (6.9–13), the mouths of the Indus and the sight of the Ocean (6.18.2–20), and the crossing of the Gedrosian desert (6.22.4–26). Each finds Alexander pushing the limits: of his capacity as general and as leader, of courage (or foolhardiness), and of the known world at the Hyphasis and the Ocean. Seen in this light it is clear that the tremendous sufferings of the army in Gedrosia form a part of Arrian's larger picture of Alexander as leader. The vivid descriptions of the Macedonians' trials are not meant to be a criticism of Alexander, but to prepare us for the final two anecdotes, Alexander's refusal to drink water which could not be shared with his men (6.26.1–3) and his marvelous ability to lead the army to water when the guides had lost their way (6.26.4–5).[75] He surpasses all conquerors, all leaders, and is only prevented from going further by his own weary soldiers.

Book VI ends with the return to Persia and Pasargadae. The king

found many acting intemperately, as though he were dead, and executed them, but Arrian fastens on one incident, the violation of the
tomb of Cyrus the Great (6.29.4–11). Aristobulus' eyewitness description of the tomb is of course interesting in its own right, but the
story of the tomb and its desecration also serves to illuminate two
motifs: the transitoriness of power and fame, and Alexander's acceptance of the duties and prerogatives of the Persian kings as their successor as Lord of Asia. Arrian's quotation of the inscription on Cyrus'
tomb is pathetic, and effective: "O man, I am Cyrus son of Cambyses,
who established empire for the Persians and was king of Asia. Do not
grudge me my monument." Now Cyrus' monument was destroyed.
Alexander had surpassed Cyrus, but what would be his power after
death? Alexander honors and emulates Cyrus the Great, but finally
will be powerless, as Cyrus is, in death.[76] The last item in the book,
the appointment of Peucestas as satrap of Persia and the comment on
his Persian ways, continues the theme of Persian kingship (6.30.2–
5).[77] In a sense it revives the question of Book IV, whether Alexander
would be spoiled by his role as king of Persia.

In the last book, the moralizing tone, always present but up to this
point usually subdued and overwhelmed by the description of campaigns and battles, assumes the major role. The narrative structure is
still that of a march, but the dynamic movement of a campaign is
lacking.[78] Without any major military action, the narrative concentrates on the various modes of viewing Alexander, slowly drawing together the threads of the conqueror's life, moving inexorably toward
his death. The first paragraphs represent a digression which establishes
the two major themes of this book—success and death. A reference
to Alexander's longing (pothos) to see the mouths of the Tigris and
the Euphrates takes the reader out of the chronological and geographical sequence of the narrative to consider Alexander's plans for future
conquest. Speculation on his possible campaigns around Africa or
against the Scythians or Sicily and Italy modulates easily into a statement about his character, that he would always have a rival, if only
himself, and would never be satisfied with what he had. This restless-
ness is revealed as a fault by the sage observations of the Indian wise
men and of Diogenes the Cynic, retold in two anecdotes reported here
far out of chronological sequence. The digression is completed by the
dramatic recital of the death of Calanus, whose willingness to die
demonstrated for Arrian the invincible strength of the human spirit
to accomplish what it desires.[79]

The episodes which follow stress Alexander's success as king and conqueror despite the undercurrent of opposition to his plans. The weddings at Susa, the openhanded payment of the soldiers' accumulated debts, and the rewards to his captains reveal him as a generous leader, willing to share his victory with his followers (7.4–6). The trip to the Persian Gulf and up the Tigris is marked by the removal of the dams erected by the Persians as a defense against a naval attack: "Alexander said that those who were superior in arms had no need of such devices" (7.7.7). The mutiny at Opis provides an excellent chance for Alexander to defend his accomplishments in a long and highly rhetorical speech and concludes with the Macedonian capitulation and request to be treated as his kinsmen. The lacuna which intervenes here in our manuscripts prevents us from seeing how Arrian treated the treasonous flight of Harpalus or the ill will of Antipater toward Alexander and of Eumenes toward Hephaestion. But as the book continues, Alexander's present success is constantly brought to the fore. After the expedition against the Cossaeans, Arrian writes, "Alexander was able to accomplish every military operation he undertook" (7. 15.3). Embassies came from all over the world to seek his friendship and beg him to arbitrate their disputes: "Then it was especially that Alexander appeared to both himself and his followers to be lord of all the East and the sea" (7.15.5). They came with gold crowns, "as if on a sacred embassy to a god" (7.23.20). Confidently, Alexander made plans for expeditions on the Caspian Sea (7.16.1–4) and against the Arabians (7.19.3–20).

But as the Indian wise men had said, "in just a short time you will die, and possess only so much land as is sufficient to bury you" (7.1.6). The theme of mortality is established by these words and the account of the death of Calanus in the opening digression, but does not become central until the death of Hephaestion at Ecbatana. The notice of the death itself is extremely brief, and Arrian focuses instead upon the grief of Alexander and his frenzied reactions in the face of an enemy he cannot conquer (7.14). The death of Hephaestion is a presage of Alexander's end, as Arrian reminds us; there were three thousand competitors at Hephaestion's funeral games, "and these a short time later, they say, competed at Alexander's funeral" (7.14.10). Two intimations of death mark his entry into Babylon: the Chaldeans' warning not to enter the city (7.16.5–17) and the evidence of the sacrifices of the diviner Pithagoras (7.18). Arrian's own comments (7.16.7–8) make of Alexander's rejection of the Chaldeans a fateful moment: "*To daimonion* led him on this road, which once having passed, it was necessary that he then die." Heaven, or the gods, were bringing him to his death, a death which is seen by Arrian, however, not as a disaster but almost as a final confirmation of the gods' favor to Alexander. "Yet perhaps it was better for him to leave at the peak of his fame and of men's desire for him, before some human misfortune should happen to him—the kind of thing which apparently caused Solon to advise Croesus to look to the end of a long life and not to declare any man happy beforehand." Thus in a way it was time for Alexander to die; in fact, Arrian notes, it was already late, for he certainly would have preferred to die before he had lost Hephaestion.[80]

The omens of death recur with the diadem lost in the swamps among the tombs of the Assyrian kings (7.22) and finally the stranger upon the throne. "The end was near," Arrian writes, and after his last omen begins the slow count of Alexander's last days. The narrative of the king's final moments makes vivid the conflict of conquest and mortality,[81] presenting the spectacle of a steadily declining Alexander, continuing to plan with his staff the conquest of Arabia.

The final book is a unit, completing Arrian's account of Alexander. The questions posed on the meaning of Alexander's life of conquest at the beginning of the whole work, and in a special way at the beginning of Book VII, are reviewed in the epilogue, 7.28–30. In this final evaluation Arrian lists the conqueror's good qualities and accomplishments and sets them off against his weaknesses, finally justifying both Alexander and his own presentation of Alexander's deeds.

6

THE *ANABASIS*:

THE PORTRAIT OF ALEXANDER

THE *Anabasis* is fundamentally an attempt to tell the history of Alexander in such a way that his true greatness will be apparent, to celebrate Alexander as Homer had Achilles. Like Homer, Arrian is aware of weaknesses in his subject but feels that they were so overwhelmed by his achievements that they faded into insignificance in the overall picture. Since he believes that Alexander is genuinely great, he wishes to elicit a true and accurate account from his sources. Only a true account without rhetorical or novelistic invention can do justice to his subject. However, Arrian is in no sense objective; he is very much involved with his subject and expresses this involvement in frequent direct comments in his own person. These comments serve to interpret the narrative which has already been fashioned from the judicious combination of Ptolemy, Aristobulus, and other writers so that those aspects are brought out which Arrian thinks reflect the true Alexander. The final portrait is very much Arrian's creation, neither the historical Alexander (whose nature is still hidden from us), nor Ptolemy's Alexander, nor that of any other writer before Arrian.

ALEXANDER THE GENERAL

First and foremost in Arrian's eyes Alexander was the personification of the ideal general, able to handle any military situation. When in the second preface he speaks of Alexander's deeds, he has in mind not administrative achievements or such abstract notions as the unification of East and West and of Persian and Greek, nor even the effect that his conquests had on world history, but the series of military operations extending from the Balkans to Samarkand and the Punjab by which he conquered the largest part of the known world. Arrian himself was a military man, commanded troops, and was interested enough in the subject to write several short works on the theory and practice of military maneuvers. His presentation of Alexander's military achievements reflects his own acquaintance with warfare and his effort to understand the factors which made Alexander such a successful general. Although he occasionally seems to misunderstand or misrepresent one of Alexander's actions, in general his description of military operations is clear and rather well thought out. It is apparent that Arrian thought he understood Alexander's military genius and tried to present it to his readers. He would have expected at least some of his readers, members of the Roman governing class who had commanded or would have to command armies in the field, to use his book as a kind of manual of generalship, as Napoleon did the memoirs of Caesar, Frederick the Great, and Maréchal de Turenne.

Arrian's praise of Alexander as commander is summarized in general terms, which borrow heavily from Thucydides' description of Themistocles, in his final evaluation:

> He had an uncanny instinct for the right course when the situation was not clear, and was very happy in drawing conclusions from what could be ascertained. In arming and equipping troops and in military dispositions he was always masterly. He was extraordinary in his power of inspiring his men, of filling them with confidence, and in the moment of danger, of sweeping away their fear by the example of his fearlessness. When risks had to be taken, he took them with the utmost boldness, and his ability to seize the moment for a swift blow, before his enemy had any suspicion of what was coming, was beyond praise. (7.27)

These words, coming at the end of the *Anabasis*, reflect the image of Alexander which Arrian has built up in the course of his narrative. Innumerable battles, sieges, and minor encounters are recorded in the *Anabasis*. These can be divided into certain general categories: the major battles (Granicus, Issus, Gaugamela, Hydaspes), sieges (Halicarnassus, Tyre, Gaza), attacks on hill forts (the Sogdian rock, Aornus), and minor campaigns and guerilla wars (against the Triballi and the Illyrians, in the mountains near Persepolis, in Bactria and Sogdiana, and in India). What amazed Arrian, and amazes us still today, was Alexander's ability to handle so many different kinds of encounters, on such diverse terrain and against such a variety of enemies, facing each new problem afresh, discovering the weakness of his opponents, and turning it to his advantage. Arrian's own achievement was to present each of these in such a way as to bring out the superior tactics by which Alexander won. It will be useful to examine a few specific operations in detail to understand his method in treating military affairs. Since the purpose of this examination is to understand Arrian, and not to reconstruct history, parallel accounts by other authors will not be considered except insofar as they give clues to Arrian's method.

Arrian's account of the campaigns in Europe in 335 B.C., set as it is between the two proemial statements boasting of the superiority of his work, can be seen as his attempt to produce a sample of the greatness of Alexander and of the excellence of his own method of presenting him. In this short passage Alexander is seen handling brilliantly an extraordinary variety of situations: his response to the onslaught of wagons at Mount Haemus (1.1.7–10), his lightning expedition across the Danube (1.3.5–4.5), the befuddlement of the Illyrians with drill exercises (1.6.1–4), the forced march to Thebes (1.7.5–7), and his victorious assault on the city (1.8).

If we consider particularly the encounter with the Thracians on Mount Haemus, we can discern a standard narrative technique in use. The Thracians had collected wagons at the top of the Shipka pass, planning to release them on the Macedonians and thus break up the Macedonian phalanx. Alexander saw the problem, saw that there was no other passage, evaluated the risk, made a plan, and issued orders to his soldiers on what exactly to do when the wagons were released. The orders are explained by a clause clarifying their purpose and Alexander's plan: the wagons are to go between or pass over the soldiers, rushing down without harm. After the wagons are released, and all goes as he had anticipated, Alexander issues a new set of orders, moving the archers to the left, with an explanation (the phalanx could be more easily attacked there), and in the ensuing engagement once more all works according to plan. The archers successfully hamper the attack of the Thracians, the enemy is routed, fifteen hundred are killed, and the women, children, and baggage are captured.

Arrian has set out the operation in terms of the situation faced by Alexander, here given both in the fact (the wagons at the pass) and in the plan of the enemy (to release them and break up the phalanx). Alexander evaluates the situation and makes a counterplan, issuing orders which specifically describe the various contingencies of the battle.[1] Here, as regularly in Arrian, events turn out as Alexander had anticipated ("and thus it happened as Alexander ordered and expected," 1.1.9).[2] The specific purpose which was behind each order is fulfilled in the battle itself.

The circumstances in the attack on Thebes are different, but the same technique is apparent, and the more recognizable since it can be compared with the account of Diodorus (17.8–14).[3] Many features differentiate the two accounts of the battle of Thebes, but the essential contrast is that of narrative purpose. Diodorus conceives the battle as a struggle of spirit: the rage of Alexander against the do-or-die courage of the Thebans. Therefore he tells us that the rebels were not daunted by all the factors telling against them—the delay of their allies (17.8.6–9.1), the proclamation of Alexander (17.9.5), or the omens of the gods (17.10)—but preferred, bravely rather than intelligently, to fight (17.10.6). The Thebans wear out the Macedonians especially by their spirit (17.11.4), and even the onset of the Macedonian reserve troops causes them to face their dangers more courageously. Only when Perdiccas was able to slip behind their defenses and liberate the besieged Macedonian garrison did they think of withdrawing (17.12.3–4). To the end they fought on nobly, never asking for pity from their conquerors. Alexander, on the other hand, acts from rage (17.9.6) and a desire to strike fear into the hearts of the Greeks (17.9.4, 14.4). With so much said of the Thebans' spirit, there is no real account of the battle; the two sides encounter and fight heroically (17.11.3–5), Alexander sends in his extra unit (17.12.1), Perdiccas breaks through a deserted gate (17.12.3), and the Thebans retreat and are cut down (17.12.5).

In Arrian, the whole tone is different; he wishes the reader to understand the battle as battle, not as melodrama. The battle began, without Alexander's order, with the attack of Perdiccas, which was followed by the commitment of other troops, those of Amyntas and the Agrianes (1.8.1–3). These forces were at first successful, then were repulsed by a Theban counterattack at the Heracleum (1.8.3–4). At this point Alexander attacked with the phalanx and drove the Thebans inside the walls (1.8.5). The battle then moved inside the city, until finally the Theban cavalry and infantry fled as best they could (1.8.6–7). Each action is explained in terms of previous action or of Alexander's plan. Amyntas follows Perdiccas *because* he was joined with him *after he saw* Perdiccas' advance; Alexander acted *when he saw* Perdiccas and Amyntas *in order that* they might not be left alone (1.8.2); Alexander attacked *when he saw* the Macedonians fleeing from the Theban counterattack (1.8.5); the Macedonians were able to enter the

gate *because* the Theban retreat had been frantic and *because* the
walls were deserted (1.8.5); those outside the walls were able to enter
because the walls were held by those who had entered the city (1.8.6);
the Thebans finally had to flee *when* the Macedonians and Alexander
attacked from every side (1.8.7). Arrian's narrative is not a succession
of individual incidents but a sequence of causally related actions in
which causal particles and participial phrases are joined with verbs of
seeing and temporal clauses to set before our eyes not only the actions
of the battle but the reasons behind them, at least on Alexander's
side. Despite the fact that the battle did not begin at Alexander's order,
he again rapidly evaluated the situation, sent troops where they were
needed, and carried the day.

A second element of Arrian's presentation of Alexander's generalship is also present in this account, an element which in other battles
frequently dominates the narrative. At Thebes Alexander is not only
the master tactician, he is in the midst of the battle. His charge routs
the Thebans and drives them within the gates (1.8.5), and finally it is
his presence seemingly everywhere which routs the Theban cavalry
(1.8.7).

These two passages give a sample of Arrian's narrative technique
when handling small military operations. His method, however, is
consistent throughout the *Anabasis*. Although each battle, siege, or
pacifying expedition has its own peculiar problems, it will be sufficient
here to consider his presentation of two of the major battles, the
Granicus and Gaugamela.[4]

As Alexander marches from Hermoton toward the Persian forces at
the Granicus, he sends ahead Amyntas with four squadrons of cavalry
as scouts (1.12.7). The notice is not casual, since the deployment of
scouts is a regular feature of Alexander's activity in Arrian's account,
although the use of advance scouts was not a normal practice of Greek
warfare.[5] After reporting the Persian decision to fight, Arrian returns
to Alexander and describes the marching formation as the army
moved through hostile territory: scouts (cavalry and light infantry)
ahead, the main body of infantry in double formation following, and
the baggage train behind. Cavalry on either side protected the flanks
(1.13.1). Again Alexander's disposition could be a textbook example;
the order is that recommended by Arrian in his *Tactics* 28–30[6] and
used in the march against the Alans (*Ect.* 1–10). The scouts serve their
function, warning of the Persian force waiting on the Granicus, before
the armies are in sight of each other. (This is not the place to consider

whether or why the Persians decided to await Alexander with massed
cavalry on the banks of the Granicus;[7] suffice it here that Arrian takes
it as certain that they did so and describes the battle from that perspective.)

Arrian's interpretation of the battle is encapsulated in the dialogue
between Parmenio and Alexander which follows the localization of
the Persian forces (1.13.3 –7). Parmenio recommends caution, out-
lining a series of difficulties:

> 1. The river is deep in many spots and its banks are steep, some-
> times almost cliffs.
> 2. Therefore our formation will not have a broad front, but will
> be disordered and will climb up the banks in column, the weakest
> battle formation.
> 3. The Persian cavalry, in phalanx formation, will be pushing
> down on the Macedonians as they climb out of the river bed.
> 4. A defeat now would be most harmful for the whole war.

Alexander recognizes the truth of all these objections but rejects the
advice.[8] The fourth objection he answers at once: the real necessity is
not to avoid disaster but to seize an immediate and complete victory;
anything else would encourage the Persians (1.13.7).

Alexander's response to Parmenio's other objections becomes apparent in the course of the narrative. The banks are indeed steep
(1.14.4); the Persian cavalry is disposed in a phalanx and intends to
attack those climbing out of the river bed from above (1.14.5). Alexander, however, sends two waves of cavalry and a squadron of infantry ahead, then leads the right wing across the river, carefully stretch-
ing out his line obliquely where it hits the current, so that it will not
emerge in column but in fact will preserve as much as possible phalanx
formation (1.14.7). The effect of the first two waves of cavalry is to
disrupt the Persian line (1.15.1), although the Macedonians suffer, as
Parmenio had predicted, from their awkward position (1.15.2). Finally, however, the Macedonians begin to win, thanks to their im-
petus, their experience, and their long cornel lances (1.15.5).[9] Alexander has successfully overcome the advantages of the Persian position.

The real strength of the Macedonians in this battle, however, was
not tactics so much as the heroic drive of Alexander. This is suggested
in his response to the careful Parmenio, "I would be ashamed if having
crossed the Hellespont so easily, we should be halted from crossing

this little stream just as we are." The heroic tone is continued in the description of Alexander just before the battle: "He was identifiable by the splendor of his arms and the enthusiastic attendance of his retinue" (1.14.4). The two armies pause; there is a moment of silence, then Alexander begins the attack. The charge across the river which determined the battle is described in one long sentence, focused on Alexander and his plans. It begins with Alexander leaping on his horse, reaches its high point with the single main verb (in the historical present) "he plunges into the ford" and ends with the explanation of his maneuver to ensure a strong phalanx (1.14.6–7). The valiant charge of his lead troops is subordinated to the vision of Alexander urging them on. Then when these troops are being beaten back, Alexander's appearance marks the turn of the tide (the word is again "plunges," in the historical present, 1.15.3). At once Arrian concentrates the narrative on the single combats of epic ferocity and vividness which were fought by and around Alexander (1.15.6–8; note the frequent historical presents, eight in twenty-three lines).[10] Finally, the Persian cavalry yields, beginning at the point where Alexander was in the forefront (1.16.1).

In Arrian's interpretation of the battle, Alexander's superior tactics combine with his heroic energy, which he communicates also to his men, to win complete victory. Furthermore, it has once more been Arrian's method to set forth the problem which Alexander faced (in this case, through the dialogue with Parmenio) and then allow us to follow in the narrative the manner in which it was resolved.

The account of the battle of Gaugamela is more elaborate, but the same desire on the part of the author to make clear the fundamental problems faced by Alexander is evident. Arrian has no inclination for the melodrama and false tension which figure so prominently in the vulgate tradition.[11]

In describing the march to the battle site Arrian is again careful, as before the battle of the Granicus, to demonstrate Alexander's generalship. He sent out cavalry scouts before him (3.7.7) and by capturing some Persian scouts was able to learn the location and strength of Darius' forces (3.8.3–7).[12] With this information, he rested his army for four days and constructed a fortified camp for the wounded and baggage. After a further advance, he met with his other commanders. On this occasion he accepted Parmenio's recommendation and delayed battle until he could reconnoiter the battlefield for ditches, hidden stakes, or other dangers.[13] As before, Alexander himself led the scout force (3.9.5; cf. 3.8.1). Alexander's caution described here reflects the value he (and Arrian) placed on accurate knowledge of the situation: not all operations were to be approached with the reliance on élan found at the Granicus.

The reported number of Darius' troops—40,000 horses, 1 million infantry, 200 scythe-chariots—amply justified caution. Moreover, the land had been leveled for the convenience of the cavalry and chariots. Alexander's personal reconnaissance could only have convinced him that he was taking a great risk and that he must move very carefully.[14] The anecdote of Parmenio's visit to Alexander's tent to suggest a night attack on the enemy, inserted as a *legomenon*, reinforces this aspect of Alexander's generalship (3.10.1–4). Arrian's version of the anecdote is similar to that found in our other sources (Curtius, Diodorus, Plutarch), and ends with the same haughty remark of the king, that it was disgraceful to steal a victory; Alexander must win openly and without guile. Unlike our other sources, however, which treat the incident as just another example of the young leader's pride, Arrian gives his own commentary on Alexander's reasons for rejecting Parmenio's advice, based not on pride, although he recognizes that element in Alexander's words, but on tactics, his precise reasoning. According to Arrian—there is no suggestion that he found the analysis in his source —Alexander would have considered (1) the risks inherent in a night battle; (2) the fact that if the Macedonians won, Darius could use the surprise attack as an excuse for the defeat and would try to fight again; and (3) that if they lost, or even barely won, they would be in great danger, a small force in the midst of a hostile country. "For these reasons [which really represent Arrian's judgment of the situation and nothing in the tradition] I praise Alexander." Moreover, his use of this anecdote permits Arrian to contrast Alexander's decision with the incompetence of Darius, who made no proper camp, and so kept his troops in arms all night lest Alexander in fact attempt a surprise attack. According to Arrian, Alexander, like the Romans, knew the importance of a fortified camp (cf. 3.9.1); the Persians, who did not, went into battle tired from their vigil, and with their morale low, eaten away by fear, "which usually arises and enslaves the mind before great dangers when it is not scattered at once, but is dwelt on for a long time" (3.11.2).[15]

The mention of the Persian army permits a transition to the disposition of their forces for battle. Their arrangement is not justified, beyond the statement that the Greek mercenaries were stationed directly opposite the Macedonian phalanx, "as being the only troops who were a match for them" (3.11.7). Alexander's dispositions, on the other hand, are interspersed with explanations which illustrate Arrian's understanding of Alexander's plans and the course of the battle. The purpose of the phalanx itself was obvious, and needed no comment,[16] but Alexander's special dispositions for this battle all involve a statement of contingencies. A second phalanx was set behind the first so as to make a *phalanx amphistomos*.[17] If the Macedonian force were to be surrounded, their orders were to face the rear and to receive the attack with their backs to the front line (3.12.1). On the right wing had been stationed at an angle contingents of infantry and archers, with orders to extend or contract the phalanx as need be (3.12.2), and troops of cavalry, to block flanking movements (3.12.4). In front of the companion cavalry half the Agrianes and the archers plus javelin-men were ranged against the scythe-chariots (3.12.3). There was also a flank guard on the left, presumably with the same orders. The Thracian infantry had the duty of protecting the baggage. All the contingencies envisioned are really one, that is, that the Persians will attempt to outflank the Macedonians. The Persians were of course numerically far superior (3.8.6) and had purposely chosen a wide battlefield to avoid the constriction from which they had suffered at Issus (3.8.7). Only the missilemen and Agrianes in front of the phalanx had a different duty, to nullify the scythe-chariots.[18]

In the course of the battle as described by Arrian, all the contingencies foreseen by Alexander do occur, and his troops, moving according to plan, are able to blunt Darius' attack and give Alexander the chance to make their cavalry attack which would mean victory. The battle is seen schematically: three attacks by Darius, three countermoves by Alexander, the last of which decides the battle (3.13–14.3). This account of the action around Alexander is followed by two incidents, the attack on the Macedonian camp and the difficulty of the left wing under Parmenio, and concluded with the pursuit of Darius.

Despite his fundamentally defensive posture, Alexander from the beginning seizes the initiative by moving toward his right, threatening to shift the battle onto ground where the Persian scythe-chariots would be unserviceable, and forcing Darius' hand (3.13.1–2). Darius responds by ordering his front-line cavalry to outflank Alexander on the right, where they are met by the cavalry of Menidas, later supported by other flank cavalry and infantry (3.13.2–4). Despite great losses, the Macedonians were able to break the Persian formation. Darius then launched his scythe-chariots; the purpose, as Arrian explains, was to break up the Macedonian phalanx (3.13.5). However, the Agrianes and javelin-men (Arrian seems to have forgotten the archers of 3.12.3, who had also been stationed in front for that purpose) succeeded in stopping the greater part of them, and the rest passed through the neatly parted phalanx with no effect.[19] The attack of the chariots took place as the Macedonian right flank was trying to stop the attack of the enemy cavalry. Behind the chariots Darius advanced his whole phalanx, but Alexander's major difficulty was still the flank attack. He sent in his last flank squadron, that of Aretes, while continuing to move to his right. Finally, as more and more Persian cavalry were sent against his right flank, the gap in the Persian line which he was waiting for opened; at once he led the companion cavalry in wedge formation[20] into the gap and straight at Darius (3.14.2). In hard hand-to-hand fighting, using heavy spears aimed at the face, the Macedonians were able to push into the Persians and terrify Darius to flight.[21]

With the attack of Alexander and the flight of Darius Arrian's account of the battle is essentially complete. He has concentrated on the principal actions of the conflict, the attack of the forces in which Darius placed most confidence, the effective countermovements of Alexander, and finally the intervention of Alexander and the companion cavalry which turned the Persians and put their king to flight. Alexander's chief problem, as envisioned by Arrian, had been to avoid being outflanked. He had met it by his motion to the right and his carefully controlled feeding of the contingents on his right wing, until the continuing Persian reinforcements to their flank attack caused a gap to appear in their line.[22] As always in the *Anabasis*, the focus is on Alexander and the moves Alexander makes to insure victory.

The remaining incidents are subordinate to the major part of the battle but are treated by Arrian in a manner distinct from that of the other extant historians. The Persian attack on the Macedonian camp, rendered so dramatically by Curtius (4.15.5–12), is succinctly narrated: the soldiers of the second line, who had been given orders in case of an attack on their rear (cf. 3.12.1), wheeled around and in short order killed or put to flight the Persian troops (3.14.4–6). The action is brief, its effect minor. A more real difficulty occurred when the Persian right wing went around Parmenio's left wing and attacked the left flank (3.14.6). Given the size of the Persian force, and Alexander's movement to his right, the movement was to be anticipated, and in fact had been when Alexander placed flank guards on the left as on the right (cf. 3.12.4). Arrian apparently either forgot this force or felt it to be ineffective. (It certainly would have been much weaker than that on the right flank.)[23] In any case, Parmenio was attacked on two sides and sent an urgent message to Alexander for help. The king abandoned further pursuit of Darius[24] and turned to attack the Persian right wing. This story is found in slightly different versions in all our accounts of the battle, but only in Arrian is there no criticism of Parmenio for this request, neither by any word or action of Alexander nor by a comment from the historian. Yet the request both delayed the pursuit of Darius and led to some of the thickest fighting of the battle when Alexander encountered the Parthians, Indians, and Persians who had attacked the Macedonian camp and were now fleeing. The melee which took place recalls that at the battle of Coronea in 394, when Agesilaus came upon a band of fleeing Thebans.[25] On both occasions, the fighting was the more fierce since the only hope of escape for the enemy was to fight their way through at any cost. Arrian notes that the Macedonians sustained their heaviest casualties in this encounter. When Alexander finally arrived at the Persian right wing, it had already begun to flee from Parmenio's Thessalian cavalry. Alexander immediately turned once more to the pursuit of Darius, pushing as far as Arbela, but succeeded only in capturing the chariot, shield, and bow abandoned by the frantically fleeing king.

Throughout his narrative of the battle and its preliminaries, Arrian has attempted to present the consummate generalship of Alexander as he understands it. In the preliminaries, we see in action his use of scouts, prisoners, and personal reconnaissance to gather accurate information, his construction of a fortified base camp, and his careful evaluation of the risks of a night battle. His troop dispositions are made with an eye toward the particular dangers he will face (flank attacks and scythe-chariots); in the event all takes place as he had planned. He does not rush into pursuit before the outcome of the battle is certain, but then pursues relentlessly.

The omissions for which Arrian has been faulted, such as his silence on the efforts of the Persian right wing under Mazaeus to outflank Parmenio, seem for the most part the result not of ignorance or confusion, or of the limited scope of Ptolemy's narrative, but of deliberate decision. Throughout Arrian concentrates on the essentials, making clear the sequence of events and the tactical genius of Alexander. He avoids completely the romantic, the spectacular, the melodramatic which so dominate our other sources. For our author, the excitement and drama of the battle is present in the simple description of the action. His restraint gives strength to the narrative and is in fact a fundamental feature of Arrian's narrative technique, as may be seen from the following list of melodramatic or rhetorical elements omitted by him from the Gaugamela campaign.

I. Preliminaries
  1. The description of the Persian scythe-chariots
     (Curt. 4.9.4−5, Diod. 17.53.1−2)
  2. The dangerous crossing of the Tigris
     (Curt. 4.9.15−21, Diod. 17.55.3−6)
  3. Alexander's luck in not being attacked at the Tigris
     (Curt. 4.9.22−23)
  4. The panic among the soldiers caused by the eclipse
     (Curt. 4.10.2−7)
  5. Darius' letters inviting the Greeks to treachery
     (Curt. 4.10.16−17)
  6. The death of Darius' wife, and his despair
     (Curt. 4.10.18−34, Diod. 17.54.7)
  7. An unexplained panic among Alexander's troops
     (Curt. 4.12.14−17)
  8. Alexander's hesitation at the sight of Darius' troops
     (Curt. 4.12.18−21)
  9. The Macedonian shout and the Persian response
     (Curt. 4.12.22−24)
  10. Darius' vigilant care and his speech to the generals
     (Curt. 4.13.11−14)
  11. The fear of Alexander and the Macedonians, Alexander's sleepless night, his delay in awakening, and his response to Parmenio
     (Curt. 4.13.14−25, Diod. 17.56.1−4, Plut. *Alex.* 32.1−4, Justin 11.13.1−3)
  12. A Persian deserter warns of caltrops
     (Curt. 4.13.36−37)
  13. Darius' speech to his troops
     (Curt. 4.14.8−26)

II. The Battle

1. Mazaeus' attack on the baggage, Parmenio's worried report to Alexander and Alexander's reply, Sisgambis' refusal to be freed, Menidas' defense of the camp (Curt. 4.15.5–12, Diod. 17.59.5–8, Plut. *Alex.* 32.5–7)
2. The terrible effects of the scythe-chariots (Curt. 4.15.14–17, Diod. 17.58.2–5)
3. The eagle omen encouraging Alexander's men (Curt. 4.15.26–27, Plut. *Alex.* 33.2–3)
4. Rhetorical description of the flight of the Persians (Curt. 4.16.10–15)

Arrian's spare narrative concentrates on military details and is the very opposite of the kind of tragic history by which Curtius and to a lesser extent Diodorus attempt to rouse the emotions of pity and fear.

Nevertheless our historian's desire to illumine the brilliant tactics of Alexander and put the young conqueror's military decisions in the best light could lead to biased or even false reporting, as is apparent from his account of the siege of Tyre.[26] According to Arrian, the whole operation, while rendered more complex than a battle by the courage and resourcefulness of the Tyrian defenders, proceeds in a series of orderly stages. The problems of the siege are succinctly stated at the beginning: "The city was an island and was fortified on all sides with high walls, and the Tyrians to all appearances had the advantage by sea, since the Persians still controlled the sea and the Tyrians themselves still had many ships" (2.18.2). Island, navy, and walls constitute the Tyrians' strength, and it is these which the king must defeat.

Alexander's first move was to build a mole from the mainland so that the city could be attacked from dry land; but the Tyrians opposed its completion from their walls and their ships, until the Macedonians had to begin again, making the mole wider so as to hold more towers than before (2.19). Having discovered the importance of sea power for the siege, Alexander then collected a navy by both a rapid expedition against Sidon and the defection of a number of Persian naval contingents to the Macedonian side (2.20.1–2). When he sails from Sidon to Tyre, the Tyrians recognize their inferiority, refuse to fight, and blockade their own harbors (2.20.6–8).

With the threat from the navy thus reduced, Alexander moved his engines onto the new, wider mole and used boats as well to reinforce the attack. From this point the sole problem remaining was the formidable city wall, exceedingly high and protected at the base by large stones. The stones after much difficulty were removed (2.21.5–7), but then the Tyrians sent their navy against the inattentive Cyprian fleet (2.21.8–9). A number of ships were lost, but Alexander counterattacked with his fleet and completely destroyed the Tyrian force (2.22.1–5). Now nothing remained to stop the relentless attack by the machines against the walls. After various attempts, a weak point was found, the wall shaken, space cleared, and the final attack on the wall and the harbors mounted. The Tyrians could resist no longer and were cut down indiscriminately by the Macedonian troops (2.22.6–24.4).

Although there are setbacks, the emphasis of the narrative is on Alexander's response to the ingenuity of the defenders as he relentlessly defeats their every effort. In our other sources, however, the picture is far different. Diodorus does not see the arrival of the fleet as such a turning point, but records that Tyrian attacks continued against the mole, including a highly successful raid on a construction party. Nature added its dangers when a storm caused severe damage to the towers of the causeway—and, according to Curtius, to the fleet as well. Losses of men and ships were especially heavy in the final stage. Diodorus counts two unsuccessful naval attacks, the first opening a breech in the wall, which was immediately repaired, the second repelled with enormous losses to the Macedonians (Diodorus 17.43.5–45.6; Arrian gives the total Macedonian loss in the whole siege as only 400 at 2.24.4). Both Curtius and Diodorus present Alexander as seriously debating whether to abandon the siege. Their account of Alexander's indecision seems a standard narrative technique to heighten the drama of the account, but at least some of these adverse occurrences omitted by Arrian should be true and may even have been in his sources. In the interests of simplifying his account, and especially of presenting Alexander as the completely resourceful general, they have been suppressed. Embarrassing difficulties have been removed, but others have been exaggerated, so as to make Alexander's final victory more marvelous; such seems to be the case with Arrian's incredible estimate of 150 feet for the height of Tyre's walls (2.21.4).[27] In such cases and certainly in others more difficult to document, Arrian's desire to demonstrate Alexander's genius has adversely affected the accuracy of his narrative.

Yet in general Arrian's laudatory purpose led him not to flights of rhetorical fancy but to a close analysis of Alexander's decisions and actions. The combination of restraint in description and detailed attention to Alexander's tactical decisions found in the battles we have considered are typical of Arrian's narrative as a whole. Whether Alexander is besieging Tyre, attacking Uxians in the mountains near Persepolis, or coping with the problems of crossing the Hydaspes and leading his men against elephants in the battle with Porus, Arrian presents him always as the ideal general, alternately cautious and daring as the circumstances demand, by good scouting and foresight interpreting the plans of his enemy, then instructing his troops in exactly those maneuvers which will insure victory. In the battle itself, he is calm while he unfolds his plan, fierce in the attack, always the leader, in both intelligence and spirit, of his men.

ALEXANDER THE MAN

If Arrian's experience with the Roman army gave him the confidence to feel that he could explain Alexander's military genius, his studies with Epictetus and his own experience of good emperors under Trajan and Hadrian encouraged him to attempt as well an evaluation of Alexander as man and ruler of men. In this effort, even more than in his treatment of his military genius, Arrian arranged, supplemented, and interpreted his sources to shape his own view of Alexander, using earlier writers yet independent of them as well.

In the first three books of the *Anabasis*, the military side of Alexander predominates, but there are special incidents through which Arrian presents other aspects of his character. Emulation of Achilles is suggested by the visit to his tomb (1.12.1–2; cf. also 7.14.4); of Perseus and Heracles by the visit to the oracle of Ammon (3.3.1). The story of his physician Philip (from Aristobulus, 2.4.7–11) revealed "that he was a firm friend to his friends, free of suspicion even in the face of death." He showed laudable self-control toward the royal women captured from Darius at Issus (2.12.3–8) and a noteworthy resolution in his letter replying to Darius' offer of half his kingdom (2.14.4–9), but a lack of good sense in burning the palace at Persepolis (3.18.12).

However, it is only beginning with the fourth book that Arrian seriously begins to examine Alexander's character and tries to give a more general view of his life. Considering the avowedly laudatory purpose of the book, stated in the second preface (1.12.3ff.), one is at first startled to discover that Arrian's first major consideration of Alexander's character is built around a series of distinctly barbarous episodes:

the mutilation of Bessus, the drunken murder of Clitus, the attempt to introduce the Persian custom of *proskynesis*, and the execution of the philosopher-historian Callisthenes and a number of pages on a charge of conspiracy (4.7–14). Our surprise disappears when we consider the aims and techniques of Arrian's treatment of this unpleasant sequence of events.

As was said when considering the structure of the *Anabasis*, this passage comes at a time when Alexander has apparently completed his conquests and achieved mastery of the Persian empire; Darius is defeated, and Macedonian armies rule from the Danube to the Nile to the Iaxartes. It is thus a fitting moment to consider the character of the man who achieved this conquest. Arrian knew as well that Alexander was a standard example in the schools of philosophy,[28] attacked for delusions of grandeur, drunkenness, viciousness, and other vices. Even his master Epictetus had cited the folly of Alexander's order to burn the temple of Asclepius after the god had failed to save Hephaestion (*Diss.* 2.22.17).[29] If his book was to show successfully the greatness of Alexander, he must do battle with this influential tradition. Arrian determined to consider at length those very incidents which the philosophers and others hostile to Alexander found most damaging, despite the fact that his two chief sources, Ptolemy and Aristobulus, appear to have been either noncommital or surprisingly uninformative on these events. These incidents have been often discussed by modern historians, who similarly see them as central to an understanding of the historical Alexander, his attitude toward his own divinity, the tension between the young leader and his men, his assumption of the ways of the lands he had conquered, and other questions.[30] Our business, on the contrary, will be to examine these chapters in the *Anabasis* to discover how Arrian as historian and writer developed his presentation of the conqueror.

First, however, it is noteworthy that Arrian has excluded one important episode, frequently seen as the first revelation of the viciousness of Alexander's character, the execution of Philotas and his father Parmenio. Whatever other sources may say, Arrian treated the death of Philotas as a legitimate execution, relying on the combined testimony of Ptolemy and Aristobulus. Moreover, in Arrian's view Parmenio was killed either because Alexander believed he must have participated in the conspiracy or because Parmenio was too powerful to be allowed to survive the execution of his son—both acceptable, if not noble reasons for a king to act. Arrian includes as *legomenon* the story of Amyntas, also found in Curtius, which demonstrated that legal procedure was followed and only the guilty punished (3.26–27.3).

Thus, for Arrian the sequence of barbaric episodes begins with the council on the punishment of Bessus (4.7.3), which is introduced as one of a number of administrative measures taken at Bactra. The decision, to cut off his nose and the tips of his ears before sending him to Ecbatana for execution, is stated briefly, but its import is elaborated by Arrian:

> I do not myself approve the excessive severity of this punishment; for mutilation of that sort is, I think, a barbarous custom. I admit, moreover, that Alexander came to allow himself to emulate eastern extravagance and splendor, and the fashions of barbarian kings of treating their subjects as inferiors; regrettable, too, was the assumption by a descendant of Heracles of Median dress in place of what Macedonians had worn from time immemorial, and the unblushing exchange of his familiar headgear, so long victoriously worn, for the *kitaris* of the vanquished Persians. I have no praise for this conduct. (4.7.4)

The decision to mutilate Bessus is seen as just one of a series of barbarian practices taken up by Alexander, which all taken together become a formidable indictment against the man, for Arrian goes on to say that the conqueror demonstrates an absence of that fundamental virtue, self-control or *sōphrosynē*. "I hold that Alexander's deeds bear witness to the fact that neither bodily strength, nor noble birth, nor fortune in war even greater than Alexander's . . . is of any use toward mortal happiness, unless the man who accomplishes such great—apparently—deeds has learned at the same time self-control" (4.7.5). With the issues of barbarism and self-control defined, Arrian sets out to explore the other incidents which had especially damaged Alexander's reputation.

These three are separate from the immediate context, as Arrian notes twice, at 4.8.1 and again at 4.14.4. They are not set at Bactra, but are included here exactly because they involve the issues raised by the mutilation of Bessus. We should note furthermore that in these incidents Arrian is supplementing extensively his two main sources with other authors, cited as *legomena*. The fourteen *legomena* notices in eight chapters[31] warn us that here Arrian is constructing a narrative which must differ considerably from that of Ptolemy and Aristobulus. The numerous citations of *legomena*, moreover, also suggest a certain lack of confidence in the accuracy of the narratives reported, an impression fortified by the repeated use of indirect discourse where we would expect direct. Use of indirect discourse tends to separate the writer from what is said, so that we are constantly reminded that the narrative is reported on the authority of others and is not to be taken as objective fact. In 4.8–14 there are very few indicatives which do not represent Arrian's personal comments. Most of the main verbs are in the infinitive, with exceptions at high points in the narrative, for example when Alexander, enraged by Clitus, calls out for his bodyguard (4.8.8), or when the plot of the pages is revealed (4.13.7). Even Callisthenes' speech shifts strangely between indicatives and infinitives.[32] The strongest statements in the passage are in fact those made outside of the narrative itself, Arrian's frequent insertions of opinion and interpretation. Like the first programmatic indictment of the mutilation of Bessus, these nine *obiter dicta*[33] are meant to push the reader to accept the author's conclusions concerning the interpretation of Alexander's behavior.

The story of Clitus develops smoothly out of the consideration of self-control immediately preceding. The scene is a drinking party; Arrian notes that Alexander had taken to drinking barbarically, but he neglects the fact that the Macedonians had drunk heavily long before they came to Persia. Flatterers began to say that Alexander had exceeded the achievements of the Dioscuri and even of Heracles; Arrian warns us that "flatterers always have and always will corrupt a king's business." Clitus is presented as being upset, like Arrian, with both the flattery and Alexander's turn toward barbarism, so that he defends the gods and heroes by noting that Alexander must share with his fellow Macedonians the glory of his achievements. Clitus is reminding Alexander that he is fundamentally equal with his subjects, a position taken by Arrian at 4.7.4. Yet here Arrian comments cautiously: "I do not commend Clitus' words, since I think it sufficient in the midst of such drunken talk to keep one's own counsel and not join the rest in flattery" (4.8.5).[34] When Clitus continues, and cannot be kept from Alexander, he is finally killed. At this point Arrian adds a variant version taken from Aristobulus, which emphasized how Clitus, after having been led away, had once more confronted the enraged Alexander, so that he was at least partially responsible for his own death. Since we are expressly told that Aristobulus had not given the origins of the affair, Arrian must have brought in from other writers the setting of barbaric drinking and flattery which so colors this incident.

But it is the end which allows us to see the whole. Clitus should not be seen as a loyal companion struck down by a tyrannical king; on the contrary, "I strongly blame Clitus for his insulting behavior (*hybris*) toward the king." Arrian rather feels pity for Alexander, "because he showed himself conquered by two evils by neither of which any self-controlled (*sōphronounta*) man should be overcome, anger and drunkenness."[35] We return to the theme enunciated in 4.7.5; the conqueror of the world has been conquered because he was not master of himself. Yet having said this, Arrian moves at once to praise Alexander: the murder was a disgraceful deed, but he redeemed himself by recognizing it for what it was and admitting that he had erred. Various acts of repentance follow, and a sacrifice to Dionysus to make amends for the one he had forgotten. The episode concludes with praise, not criticism, for Alexander had in fact learned that Clitus was right and the flatterers were wrong: he was a man, not a god. "In this I especially praise Alexander, that he did not brazen out his crime, nor add to his guilt by becoming champion and advocate in his own defense, but admitted that he had done wrong, being after all a man." The story, which had begun as a demonstration of Alexander's lack of self-understanding, shifts to a more positive approach as Alexander comes to a new awareness of who he is.

Alexander's realization that he is only a man is contrasted in the next episode with the sophistic flattery of Anaxarchus, who in comparing the king to Zeus, once more attempts to break down the line between gods and men, between *hybris* and *sōphrosynē*. Such consolation, Arrian notes, is a greater evil than the original murder, for it leads a king to consider himself the only standard of justice. The setting is similar to that of the Clitus scene—flatterers preying upon the king's love of glory. From this false consolation Arrian finds it an easy step to Alexander's interest in *proskynesis*, the Persian obeisance before the king, which is seen again as barbarism and a surrender to flattery, and from there to Callisthenes' elaborate speech distinguishing the proper honors for gods and men and attacking the practice of *proskynesis*. As before, the fundamental consideration in the speech of Callisthenes is the awareness of a limit set for men, which it is barbarism to trespass. Alexander as a descendant of Heracles should be satisfied with Greek ways and not imitate barbarians. In a highly effective final sentence, Callisthenes recalls the examples of Cyrus, Darius I, Xerxes, Artaxerxes, and Darius III, all of whom had been humbled (esōphronisan; literally, made to be sōphrōn) by free peoples, Greeks and Scythians, who did not practice proskynesis. Excess leads to disaster.

Arrian clearly shares Callisthenes' sentiments and presents them as persuasively as possible. On the other hand, he carefully disassociates himself from the speaker. Earlier (4.10.1–4) he had noted that although Callisthenes' opposition to Anaxarchus was correct, the man himself was a boor, and quoted two stories which put him in an unsympathetic light. In the first, Callisthenes boasted that his history, not Alexander's deeds, would be responsible for any fame or share in divinity which Alexander might come to have—a vain attitude quite different from Arrian's own as an Alexander historian. In the second, he praised tyrannicide, hardly a tactful position at the court of an absolute monarch. To complete the picture, Arrian places after Callisthenes' speech, as legomenon, the story of the loving cup and the lost kiss,[36] which while witty is in context distinctly uncomplimentary to Callisthenes. Alexander reveals hybris, but the rudeness of Callisthenes is equally deplorable, in Arrian's opinion. "It is enough, I think, that a man should behave himself in a seemly manner, while at the same time, if he has consented to enter a king's service, exalting his master as much as he can" (4.12.6). The subject has duties as does the king, and therefore Alexander was right to be angry with Callisthenes. Alexander held back, and did not insist on proskynesis, but Arrian's criticism of the philosopher's foolish arrogance provides a smooth transition to the last episode, the conspiracy of the pages, in which Callisthenes lost his life. Knowing his attitude, Alexander was the more willing to believe that he was a conspirator.

The account of this final incident begins with a straightforward historical summary on the institution of the pages, but then cites legomena for the grudge of Hermolaus and the plot. The story of Aristobulus is then introduced, according to which Alexander was warned not to return to his tent by an inspired Syrian prophetess, an intimation that the king was being protected by the gods. The discovery of the plot follows, narrated in historical presents, vivid and rapid. Arrian accepts as fact the guilt of the conspirators, among whom both Ptolemy and Aristobulus included Callisthenes, but he includes the story of the plot in this context because many writers ascribed the punishment of Callisthenes to Alexander's ill will. Arrian himself does

not actually accuse Callisthenes, but he reports as *legomenon* Hermolaus' confession, a speech which also repeats the charges voiced by
Arrian in 4.7.4–5, adding the execution of Philotas and Parmenio:
"He listed everything: the illegal death of Philotas and still more illicit
killing of Parmenio, and of the others who had died at that time, the
drunken murder of Clitus, the wearing of Median costume, his wish
for *proskynesis*, still not abandoned, and Alexander's drinking and
sleeping" (4.14.2). The charges are the same, but our attitude toward
them has been changed by Arrian's narrative. When Hermolaus pro-
claims himself a tyrant-slayer, it does not prove Alexander a tyrant
but confirms Callisthenes' involvement in the guilt of the conspiracy,
recalling his words in praise of tyrant-slayers reported earlier by
Arrian (4.10.3–4).

   In this sequence of incidents (4.7–14) Arrian has raised the question of Alexander's *sōphrosynē*, implied an opposition between world-
mastery and self-mastery, and revealed Alexander's weaknesses in his
desire for glory and his tendency to imitate barbarians and forget the
limits his humanity sets upon him.[37] Yet he has simultaneously argued
that Clitus was looking for trouble, that Callisthenes said the right
thing in the wrong way, and that there was a real conspiracy for which
Callisthenes was at least partially responsible. Arrian's presentation
has been strongly colored by his idea of a proper relation between
subject and king, even when the subject is a lifetime companion as
Clitus was. Flatterers would always attempt to spoil kings (4.8.3), but
a wise man, especially when drinking is going on, need merely keep
his thoughts to himself (4.8.5), and it is insulting to belittle the achievements of the king, or even to set oneself above him, as did Callisthenes,
rather than glorify him in every suitable way (4.12.6). Arrian's understanding reflects the life of the imperial court under Trajan and Hadrian, when the tyranny of a Nero or Domitian was a thing of the
past, but the emperor was still emperor, to be respected and praised.
The letters of Pliny to Trajan, his panegyric, or the praise of Hadrian
by Arrian himself (*Per.* 2.4, *Tact.* 44.3) are our best commentaries
on these passages. Furthermore, even before Arrian enjoyed the company of princes, he had been taught by Epictetus to pity a man who
did wrong, even if a tyrant (*Diss.* 1.18.3; cf. *Anab.* 4.9.1), and see
the importance of recognizing one's faults (*Diss.* 2.21.1–7). Epictetus
also had seen the danger of the flatterer and the importance of keeping
oneself independent when in the service of the great (*Diss.* 3.24.44–
57). In the final analysis, Clitus and Callisthenes are convicted of

violating the sensible relation of subject to monarch, but Alexander is discovered to have found that self-knowledge which it was the object of philosophy to encourage. Alexander's strength has been to see and admit that he did wrong in killing Clitus, and to forego the *proskynesis* ceremony, in both cases recognizing that he was only a man. Thanks to Arrian's manner of presenting these incidents, the question to be resolved in the remaining history is no longer whether Alexander is a vainglorious barbarian, but how he will reconcile his extraordinary desire for glory with the limitations of his humanity.

The sequence in 4.7–14, while concentrating on certain incidents of the expedition which were commonly presented as evidence of bad traits in Alexander's character, recalls other motifs which are combined in Arrian's portrait of Alexander. At 4.7.5 Arrian contrasted being master not of Asia, but of all three continents, with being master of oneself. Alexander's conquests imply not only military genius but that tremendous desire for achievement which was one of the outstanding characteristics of the man. Through the first three books the goal is the rule of Asia, where Asia equals the Persian empire. The fourth book begins an extension of that motif: Alexander's plans for the conquest of the rest of the world. At 4.1.3 he is thinking of invading Scythia beyond the Tanais (Iaxartes); at 4.7.5 Arrian states that he planned to sail around Asia and Africa, conquering them both. While still in Zariaspa, Alexander receives the Chorasmanian king Pharasmanes, who invites him to invade Colchis and the tribes around the Black Sea. Alexander replies that he first intends to subdue India, thus gaining all Asia, and then to return to Greece, from which he could make an expedition to the Black Sea (4.15.6). The enormous size of India is described so that we can properly appreciate Alexander's conquests there (5.5.2–6.8). The speech to the officers at the Hyphasis both recalls the great conquests of the past (5.25.4–5) and presents a panorama of the conquests to come—the Ganges, the Eastern Sea, and all Africa, so that "the boundaries of our rule will be the boundaries God has set for the earth" (5.26.1–2). Coenus humbly suggests that Alexander get new men from home before conquering what lands he likes—the tribes beyond the Hyphasis, those on the Black Sea, or in Africa (5.27.7). Book VII, of course, begins with the elaborate refusal to speculate on what Alexander's plans might have been, set into the context of the philosophic renunciation of the world typified by the Brahmins, Diogenes, and Calanus. The speech at Opis does not speak of further conquests but recalls in two magnificent lists those which have already been made (7.9.7−8, 10.5−7). The roll of ambassadors at 7.15.4−5 suggests that the world is submitting to him of its own free will: from Africa came Carthaginians, Libyans, and Ethiopians; from Europe, Italians, Celts, Iberians, Scythians, perhaps even Romans. But Alexander is still planning expeditions on the Caspian Sea (7.16.1−4) and against the Arabs (7.19.6). "The truth is, as it seems to me, that Alexander was always insatiable in winning possessions." Yet Arrian saw another aspect to this insatiable desire.

Clitus had argued that Alexander's achievements were not his own, but in large part the work of his Macedonian comrades (4.8.5). Callisthenes had recalled that Heracles had won honor for his labor after his death (4.11.7). The motif of toil (*ponos*) thus emerges as that which will distinguish Alexander from other men and win him the honor he craves. Heracles, as an ancestor of Alexander, was the natural focus of this motif. At the siege of Tyre, certainly one of Alexander's most difficult military operations, Alexander had dreamed that Heracles had stretched out his hand and conducted him into the city. The seer Aristander had interpreted the dream to mean that Tyre would be taken, but with labor, for the deeds of Heracles had been achieved only with labor (2.18.1).[38] A new omen of the same import came to Alexander shortly after leaving Zariaspa; a spring of oil was discovered near his tent, which Aristander interpreted as a sign of labors but also of victory after the labors (4.15.7−8). Alexander accepted this message willingly and in the speech at the Hyphasis, according to Arrian, pronounced a kind of panegyric of labors, in which his attitude is expressed unequivocally: "For a man of spirit, there is no limit to labors, I feel, when the labors lead to fine deeds, except the labors themselves" (5.26.1).

At the Hyphasis Alexander was checked, but he would not be held back from the glory toils could bring. While attacking the town of Mallians, thinking that his troops were not energetic enough, he pushed forward to the top of the wall, where he found himself alone and unprotected. "He decided that it was risky to remain there, yet he would display nothing worth talking about, whereas if he jumped within the wall he might by this act terrify the Indians, or if not, since he must needs be in danger, he would die not without effort, having performed great deeds, worthy to be heard by those coming after" (6.9.5). Arrian here compares Alexander's decision with the individual heroism and striving for glory of the Homeric heroes (made more present by the double mention of the sacred shield brought from Troy,

6.9.3 and 10.2, and the echo of Hector's words when drawing his sword on Achilles),[39] but he also stresses the element of personal risk and effort which was proper to Heracles as well. The moral is pointed when Alexander's friends rebuke him for risking his life. Arrian admits that the criticism is just but notes that Alexander loved glory and was not able to hold back from risks, and he quotes the words of an old man which won Alexander's approval—"Deeds are the work of men" —with the addition that a man who acts must suffer (6.13.4−5). In his speech at the Hyphasis and his actions among the Mallians, Alexander goes well beyond his men in his willingness to undergo toils, hoping to win lasting glory.

Arrian, always a philosopher, is aware of two other views of such efforts. The one is uttered by the Brahmins: Alexander is restless and wretched, roaming far from home, making nothing but trouble for himself and others (7.1.6). The other is expressed by Alexander himself, in his speech at Opis: his efforts, greater than those of any of his men, have been all for their sake, so that they could rule and be rich. He is sleepless, so that they can sleep (7.9.6−10.4). Philosophically, there is no justification for heroic labors or conquest unless they do some good, unless they do more than assert one's dominance over another. In this speech, Alexander argues that in fact his conquests are not for himself, but for the Macedonians.

His argument in this speech, moreover, represents a response to another criticism expressed immediately after the decision to mutilate Bessus: Alexander's acceptance of the barbarian custom of not sharing the way of life of his men (4.7.4). Not only in this speech but generally throughout the *Anabasis* Arrian argues the opposite, that any desire of Alexander for barbarian aloofness was an aberration and that his true character was to share life with his subjects and be attentive to their needs. This appears in small things, such as allowing newly married husbands to return to Macedonia to their wives, on which Arrian comments that Alexander gained as much popularity among the Macedonians by this act as by any other (1.24.2). His relations with his troops were generally excellent, and he joined their work to encourage and reward them (e.g., at Tyre, 2.18.4, 2.23.4). Arrian singles out as Alexander's finest deed a simple act demonstrating the king's willingness to share the labors of his men. In the Gedrosian desert, when all were suffering greatly from thirst, some soldiers found a muddy water hole, and collecting some water, brought it in a helmet to Alexander. He thanked them, but poured the water out in the sight

of the troops (6.26.3). Such a leader the soldiers would follow anywhere. The revolt at Opis is seen as prompted more by a feeling of
exclusion than of independence. It is resolved with the dialogue between Callines and the king, when the men ask merely to be called
his kinsmen, and receive a kiss (7.11.6–7). How far removed we are
from Callisthenes' disinterest in a kiss (4.12.5)! The troops cheer him
on his recovery from the Mallian wound (6.13.2), and on his deathbed
all filed past to see him one last time (7.26.1).

Finally the barbaric treatment of Bessus is set off against the great
number of acts in which Alexander behaves generously toward his
foe. The outstanding case is his treatment of Porus, which Arrian reports as a *legomenon*. On being asked by Alexander how he wished
to be treated, Porus replied only, "Treat me as a king." Alexander,
much pleased, gave him back his kingdom and more besides (5.19.2–
3). The Persian royal family was given all the respect due their station,
both Darius himself (after his death) and the captured Persian women,
as were other defeated leaders and cities. On his generous treatment of
the Ephesians, Arrian comments, "Alexander won as much popularity
by what he did in Ephesus as on any other occasion."[40]

At the end of the *Anabasis*, Arrian summarizes his view of the
strengths and weaknesses of the man and reunites these and other
facets of Alexander's character which he has brought to the surface
in the course of his history: "Physically he was extremely handsome
and enduring of labor; mentally he excelled in quickness, bravery,
love of glory, and love of risks, and was most careful towards the
gods. Most temperate in the pleasures of the body, his passion was
for praise only, and of that he was insatiable. . . . Both his word and
his bond were inviolable, but no cheat or liar ever caught him off his
guard. Spending but little on his own pleasure, he poured out his
money without stint for the benefit of others" (7.28).

A paragraph follows, considering Alexander's weaknesses, excusing
them one by one: (1) he had a tendency toward barbarian arrogance,
but he was young, successful, and a prey to flatterers, and moreover,
he admitted his error, which is the important thing; (2) he claimed
divine origin, but this may have merely been a device to impress his
subjects, and other great men of the past had done the same;[41] (3) he
adopted Persian dress, but that too was a device, to appear less strange
to the barbarians and relieve Macedonian rashness, as was his incor-
poration of Persian troops into Macedonian units; (4) his drinking,
according to Aristobulus, was from a love of companionship. All these

faults, it will be noticed, are those imputed to Alexander in the passage 4.7–14, the most important of which, in Arrian's mind, clearly was the murder of Clitus. Arrian does not attempt to evaluate other moments of weakness such as the unwise decision to burn the palace at Persepolis (3.18.11–12) and the carte blanche letter to Cleomenes in Egypt (7.23.6–8), which he had criticized in the course of his history.

The indictment based on the actions of 4.7–14 was sufficient, if valid, to condemn Alexander, but Arrian's analysis, borne out by the narrative of the remaining books, demonstrates the weakness of the accusations. In Arrian's view, the man must be evaluated as a whole, not for a few moments in his life. Alexander's virtues were great, his faults minor. The extraordinary deeds he accomplished have justly spread his name over the known world. Even the gods, through omens and dreams, have sanctioned his praise, and Arrian is not ashamed to admire Alexander (7.30).

Arrian combined in his portrait of Alexander elements of the Homeric hero, of the Stoic Heracles who won glory through labors for mankind, of the ideal king who rules justly and without asserting himself over his subjects, of the military leader, masterful in every situation, of the conqueror of the world, and of contemporary Roman emperors. He could rightly feel that he had fulfilled his purpose, "worthily to celebrate Alexander and his deeds."

7

THE BOOK ON INDIA

INDIA was the most distant and most exotic of Alexander's conquests. Long before his expedition, its remoteness had generated marvelous tales of strange animals and unlikely customs. Herodotus had passed on stories of ants which dig gold and men who eat their fathers when they die; still more fantastic accounts were elaborated by Ctesias of Cnidos in his *Indica*.[1] These writers established a tradition of the fabulous East which was enhanced, not diminished, by Alexander's brief subjugation of the country. Both the historians of Alexander and writers of independent books on India (*Indica*) wrote at length on the wonders of the country. Arrian like the others felt the attraction of these marvels, and he apologizes in his *Anabasis of Alexander*, at the moment when Alexander crosses the Indus, for his refusal to yield to their lure.

I have not included in this book an account of the Indian way of life, or any description of the strange animals to be found, or of the variety and size of the fish and other aquatic animals in the Indus, the Hydaspes, the Ganges, and elsewhere. Nor have I mentioned gold-mining ants and gold-guarding griffins[2] and other queer things which people have invented rather for diversion than for serious history, in the belief that none of the absurd stories they tell about India were likely to be brought to the test of truth. Actually however, most of these fables were indeed proved or disproved by Alexander and his men—except in a few cases where they themselves were guilty of invention. They proved, for instance, that the Indians have no gold—at any rate the very considerable part of them which Alexander visited in the course of his campaign—and that their domestic arrangements were far from luxurious. The men are taller than any other Asiatics, most of them being over seven feet, or not much less; they are darker-skinned than any other race except the

Ethiopians, and were the finest fighters to be found anywhere in Asia at that time. . . . However, about India it is my intention to write a special account based on the most reliable reports from Alexander's expedition and the discoveries of Nearchus, who sailed along the northern coasts of the Indian Ocean, and including facts recorded by the two distinguished writers, Megasthenes and Eratosthenes. My account will cover the Indian way of life, any strange creatures to be found in the country, and the actual coastal voyage in the Southern Ocean. (*Anab.* 5.4.3 – 5.1)

Proportion prohibited a long digression on India in the *Anabasis*,[3] but Arrian decided to have his cake and eat it too by writing a separate book on India which would be a complement to his history of Alexander. The title that he chose, *Indike*, suggests that he intended it to be different from the usual accounts of India, *Indica*.[4] The basic outline of the *Indike* had already formed in his mind while writing the *Anabasis*, and Arrian refers to it several other times in the course of that work.[5] Both works are about Alexander: "This book, like the present one, will be a Greek history written in Alexander's honor. It will be a work for some future date, when my spirit and heaven move me to it" (*Anab.* 6.28.6).[6] As this passage shows, the *Indike* was written after the *Anabasis*. Frequent cross-references to events narrated in the Alexander history tie the *Indike* to the earlier work.[7]

Several distinctive features of Arrian's book on India are stated or implied in the first passage quoted, which in the absence of a prefatory statement in the *Indike* may be taken as a kind of proem to that work. Most evident is the influence of Herodotus, who included a number of major ethnographical digressions in his history.[8] While the most notable are those on Egypt (which occupies the whole of Book II), Scythia (4.5–82), and Libya (4.168–99), he also had a brief section on India, including the gold-mining ants. Arrian's decision to write the *Indike* in the Ionic dialect may be interpreted as homage to Herodotus and to the Ionian ethnographic tradition. For this work he abandoned the artificial Attic Greek which was dictated by the literary standards of his day. His Ionic is equally an archaizing reconstruction, in no way dependent upon the spoken language of his own day, using words and a limited number of forms culled from Ionian authors, especially Homer and Herodotus. Lists of such Ionisms had been drawn up by grammarians as part of the same revival of the ancient ways which determined the Atticist movement, but we need not doubt that Arrian profited as well from his own thorough knowledge of Herodotus. In any case, he does not attempt a pedantic and lifeless recreation of all the peculiarities of the old dialect, but chooses a middle road, combining the Ionic features freely with standard Attic usage. The result is a charming recreation and reminder of early ethnography.[9]

The use of Ionic, the emphasis on Alexander, and the explicit reference to literary sources indicate that Arrian did not intend his account of India to reflect the situation in his own day. He did not imitate Herodotus in traveling and making inquiries, for his work was basically a digression from his Alexander history and was meant to describe the India which Alexander found. There was in fact an active commerce between India and the Roman empire in Arrian's day, which was important enough to encourage some modern scholars to argue that the major factor behind Trajan's Parthian war was a desire to control the traffic with the East,[10] and Trajan himself, when he reached the head of the Persian Gulf, expressed a desire to sail to India.[11] There was a regular trade route between the ports of the Persian Gulf and India along the route taken by Nearchus and his fleet, and for at least half a century Roman merchants had traded directly with India, using the monsoons to sail from the Red Sea to the east coast of the subcontinent.[12] None of this filters into Arrian's account, which is resolutely traditional; Roman acquaintance with Indian products or animals is mentioned only sporadically.[13] Later historical events are omitted as well. When he states (*Ind.* 5.7) that only Alexander had made an expedition against India, he does not consider Seleucus I, Antiochus III, the Parthians, or the Kushans. The *Indike* is in no sense an account of India in Roman times.[14]

Nevertheless, Arrian had no desire to retell the fables of the past. In his statement in the *Anabasis* he emphasizes his rejection of these stories, and the salutary effect of Alexander's expedition in putting them to the test. Like the preface to the *Anabasis*, this proemial paragraph stresses the author's choice of reliable informants: in this case Nearchus, admiral of the fleet sent by Alexander from the Indus to the Persian Gulf; Megasthenes, ambassador to the founder of the Mauryan dynasty, Chandragupta, about 302 B.C.; and Eratosthenes, the learned Alexandrian geographer and polymath. Even the choice of these men did not free Arrian from difficulty, as shall be seen, but his intention is clearly to present thoughtful and truthful reports rather than fiction. Nor was he deceived in the result; his monograph is undoubtedly the most sober and credible account which has come down to us on India, exceeding even the skeptical Strabo in its firm exclusion of the fabulous. It is a sign of the genius of Arrian that this exclusion does not dull its interest or its charm.

From the statement in the *Anabasis* we learn that Arrian from the beginning had determined on the bipartite work which we now possess. He in fact conceived of his work as two disparate halves with no intrinsic unity—a compositional technique he found useful elsewhere.[15] In a sense, he combines two separate digressions from the *Anabasis*, the first (*Ind.* 1–17) an ethnography of India which might have been inserted, as were those of Herodotus, at the point where the country was attacked, the second (*Ind.* 18–43) an account of the voyage of Nearchus. It was not Arrian's practice in the *Anabasis* to narrate subordinate actions: with few exceptions his history follows Alexander's movements and activities. Thus the account of Nearchus' movements from the time he left Alexander at the Indus until he rejoined him at Susa had no proper place in the *Anabasis*, no matter how interesting the narrative. In the *Indike* the two accounts are combined into one work, within which Nearchus' expedition was the major interest, and the ethnography a sort of introductory excursus.[16]

The structure of the first half is similar to that of many other ethnographic accounts:[17]

The Country (1–6)
    Exclusion of the land west of the Indus (1)
    The boundaries of India and their measurement (2–3.8)
    The rivers of India (3.8–4.16)
    Digression on the credibility of the accounts of India (5.1–6.3)
    Cause of the river floods (6.4–9)
History (7–9)
    History by kings (7–9)[18]
        Dionysus (7.5–9)
        Heracles (8.4–9.9)
Customs (10–17)
    Burial, cities, slaves (10)
    The seven castes (11–12)
    Elephants, especially elephant hunting (13–14)
    Other unusual animals: tigers, ants, parrots, apes, snakes (15)
    Clothes and armor (16)
    Other unusual facts (17)

The threefold division echoes Herodotus' division of his Egyptian account into the country, customs, and history,[19] although the immediate source of the pattern is Megasthenes, Arrian's chief informant for this portion of the *Indike*. Megasthenes' *Indica* in three or four books was used extensively by Strabo as well as by Arrian, and Diodorus provides a useful summary of much of his work.[20] From these we can determine that Arrian followed for the most part Megasthenes' arrangement[21] and that Megasthenes himself must have been influenced by Herodotus, although the exact extent of this influence is impossible to determine. Before Arrian, Megasthenes also wrote of the causes of the river risings, treated history according to a king list, wherein some kings are passed over rapidly, while others are considered at length, and showed an interest in unusual animals and customs. These features in Megasthenes are all derived from Herodotus and give a generally Herodotean flavor to this part of Arrian's book.

The element which dominates our author's presentation in this section is the desire to achieve a credible account, already apparent in the proemial statement in the *Anabasis* (5.4.3–4). He is torn between the wish to present the most interesting facts about India and an awareness that his sources frequently lied. He had noted that "most of these tales were proved or disproved by Alexander and those with him—except in a few cases where they themselves were guilty of invention" (*Anab.* 5.4.4). But Alexander had only gone as far as the Hyphasis; the source which described most comprehensively and circumstantially the country was a book written by a traveler beyond the Hyphasis, Megasthenes, who would have been an ideal informant, except that he combined personal, generally reliable observation with fabulous hearsay.[22] For this reason he was attacked by the most rationalistic of the geographers, Eratosthenes, whose strictures had impressed the learned Augustan writer Strabo.[23] Strabo himself dealt with India in his fifteenth book, and ran into the same difficulties as would Arrian: "All who have written about India have proved themselves, for the most part, fabricators, but preeminently so Deimachus [another ambassador]; the next in order is Megasthenes; and then Onesicritus and Nearchus and other such writers, who begin to speak the truth, though indistinctly. . . . Especially Deimachus and Megasthenes deserve to be distrusted."[24] From Strabo we discover that Megasthenes was willing to give a place in his *Indica* both to a detailed description of Chandragupta's capital city Palibothra (Pataliputra, now Patna) and to tales of "the men who sleep on their ears," "the noseless men," "the mouthless men," "men with one eye," and —an early version of the abominable snowman—"men with back-ward toes."[25] Little wonder, therefore, that Arrian, like Eratosthenes and Strabo, was skeptical of Megasthenes' book.

Arrian's difficulty in reporting accurately on India is apparent in his description of the physical features of the country. For the dimensions of the subcontinent, he relies on Eratosthenes: "To me he is more trustworthy than another, since he made a study of geography" (3.1).[26] Concerning three sides of the trapezoid of India, the Alexandrian scholar was comfortingly precise. For the northern side, however, he had admitted that he had accurate measurements only from the Indus to Palibothra: "beyond that point one could not be so exact" (3.4). Eratosthenes had given an estimate based on reports, then criticized others—Ctesias of Cnidos and Onesicritus, both of whom wrote nonsense, Nearchus, and Megasthenes, who gave the most detailed figures but described an India much larger than that of Eratosthenes (3.5−8).[27]

Finding even the general dimensions of the subcontinent in dispute and his surest guide, Eratosthenes, uncertain, Arrian turns to the other topic standard in geographical accounts, and especially necessary in a description of India, the rivers (3.9−6.9).[28] His presentation is repeti-tive again because of his doubts on the veracity of his sources.[29] He begins firmly enough, with the assertion that the rivers of India are greater than any in Asia; he names the Indus and the Ganges, com-pares them with the Nile and the Danube, and even ventures to suggest that the Acesines, a tributary of the Indus, is larger than the Danube. But the paragraph concludes with a note of uncertainty: "Perhaps there are other greater rivers in India." Since Alexander had gone only as far as the Hyphasis, a tributary of the Indus, and never reached the Ganges, Arrian wishes to be cautious. Still, Megasthenes had seen the Ganges, and on his authority Arrian describes that river and its tributaries (4.3−7) and then the Indus and its affluents (4.8−12). These lists justify his renewed assertion that these rivers were in fact much larger than the Nile or the Danube, neither of which had so many tributaries.[30] For the Danube, Arrian is proud to adduce his own knowledge; he himself knew of and had seen only two navigable tribu-taries, the Save and the Inn (4.15−16).[31] Thus he comes full circle to his starting point: the rivers of India are indeed greater than the Nile or the Danube (3.9−10 = 4.13−16).

The chapter which follows attempts to clarify the problems of reliability. It is introduced by the statement that the explanation of the
magnitude of these rivers must be hearsay (5.1) and concludes, "This
digression was written so that the stories told by some about the Indians beyond the Hyphasis can be seen to be unreliable" (6.1).[32] One
would expect an attack on Megasthenes, as is implied also by the
statement that Megasthenes did not travel much in India (5.3). But the
point of contention shifts as Arrian summarizes Megasthenes' argument that there was no foreign conqueror of India between Dionysus
and Alexander. Strabo had used the same account (15.1.6 = *FGrHist*
715 F11a) to reveal the mistakes of the Alexander historians, notably
Nearchus. Both authors reflect Eratosthenes' use of Megasthenes to re-
fute the flattering inventions of those who traveled with Alexander.
Eratosthenes had in fact rejected the stories both about Dionysus and
about Heracles. Arrian, however, seems tentatively to accept Megasthenes' account of Dionysus in India[33] but rejects with Megasthenes
the supposed expedition of Heracles, which in the *Anabasis* he had left
uncertain.[34] Still Eratosthenes had convinced him of the danger of
hearsay report, so that he concludes that beyond the Hyphasis little
is certain, while up to that river the companions of Alexander are
"not completely unreliable."[35] The judgment is confirmed by a part-
ing shot at Megasthenes; he speaks of a certain river Silas, in which
nothing floats (6.2–3). No comment is needed to explain that Arrian
finds this just the sort of story which makes him distrustful of hearsay
reports.[36]

Arrian then resumes the subject broached in 5.1, the cause of the
size of the rivers. True to the principle enunciated, he relies on a companion of Alexander. Both Aristobulus and Nearchus had described
the rains in India and the subsequent rise of the rivers,[37] but Nearchus is surely the source of the following argument.[38] "In the summer
there is rain in India, especially in the mountains, the Parapamisus,
Hemodus, and Imaus, and from them the rivers flow great and
muddy" (6.4). The value of this fact is that its discovery finally resolved the problem of the Nile floods, as Arrian points out. Since
Herodotus had made a point of considering the Nile problem (Hdt.
2.20–27), the explanation took on a special importance. Furthermore, the comparison of the two rivers gave Arrian an opportunity
to note some of the other similarities between Ethiopia and India
(6.8–9), a standard feature of Greek accounts of India.

The discussion of the physical characteristics of the inhabitants of the two countries provides an easy transition to the second section of the ethnography, the history of India. For this account Arrian relies on Megasthenes but continues his own skeptical approach. Megasthenes said there were 118 Indian tribes; "I agree there are many, but I do not know how he could have discovered the exact number, since he did not visit the greater part of India, and there is little contact between the tribes." The argument is not pursued, but Arrian has asserted, at least to his own satisfaction, his independence from Megasthenes as well as his own preference for autopsy. The sentence no doubt is an allusion to the many fabulous tribes described by the credulous ambassador (cf. *FGrHist* 715 F27–30). In the historical sketch that follows, Arrian concentrates on Dionysus (7.5–9) and Heracles (8.4–9.8), although Megasthenes listed other kings as well. The most novel information here is that this Heracles, according to Megasthenes, was not a foreign conqueror but a native, one of the local kings. The Heracles story, moreover, was extended by the account of Heracles' daughter Pandea, the country which she ruled, and her children by her father. According to one Indian folktale, Heracles had also discovered the pearl: "When Heracles had traversed all the earth and sea, and purged it of every evil monster, he discovered in the sea an ornament for women. This it is which even today [here Arrian adds his own note] those who bring the products of India to us purchase eagerly and export, and all the rich and prosperous, once of the Greeks and now of the Romans, buy still more eagerly: the sea pearl, as it is called in the Indian language. Heracles, since the jewel seemed lovely, collected this kind of pearl from all the sea to India, to adorn his daughter" (8.8–10). Such is the legend, but Arrian, following Megasthenes, also describes oyster-fishing with nets.

In treating the customs of India, the third major division of the ethnography, Arrian has a few words on many subjects—funerals, cities, slaves, various animals. But the major focus is given to two peculiar features of Indian life, the hereditary division of occupation (11–12),[39] and elephants (13–14). Although he is not cited explicitly for the first, comparison with the fragments in Diodorus and Strabo show that Megasthenes again is the source.[40] Arrian allows himself to consider the highest class of Indians, the Brahmin wise men, at greater length than the others. However, the remarkable feature of his account of the Brahmins and their role in the community is his restraint, as is apparent from comparison with other writers.

A large part of Strabo's account of India discusses these men, drawing on the notices of Megasthenes, Aristobulus, Onesicritus, and Nearchus.[41] The meeting of Alexander with these naked philosophers became a standard subject of Cynic diatribes as well as a favorite element of the Alexander romance.[42] Arrian could not have been ignorant of this extravagant development, but he chose to present the minimum which could give a true view of these men and fulfill his promise in the *Anabasis* to explain the wisdom of the Brahmins, "if such it was."[43] He had already presented the meeting of Alexander and the gymnosophists, and the story of Calanus, succinctly but remarkably effectively, in the *Anabasis* (7.1.5−6, 7.2.2−3.6). Although a student and admirer of Epictetus, honored by his friends and fellow citizens as a *philosophos*, Arrian refused to overdramatize his presentation of this extraordinary race of philosophers.

Next to naked sophists, elephants. The elephant has always fascinated on account of its bulk and great strength, and Arrian, no less a huntsman than a philosopher, was especially intrigued by the means by which it was caught, "unlike all other kinds of hunting, as these animals are unlike all others" (13.1). The descriptive passage is a model of clarity, as our author devotes himself wholeheartedly to Megasthenes' presentation, putting aside for the moment all doubts as to his veracity. He allows himself to intrude only once, when to support the report of the elephant's intelligence he describes his own experience of watching elephants dancing and playing the cymbals (14.5−6).

When he turns to other animals, skepticism revives, and Arrian prefers to rely on Nearchus (15).[44] Pride of place, of course, is taken by the gold-digging ants made famous by Herodotus.[45] Nearchus had tried to be cautious; he had not seen the ants themselves, but many of their skins had been brought into the Macedonian camp (15.4). Megasthenes on the other hand modified some details of Herodotus' fabulous story, but retold it with a straight face. Whatever modern opinion of the credibility of Nearchus' autopsy, Arrian prefers it to Megasthenes' story: "Megasthenes reports hearsay, and I, since I have nothing more certain to write, am glad to abandon the subject of these ants" (15.7).[46] The other animals described by Nearchus, parrots and apes, had by Arrian's day become common in the Roman world, and he declines to describe them.

Arrian continues with Nearchus in the following chapters, which describe the clothing of the Indians, their military equipment for men and horses, and miscellaneous customs. The emphasis, of course, is on all that is different from Western usage—cotton cloth, ivory earrings, beards dyed in various colors, parasols, platform sandals. Paying his respect to the tradition of Greek ethnography, in which sexual customs were a regular feature, Arrian reports that the women are extremely chaste but may be seduced by the gift of an elephant, to which they yield without shame. "It seems awesome to the women that one should appear so beautiful as to be worth an elephant" (17.3).

This presentation of the geography, history, and customs of India, however, was only a preface to the major part of the *Indike*, the account of the voyage of Nearchus and the fleet of Alexander from the Indus River to the head of the Persian Gulf. The narrative of this voyage occupies the last three-fifths of the book and is based on Nearchus' own account of the journey. In this half of Arrian's book no longer do we find the ambiguous attitude toward his source which characterized the ethnographical section. Now Arrian can entrust himself to "whatever is most reliably narrated . . . by Nearchus, who sailed around the part of the sea off India" (*Anab.* 5.5.1).

Nearchus might well inspire confidence. He had been one of the first friends of Alexander, going into exile with him before the death of Philip II. He was recalled after Alexander's accession and later made satrap of Lycia, perhaps because of a special knowledge of ships. He rejoined Alexander, however, and became first a chiliarch of the elite infantry body, the hypaspists, then commander of the fleet Alexander was building on the Hydaspes. After his famous voyage of exploration he remained close to Alexander, planning other expeditions. He was one of the friends who saw the king regularly while he was dying, and continued to play an influential, though not major, role in affairs after his death. His account of the expedition he led, although undoubtedly intended to glorify himself and stress his connection with Alexander, was extremely valuable as the personal observations of an intelligent and responsible figure, one of the leaders of Alexander's army.[47]

Arrian, however, did not simply copy Nearchus. A generation ago Hermann Strasburger noted that Arrian was not an excerptor but a narrator.[48] The fundamental question in the present context must be not how accurate are his excerpts, but what did Arrian hope to accomplish with his narrative? Even if he found Nearchus exciting, that was not sufficient reason to write the *Indike*. Nearchus in Arrian's day was like Ptolemy and, to a lesser extent, Aristobulus, an obscure writer, who had not found his way into the standard literature on

Alexander.[49] We know practically nothing except what can be deduced from Arrian of the form and content of his book. But we must guard against assuming that it was a literary masterpiece, since it never appeared that way to Greek writers. Even Arrian praises its reliability but not its style. It is reasonable to think that Arrian found Nearchus' directness and originality appealing and the first-person narrative an invaluable supplement to the history of Alexander, but felt that his own presentation would be more artful than that of Nearchus. He could in fact contribute two factors which would make Nearchus' narrative a fitting companion to his history of Alexander: selectivity and style. Arrian's excellence as a Greek stylist is both asserted and demonstrated in the *Anabasis*; we need not doubt that his *Indike* was an improvement on, not simply an excerpt from Nearchus.[50] Part of his contribution would have been the decision to write in Ionic. Although it has been suggested that Nearchus used that dialect,[51] none of the fragments shows any indication of it, and even the Herodotean expressions noted by Pearson are probably Arrian's, since they are not found in the parallel passages in Strabo.[52] Nearchus, a Cretan raised in Macedonia, more likely wrote in the *koinē* of his day. He may have read Herodotus and been influenced by him, as Pearson argues, but was his education sufficiently literary to permit him to write Herodotean Ionic effectively? The artificial recreation of the Ionic dialect seems rather to be characteristic of the second-century Greek revival, a concomitant of the Atticizing movement, than of the companions of Alexander. Thus Arrian may have hoped to add literary distinction to Nearchus' account by transferring it from an unpretentious *koinē* to an elegant archaizing Ionic, fit for the high literary standards of his own age.

It is evident as well that Arrian severely edited Nearchus' narrative. The length of the book is unknown, but it apparently began with the formation of the fleet on the Hydaspes and continued at least until Nearchus' reunion with Alexander at Susa.[53] The trip down the Indus had been described in the standard Alexander historians, and Arrian had incorporated what he thought suitable of Nearchus' narrative of it into the *Anabasis*. It need not be repeated in the *Indike*.[54] But even the account of the dangerous coastal exploration was edited with a firm hand. The underlying structure of Nearchus' book was that of a coastal voyage, a *periplus* of the same genre as Arrian's own *Periplus of the Black Sea*. Each locality was recorded in turn, with its peculiar features, the behavior of the inhabitants, etc., then the next locality and the distance traversed. Arrian preserves this rather dry but utilitarian system, but makes sure that full prominence is given to selected incidents of particular interest, which may be listed as follows:

1. The establishment of the navy, with a full list of officers (18.1–10)[55]
2. Alexander's desire (*pothos*) to explore the coast, and the conversation with Nearchus which results in his choice as admiral (20)
3. The official departure from Pattala (21.1–2)[56]
4. The battle with the Oreitae (24.1–9)
5. Observation of shadows, and Arrian's comments (25.4–8)
6. The attack on the town of the fisheaters (27.8–28.9)
7. The description of the fisheaters (29.9–16)
8. The meeting with the whales (30)
9. The island of the sun (31)
10. Nearchus' rebuttal of Onesicritus' proposal not to enter the Persian Gulf (32.7–13)
11. The reunion with Alexander (33.3–36.9)
12. The climatic divisions of Persia (40.2–5)
13. The final reunion with Alexander (42).

It is one of the features of a journey narrative, whether *periplus* or land journey (such as those of Xenophon and Alexander), that it may be expanded at will at any point. Arrian has preserved the underlying voyage framework but brought these incidents into prominence. If we consider particular cases, the nature of Arrian's presentation will be seen more clearly.

When Nearchus approached the town of the Oreitae at the mouth of the Tomerus River (24.1), the natives met his little fleet on the beach with spears ready to drive them off. Nearchus responded by halting his ships offshore and having his light-armed troops swim in toward shore until they could touch bottom, but wait to attack until a phalanx four deep could be formed. Then, on a signal, the ships bombarded the natives with javelins and catapulted missiles while the compact phalanx charged with a loud shout. The artillery disoriented the natives while the phalanx advanced slowly through the water to the shore, and the natives fled in terror.[57]

It is common to ascribe the effectiveness of this account to Nearchus; it is more likely, however, that Arrian himself is responsible for those vivid touches which place the action so clearly before our eyes. The battle description is similar to many of Alexander's operations as found in the *Anabasis*: first the enemy position, then the commander's careful observation of the situation (in this case noting the heaviness of the native spears, which precluded their being thrown against the infantry phalanx as it was forming), the rapid execution of a complex maneuver (swimming up to form a phalanx), and the decisive action which brings victory. This amphibious attack on a defended shore was a unique military exercise, and Arrian presents it with the clarity and the drama he had already demonstrated in the *Anabasis*.

A similar skill is apparent in the narrative of Nearchus' stratagem at an unnamed town of the fisheaters (27.7–28.9). Nearchus deduced from the reeds which he could see near the beach that this town grew grain. However, it would be necessary to surprise the inhabitants: they would hardly surrender their grain voluntarily; a direct attack would be impossible, a siege too long. Therefore, leaving the other ships at anchor, he went with one ship "to visit the city." The unsuspecting inhabitants allowed Nearchus and his escort within the walls, whereupon he at once ordered two archers to seize the gate, and himself mounted the wall and signaled to the ships. At this point Arrian reveals that the men on the ships had been warned to await this signal to attack. The Macedonians land at once. After a brief resistance, the townspeople yield, agreeing to save their city by surrendering their store of food. The whole operation is a model of military efficiency, although in the event Nearchus' expectations were deluded; the natives' storehouse contained chiefly fishflour.

More indicative is the contrast between two versions of one of Nearchus' best stories, the encounter with the whales, found in the *Indike* and in Strabo (*Ind.* 30, Strabo 15.2.11–13). The story is introduced differently in the two authors. Arrian includes it as one of several items inserted after the land of the fisheaters and before Carmania[58] and presents it as an example of new things learned by the explorers: "Large whales live in the outer sea, and fish which are much larger than those in the inner [Mediterranean] sea. In fact, Nearchus says. . . ." Strabo, on the other hand, presents this narrative after the expedition had reached the Persian Gulf, as one of the trials it had endured. The geographer complains that sailors frequently exaggerate their troubles, but admits that this difficulty was real enough, although in fact more in anticipation than in the event. In both versions the fleet is frightened by the appearance of the whales, although their native guides were accustomed to them. But Arrian omits one phrase found in Strabo: the guides explained to Nearchus that the whales would go away when trumpets were blown. The omission is conscious, for it permits Arrian to develop with some suspense the following encounter, as Nearchus, apparently quite intrepid, urges his men to row toward the whales, as if for a battle, and to make as much noise as possible. For the reader of Arrian, the effect of this maneuver on the whales is unpredictable, so that when they plunge into the sea and emerge behind the ships we are surprised and pleased, and join the sailors in their cry of praise for Nearchus' courage and cleverness. In Strabo's version, on the other hand, there is no suspense as the fleet approaches the whales, for we have been told that they will flee. On the contrary, the sailors are terrified when the whales reappear behind them, for this action makes them fear a sea battle! That is, they are afraid that the whales are executing one of the normal maneuvers of sea warfare, sailing through (or here, under) the enemy squadron and then attacking its defenseless rear. Their fear is relieved when the whales swim off. The accent in Arrian's version is on the courage and sense of Nearchus when set face to face with these strange beasts; in Strabo on the fear they provoked, although there was no real danger. Strabo had no reason to rewrite the story for his *Geography*, and we may credit Arrian with the conscious omission of the advice of the native guides and the shift of the notion of the sea battle from the reappearance of the whales to Nearchus' first maneuver.

Similar differences are apparent between the versions of Strabo and Arrian of the visit to the island of the sun (*Ind.* 31, Strabo 15.2.13). The point is the same in both, that Nearchus by his landing and return is able to prove false the legend which said that all who landed on the island would disappear. But Arrian develops the sense of mystery connected with the island by a triple repetition of the central phrase, "disappear from sight," at the end of three successive sentences (*Ind.* 31.2–3) and rearranges the narrative to heighten the role of Nearchus as the rationalistic Greek opposing the superstition of natives and sailors. The contrast is most notable in the two accounts of Nearchus' landing on the island. In Strabo, the emphasis is on searching the island for the lost seamen; for Arrian, the object of his visit is the refutation of the legend—nothing is said of what he did on the island, the entire focus being on his return.

One passage from Nearchus is used twice by Arrian; *Anab.* 7.20.9–10 is the same as *Ind.* 32.8–13. From a parallel presentation one can readily discern Arrian's freedom in narrating Nearchus' story of an argument between Onesicritus and Nearchus.[59] Onesicritus had suggested that they sail across the mouth of the Persian Gulf. Here is Nearchus' reply in the two versions:

Ind. 32.10–13	*Anab.* 7.20.9–10
Nearchus replied that Onesicritus was a fool if he did not know why the expedition *had been sent* by Alexander.	But Nearchus said that he forbade it, so that he could report to Alexander, after *sailing around* the Persian Gulf, on the object for which he *had been sent* by him.
For he did *not* send out the ships because he was at a loss how to preserve the infantry entire, but because he wished to observe thoroughly the shores along the voyage	*For* he had *not* been sent out to sail the great sea, but to learn thoroughly the land along the sea
and the *anchorages* and the islands, and to *sail around* any bay which might reach inland, and [to observe] the cities on the sea	and the men inhabiting it and the *anchorages*
	and the fresh water and the customs of the men
and if any ground was fertile, or any desert.	and if any land was good for bearing fruits, and any bad.
They should not, therefore, destroy their work, when they were now at the end of their labors, especially when they were as yet in no need of supplies for coasting. He was afraid that the promontory extended to the south, and that they would discover this land to be desert, waterless, and scorched.	

He won, and I think that
Nearchus clearly saved the
expedition by this decision.

And this, therefore, was the
reason why the fleet was
saved for Alexander.

While the general tenor is the same, only the few underlined words appear in both versions.[60] Some expressions are paraphrased, on the fertility of the land and the preservation of the fleet. But note the difference of the two phrases giving Nearchus' reasons, beginning "For he. . . ." The *Indike* passage is fuller, as we might expect, but there is no reason to think its words are closer to Nearchus' original. The words, and the choice of emphasis, are in both cases Arrian's.[61]

Most noteworthy in Arrian's choice of incident is the attention given to Alexander. Both Strasburger and Pearson have noted[62] that Nearchus' reports on his relations with Alexander are exceptionally valuable for our understanding of the king's personality; what has not been observed is that only Arrian preserves these notices.[63] The artfully composed dialogue between Alexander and Nearchus (*Ind.* 20) —with its evocation of Alexander's longing (*pothos, epithymiē*) to explore and accomplish new and unusual deeds, the various reasons for excluding other leaders, and Nearchus' earnest promise to bring the fleet safely to Persia—no doubt reflects Nearchus' pride in his undertaking, but also reveals Arrian's own fascination with Alexander's ability as leader to persuade men to achieve the impossible. The expedition sets out with all the men "confident in Alexander's extraordinary good fortune generally, and sure that there was nothing which he could not dare and carry to its conclusion" (20.11). Alexander thus is the figure behind the voyage, and when at midpoint the fleet and the army are temporarily reunited, the spotlight is once more on Alexander. The local governor's announcement of Nearchus' impending arrival is a narrative device to permit this shift of attention to Alexander and his fears for the safety of his expedition. The reunion of the two men after Nearchus' hardships along the coast and the king's disastrous march through the Gedrosian desert forms the longest and most dramatic scene in the *Indike*. Certainly Arrian used his own literary gifts to heighten Nearchus' story, but no parallel versions exist which permit us to evaluate his contribution. The very absence of such accounts may suggest, however, that other writers did not find in Nearchus the same drama which we find in Arrian.[64]

The last two chapters of the *Indike* return once more to Alexander as the fleet again rejoins the king: "Thus the expedition which had set off from the mouths of the Indus returned safely to Alexander" (42.10). Surprisingly, Arrian does not end his *Indike* at this point but briefly considers the possibility of circumnavigating the Arabian peninsula. The subject is not so unrelated as it might appear; the *periplus* of Nearchus from the Indus to the Euphrates was one of the great achievements of Alexander. On his deathbed, the restless king was projecting still another voyage of conquest and exploration against Arabia, in which Nearchus would again have a prominent role.[65] Although Jacoby excludes this chapter from the fragments of Nearchus,[66] I think it likely that Arrian derived it from the commander of the fleet. Nearchus certainly had discussed the problems of sailing along the Arabian coast with Alexander and was familiar with, if he did not instigate, the small exploratory missions described in *Anabasis* 7.20.7–8.[67] The description of Arabia given here fits much better the state of knowledge when Nearchus was writing than Arabia as Arrian would have known it, when the northwestern part had been annexed as a Roman province and the peninsula was regularly circumnavigated by traders.[68] The last historical event mentioned in the chapter is the dash across the desert to Babylon made by the men of Ptolemy I, probably in 302 B.C.[69] No doubt Nearchus concluded his book with a vision of yet another great expedition which Alexander had hoped to launch. Arrian pleased to end his *Indike* in the same way; like the rest of the work, this chapter is a celebration of Alexander's greatness rather than an up-to-date statement of geographical knowledge. The key to Arrian's thought is the assertion at 43.10: "It seems to me that had this been navigable or passable, it would have been proved navigable and passable by Alexander's energy." Here as elsewhere, our author dwells particularly on that part of Nearchus' account which glorifies Alexander's restless search for new worlds to conquer.[70]

Without Nearchus' text it is impossible to evaluate precisely the scope of Arrian's omissions. He did not use in the *Indike* the voyage down the Indus, nor (if Nearchus actually included it) Alexander's march across the Gedrosian desert.[71] He omits some of the notices of plants and animals seen (cf. *FGrHist* 133 F27) and perhaps some of the notices of distances and the exact configuration of the shore and harbors which might be expected in a *periplus*.[72] One incident has clearly been abbreviated—the visit to the island of Mitropaustes, described slightly more fully by Strabo, using Nearchus (*FGrHist* 133 F27 and 28).

It has been suggested that an extraordinary astronomical report has been garbled through omissions or other changes.[73] Arrian tells us (*Ind*. 25.4–6) that Nearchus reported that he saw shadows which fell toward the south, that at midday there appeared to be no shadows, and that the stars were different as well. The phenomena would require that Nearchus be south of the Tropic of Cancer, but since he appears to have always remained relatively near the mainland and thus far north of the tropic, either Nearchus has observed badly or Arrian has garbled his account. Yet Arrian was interested enough in the observation to compare it with Eratosthenes' observations at Syene in Egypt, which was on the tropic (25.6–7). It is more reasonable to think that Nearchus allowed his own expectations to affect his interpretation of what he saw.[74]

In the sense that he did no original research and had no personal contact with India, but depended upon the books of Eratosthenes, Megasthenes, and Nearchus, Arrian's work on India was derivative. But Arrian would claim for himself, justly, a different kind of originality, one lying in the charm of his presentation and the effectiveness of his selection. The former is apparent to every reader, but the latter reveals itself only by comparison with our other accounts. Megasthenes wrote four books of *Indica*. Arrian has distilled them to a few chapters, yet manages to convey a vivid sense of the uniqueness of the country. Always conscious, in the Herodotean tradition, of the danger of hearsay report, he has given his reader a sense of the difficulty of describing India accurately, yet filtered out a series of accounts which inspire trust. His most effective criticism of the stories current on India is his silence, his refusal to retell the tales of fantastic beasts and people first set down by Ctesias and repeated by Megasthenes and others. We must go elsewhere to hear of men without mouths who nourish themselves on the vapors of cooked meat and fruit and the perfume of flowers.[75] Nearchus he rewrote and edited, developing with his own peculiar narrative ability the scenes recorded by the admiral. A judicious omission here, a slight change of emphasis there allowed him to compose from Nearchus' narrative a work which might be a suitable companion to the *Anabasis of Alexander*.

8

THE LOST HISTORIES

THE *Anabasis of Alexander* and the *Indike* reveal the clarity and competence of Arrian as a writer and historian, his straightforward narrative, and his judicious selection of sources. But for a true evaluation of the breadth of his interests, the variety of his works, and his preeminence among the writers of his generation we must examine also those works no longer preserved, but which were equally well known in antiquity and the Middle Ages, and whose quantity and excellence established his reputation. The *Bithyniaca* in eight books, the *Parthica* in seventeen books, the *Events after Alexander* in ten books, the *Alanike*, *Dion*, *Timoleon*, *Tillorobus*—an impressive mass of history on the most disparate subjects, treated with an extraordinary virtuosity according to a variety of historical genres. Three works are longer than the *Anabasis* and reveal a perspective quite different from that apparent in an Alexander history. The *Parthica* in seventeen books considers the relations between Rome and Parthia, a question of vital interest to the empire in Arrian's time, giving special consideration to the most recent Roman expedition under Trajan. Here there is no glorification of the Greek past, but a historical exploration of significant contemporary events. The *Bithyniaca* falls at the other extreme. Its eight books were devoted to the glorification of Arrian's native land, with emphasis on its mythical and legendary past. Somewhere between excursuses on myth and contemporary wars we may place the ten books of the *Events after Alexander*, a dense account of the first years after Alexander's death, when Perdiccas strove for control of the empire against the other generals. Such variety defies classification. Felix Jacoby's decision in his *Fragmente der griechischen Historiker* to place Arrian's fragments among the historians of the period of the Successors in II B is justifiable, but arbitrary, since they could as well be grouped with the writers of *Bithyniaca* or *Parthica* in III C. The

scope of Arrian's interests requires that each work be considered separately before a synthetic view can be attempted.

These three major histories, the *Parthica*, the *Events after Alexander*, and the *Bithyniaca*, although now lost, survived well into the
Byzantine period, and enough is preserved in summaries, quotations,
and paraphrases by Byzantine scholars (some 180 fragments) to allow
us a glimpse of their individual qualities.[1] The ninth-century scholar
Photius, later patriarch of Constantinople, summarized each of these
histories, along with the *Anabasis*, in his *Library*.[2] Later, as part of the
vast collection of historical excerpts made under various headings for
the emperor Constantine Porphyrogenitus, selections were made from
the *Anabasis*, the *Parthica*, and the *Events after Alexander*.[3] Although
most of this collection has also been lost, it was used in the great
literary-historical encyclopedia, the *Suda*, which thus preserves numerous bits and pieces, usually frustratingly short and difficult to
locate in the context of a work or even to ascribe with certainty to
a given work.[4] Later still, Eustathius, before being appointed bishop of
Thessalonica in 1174/75, cited the *Bithyniaca* frequently and often at
length in his commentaries on Homer and on the geographer Dionysius Periegetes.[5] These three sources provide us the bulk of our information, though a few citations come from other writers.[6]

For both the *Parthica* and the *Events after Alexander*, Photius'
summaries are our best guide. Nevertheless, they must be used with
caution. Photius composed his summaries from notes, often made long
before, and his memory; normally he did not have the works themselves before him. In summarizing, he occasionally adds his own comments or modifies the original order. He feels free to add material
from marginal notes or scholia.[7] The summary of the *Anabasis* provides a useful sample of his work: the coverage is uneven (e.g., *Anab.*
1–3.22 in fifteen lines, 6.29–7.30 in forty lines); there are many omissions (such as the campaigns in Europe, the sieges of Tyre and Gaza,
the Egyptian campaign); the mutilation of Bessus is described out of
order, immediately after his capture; he states that the Indus was
bridged by boats, although Arrian expressly says he does not know
how it was bridged; and he refers to the "seven wounds" of Alexander, although Arrian never gives the number of his wounds. Thus,
although generally accurate in reporting facts, these summaries are not
always so useful in preserving the author's presentation or interpretation.

In all cases, the particular interest of these Byzantine writers is responsible for the type of fragments which are preserved, and this fact must be considered when attempting to construct a picture of these works.

THE PARTHICA

The *Parthica*, as the longest work and one with strong personal relevance to Arrian, may be considered first. The Parthians had begun as one tribe among many in the vast empire of the Seleucids, who inherited what they could of Alexander's eastern conquests.[8] Profiting from Seleucid weakness, the Parthians established their independence and gradually extended their sovereignty westward from their homeland in northeastern Iran and southern Turkmenistan. By the time of Sulla, when the Romans first encountered them, they ruled a vast territory extending from Mesopotamia to the frontiers of India. How much the triumvir Crassus knew of the Parthians when he set out in 54 B.C. to conquer them is not known, but the annihilation of his army at Carrhae (Harran) in the following year made an indelible impression on the Roman consciousness.[9] From an obscure kingdom on the frontiers of the empire Parthia became for the Romans a menacing power, challenging Rome's rule of the world. From that date until the eventual collapse of the Parthian kingdom in the third century A.D., Parthia was Rome's leading opponent in the East, and a major thrust of Roman foreign policy was the establishment of suitable relations between the two countries, whether by war or negotiation. Major expeditions were launched by Mark Antony, Nero, and Trajan, the peaks in the continuous tension between Rome and Parthia.

When Arrian decided to write on Parthia, therefore, various possibilities were open to him.[10] He could write a historical ethnography of Parthia and the Parthians, designed to acquaint Romans more exactly with their opponents. According to the canons of this well-established genre, he would describe the geography and climate of the country, give a general account of the people, their origins, traditions, customs, religion, and diet, and then narrate the most interesting facts concerning their kings and wars. The type is best represented by Herodotus' book on Egypt but was followed with variations by Herodotus in other digressions and by many famous writers, such as Ctesias in his *Persica*, Manetho in his *Egyptiaca*, and Berosus in his *Babylonica* (*FGrHist* 688, 609, 680). Arrian followed a compressed version of this scheme in the *Indike*, 1−17. Such apparently were the *Parthica* of Apollodorus of Artemita and Seleucus of Emesa (*FGrHist* 779 and 780).[11] Or he could have written a monograph on one of the Seleucid or Roman campaigns against Parthia, a detailed treatment of a single military venture, such as that of Crassus or Corbulo. The works of Julius Polyaenus and Q. Dellius on the campaigns of Ventidius and Mark Antony (*FGrHist* 196 and 197) seem to follow this pattern. Again there is a long tradition of such works (collected by Jacoby in *FGrHist* II B), including not only the historians of Alexander but writers on the Italian campaign of Pyrrhus of Epirus, the Hannibalic War, or, closer to Arrian, the swarm of writers on the Parthian war of Lucius Verus mocked by Lucian (*FGrHist* 203−10) and the rhetor Cornelius Fronto, who promised Verus a history of the war.[12] If, as I believe, Arrian took part in Trajan's expedition, he might have written memoirs of his own experiences, following the good Roman examples of Sulla, Lucullus, Caesar, and Cicero, although considering his youth, he may have been more inclined to write an encomiastic account of Trajan's triumphs.

Arrian's final decision combined certain elements of each of these types of history into a new framework. Photius tells us, and he is supported by our other fragments, that Arrian "in this work narrates the wars which the Romans and Parthians fought" (P1 = F30). Arrian attempted to put the Roman-Parthian conflict into some kind of historical perspective by tracing its course through the one hundred seventy years from Crassus to Trajan, from the disaster of Carrhae to the crowning by a Roman emperor of a Roman client-king in Ctesiphon.[13] Arrian's initiative resembles to a degree the attempt of Appian to treat Roman history as a series of external and internal conflicts, named according to Rome's chief opponents, but differs in presenting an exhaustive treatment of a single enduring tension over a period of almost two centuries.[14] Considering the disproportion between the history of the earlier campaigns and the ten books devoted to Trajan, the earlier history of the attempts to deal with the Parthians should probably be regarded as historical background meant to reveal the magnitude of Trajan's task in finally conquering Parthia.[15]

Arrian intended to combine detail with broad scope, and thus created his longest work, in seventeen books. The fragments tell us little about the organization of the material, other than confirming the natural hypothesis that the campaigns were taken in chronological order: Book II for Crassus' expedition of 54 B.C (P2 = F33), Book IV for Antony's of 36 (P3 = F34), Book VI for Corbulo's in A.D. 53 (P4 = F35). Ten books, over half of the whole, were given over to the campaign of Trajan, 113–17, with which the work ended.[16]

The first book was reserved for an account of the Parthians before their first encounter with Rome in the time of Sulla.[17] Here, if at all, would have been found the usual ethnographical material on religion, customs, and geography, but none of this is preserved. Arrian did trace their origin back to the distant past, when their Scythian ancestors were reported to have migrated from the north into the satrapy of Parthia in the northeast of the Persian empire at the time of the invasion of Asia by Sesostris of Egypt and the return attack of the Scythian king Iandyses. The derivation of the Parthians from a migrant Scythian tribe was common, and is probably correct,[18] but Arrian also places it in the Hellenic framework of the great military campaigns which in legendary times were said to have swept from one continent to another.[19]

Their emergence as an independent nation appears in Photius' summary as follows: "[The Parthians] had long before been enslaved by the Macedonians, at the time when the Persians were conquered, but they revolted for the following reason. Arsaces and Tiridates were two brothers, Arsacids, the descendants of Phriapitus the son of Arsaces. When Pherecles,[20] who was appointed satrap of their country by Antiochus Theos [261–246 B.C.], shamefully tried to violate one of the brothers, these Arsacids did not endure the insult but killed him. Then, joining with five other comrades they led their tribe in revolt from the Macedonians and ruled independently" (P1 = F30). The story, as given here by Photius and with minor variations by Syncellus (P1b = F31), is in the Herodotean tradition. Actions are seen as resulting not from the discontents of a people or a ruling class, nor from contrasts in ways of thinking or from interests of power, but from direct personal involvement. The origin of Parthian freedom, like that of Athens and innumerable other cities in Greece, began with the violent erotic impulses of a tyrant. Arrian accepts the Parthians' attempt to legitimize their rule by tracing the Arsacid to an Achaemenid, Arsaces, whose throne name was Artaxerxes II (king 404–358 B.C.).[21] The association of five other men in the conspiracy is a striking parallel to the seven conspirators who put Darius the Great on the throne (Hdt. 3.71ff.). "Thus does Arsaces I conform to the 'legend' of the founder of a dynasty in Iran."[22] Syncellus continues Arrian's narrative of the brothers, telling us that the one brother, Arsaces, ruled for two years, then died and was succeeded by his brother Tiridates, who ruled for thirty-seven years. Although the story has been challenged and Tiridates dismissed as an invention, it may be true.[23]

The fragments of Books II–VI are meager and tell us little. Arrian portrays Antony as "ruined by his love for Cleopatra" (P23) and not interested in negotiating (P28), but sees the victory of Ventidius in 38 B.C. as counterbalancing the defeat of Crassus fifteen years before (P24). Books VIII–XVII, Trajan's Parthian war, furnish the bulk of our fragments.[24] These are sufficient to preserve a dim outline of Arrian's presentation of this expedition, so important in terms of the number of men involved, the area overrun if not subdued, and the risk to the empire. They also raise questions as difficult to resolve as they are interesting. What was Arrian's attitude toward Trajan? What were his sources? When did he write? What is the relation of this work to the *Anabasis of Alexander*? Two points should be noted at once. Arrian devoted ten books to the Roman conqueror as against seven to the Macedonian, although Trajan's campaigns occupied little more than three years, and Alexander's almost twelve. Moreover, although basically favorable to Alexander, Arrian was ready to admit that he had weaknesses. He may have seen weaknesses in Trajan as well.

Despite the negative bias of some modern assessments of the war and its results, there is no doubt that Arrian conceived of it as a success. Photius ends his summary, "The emperor of the Romans, Trajan, humbled the Parthians by force and left them under treaty, having himself crowned a king for them" (P1 = F30). Arrian shared the vision of the expedition that had been heralded on Trajan's coins with the slogans "Parthia capta" and "Rex Parthis datus."[25] He appears to have felt that Trajan's establishment of Parthamaspates as king represented a respectable achievement which was not rendered meaningless by any of the actions subsequently taken by Hadrian to stabilize the eastern frontier after Trajan's unexpected death. Although Arrian does consider the revolts of 116–17, which seriously undermined Trajan's conquests, Lepper has shown that he treated them only in Book XVII, in which were compressed both these revolts and Trajan's final retreat. The account of these difficulties was not allowed to overwhelm the narrative of Trajan's victories, as had previously been supposed.[26]

The focus of these ten books was Trajan: his actions, decisions, and feelings. The extant fragments do not discuss the problem of the causes of the war, which Dio Cassius reduced to a desire for personal glory (*doxēs epithymia*, 68.17.1), and modern writers to a need to control the caravan route to the East or "regularize" the eastern frontier.[27] Arrian does tell us that the war was begun after an attempt at peace: "He decided not to leave the opportunity untried, if Osroes in some way would admit his mistake and submit to the just demands of the Romans and himself" (P33 = F126). He defends the assassination of the Armenian king Parthamasirus after his deposition, reporting Trajan's words that "as far as Parthamasirus is concerned, the decision was not Axidares' to take, but his own, since Parthamasirus was the first to break the agreement, and received his punishment" (P40 = F51). Someone, probably Trajan, is quoted giving the Roman position: "There seems to me to be no question that Axidares should rule Armenia" (P37 = F120).[28] We may ask, however, whether Arrian ever really felt it necessary to explore the deeper causes of the war. He carefully avoids doing so in the *Anabasis*, where he treats Alexander's desire to conquer Persia as a simple fact, not requiring explanation, and presents the expedition as a series of military campaigns without attempting to motivate them. Far from questioning the war, these books were laudatory. Trajan's operations were successful, and his motives honest. On a personal level as well Trajan was admirable. As a good general he was in close contact with his troops. "Trajan lightened the toil of the troops by sharing in the work" (P41), and showed sympathy with their distress: "Many of the Romans were killed, and Trajan was angry at what had been done" (P82).[29]

Both to contemporaries and to posterity Trajan's expedition was comparable to Alexander's. The image of Alexander the great conqueror was always present in the Roman mind, prompting many to assert, as Livy did (9.17–19), that Alexander would have met his match in Rome, or to compare his achievements with those of Roman conquerors, notably Pompey and Caesar.[30] Thus Trajan as emperor and successful general could readily be compared with Alexander, as Dio Chrysostom does by implication in his second and fourth discourses on kingship. The resemblance was all the more apparent when Trajan mounted a war against the Parthians, the successors of the Persians. Every rhetor, every educated man would naturally think of Alexander. This being the case, it is remarkable how little actual testimony we have of Trajanic *imitatio* of Alexander.[31] There seems to be no suggestion of Alexander on the coins, which rather emphasize the labors and virtue of Heracles.[32] The extant fragments of Arrian's *Parthica* makes no direct reference to Alexander.

Dio Cassius' history, on the other hand, even in its lacerated form, suggests the parallel at several points. Describing the moment when Trajan arrived at the head of the Persian Gulf, Dio wri·es, "When he had seen a ship sailing to India, he said, 'I shoul ˙ certainly have crossed over to India, too, if I were still young.' Fc˙ he began to think about the Indians' affairs, and counted Ale:.ander a lucky man" (68.29.1−2). Dio goes on to say that nevertheless Trajan boasted that he had gone further than Alexander, although in fact "he could not hold the territories he had subdued." He was honored with the highest honors but never reached Rome to enjoy them (68.29.2−4). Trajan visited Babylon, Dio adds, "because of Alexander, to whom he offered sacrifice in the room where he had died" (68.30.1). The comparison with Alexander in these passages is melancholy, not glorifying either emperor but rather commenting on their ultimate defeat by death.

Dio apparently depended heavily on Arrian's *Parthica* for his account of this war,[33] and this presentation of Trajan might be derived from Arrian. True, Dio, from the perspective of several generations and of other wars against the Parthians, might more easily evaluate Trajan's achievements objectively than Arrian. Yet there are close associations between Dio's account and the picture presented by Arrian of Alexander's visit to the Persian Gulf and his plans there (*Anab.* 7.1). Roos argues that P73 (= F131), "those who write not only the deeds but also the plans of Trajan," belongs to the same scene on the Persian Gulf, when Arrian would have treated the plans of Trajan.[34] In the *Anabasis*, Arrian, like Dio in the case of Trajan, used the consideration of Alexander's plans to introduce his most extensive philosophical evaluation of the desire for conquest (*Anab.* 7.1−3). If, as seems likely, Dio derives from Arrian, then we may conclude that Arrian, the student of Epictetus, could not resist making some observations on the contrast between Trajan's urge to conquer and his defeat by sickness and death, the ultimate enemy. Such comments, as in the case of Alexander, would have heightened the heroic presentation of Trajan's achievements and been congenial to Hadrian, the intellectual and admirer of Epictetus. Death remains the final boundary of mortal achievement.[35]

There are other possible grounds for comparison with Alexander which might have been exploited by Arrian. Dio, in describing Trajan's conquest of Adiabene, recalls that this district includes Gaugamela (68.26.4), where Alexander defeated Darius. In describing Trajan's character, Dio remarks that he drank heavily yet remained sober

(68.7.4), perhaps a silent comparison with Alexander's drunken murder of Clitus. Arrian may therefore have made an implicit or explicit comparison with Alexander, and even raised questions about the value of an unlimited desire for conquests and the glory they bring. But as with Alexander, whatever his reservations, the final picture drawn by Arrian of Trajan and the Parthian expedition as we see it in the fragments is favorable. Trajan was the great leader who humbled the Parthians.

The contents of the *Parthica*, as far as we can tell, were political and military events, with little attention given to other matters which might make the history more novelistic or exploit the exotic aspects of a campaign far beyond the imperial boundaries. In military matters, as in the *Anabasis*, the coverage is careful. It includes the planning before an engagement: "[The Parthians] had decided that when the Moors should rush against them, the troops facing them would flee as if terrified, but those stationed on either side would attack on the flanks of the pursuers" (P53 = F140). There are numerous descriptions of the operations themselves: a march against a hostile country (P55), the flight of a king (P56 = F167), the bridging of the Tigris (P57 = F165), a defensive action against invaders (P21). Noteworthy in the *Parthica* is the vivid treatment of numerous embassies to Trajan. The reason for the large number of fragments of this sort lies in part with one of our intermediate sources, the Constantinian excerpts *On Embassies*, but also in the real situation in Parthia, which was not a strongly centralized state but a collection of petty kingdoms ruled by men who were vassals to the Parthian King of Kings.[36] The success of the campaign depended on whether Trajan could win some of these vassals to the Roman cause, and negotiations thus represented an important part of his total activity. Unlike the faceless embassies we find in the *Anabasis*, the kings and princes who came before Trajan are described as individuals: Arsaces (P19), Arbandes, "handsome and tall and in the bloom of youth" (P43), Sanatruces (P77), and others whose names are lost (P89 = F123, P99 = F157). Although the fragment is not explicitly ascribed to Arrian, the description of Sanatruces is worth quoting: ". . . the king of Armenia, who was moderate in stature, but extraordinary in judgment toward everything, not least toward military matters. He seemed to be a careful guardian of what was right and in his way of life as restrained as the best of the Greeks and Romans." Here again we see Arrian the student of Epictetus, admiring the man, although a barbarian, for his self-control. On the other hand, the judgment of the unknown leader in P89 (= F123) brings out the weaknesses of a bad leader, "a man reckless because of his youth, foolish because of his inexperience of affairs, persuasive to the multitude because of his physical strength and rashness in battle. He wanted plans about even the most important matters to be deliberated in the whole crowd rather than among a few of those who especially showed forethought, and desired that those who opposed too long should be bound, and yet should follow in their bonds."

When Arrian does describe Parthian ways, it is usually because they have a military relevance, as when he describes Parthian armor (P20; cf. the descriptions of foreign military dress in his *Tactics*), the native use of snowshoes made of willow withes to cross sixteen-foot snow (P85 = F153), and the native wild horses (P88 = F138). The description of Semiramis' tomb, which was seen by Trajan in Babylon (P74), was no doubt introduced as part of the continuing comparison of Trajan with great conquerors of the past.[37]

The narrative of embassies and battles was relieved by a number of orations and letters. Some fourteen fragments appear to belong in this category, most of them not direct quotations but indirect reports of what someone wrote or spoke. Of those reported directly, several appear to be only a line of dialogue introduced into the narrative, rather than a fragment of a full oration. This technique, also found in the *Anabasis*, is well exemplified in P46: "Trajan said to Augarus' son [Arbandes], 'You were wrong not to have come sooner to join my expedition and share my efforts, and for this reason I would gladly pull off one of these earrings of yours,' and at the same time he grasped one of his ears. Both of Arbandes' ears were pierced, and gold earrings hung from both."

In the preface to the *Anabasis*, Arrian writes that he intends to rely on Aristobulus and Ptolemy, because they seem more trustworthy in that both accompanied Alexander on the expedition, yet wrote only after his death, when there was neither need nor profit in writing other than as it occurred. Since the Parthian war only ended with the death of Trajan in 117, there is no doubt that Arrian also wrote after the death of his protagonist. Moreover, he had almost certainly been a participant in the Parthian war.[38] The frequent argument that P73 (= F131), "Those who write not only the deeds of Trajan but his plans as well," proves that Arrian had no personal experience in the war but derived his knowledge from earlier authors[39] has little to recommend it. The use of written sources is not incompatible with autopsy. Lucian's comments on the writers of Verus' Parthian war show us, first of all, that many histories of such wars were produced almost at once, so that we may presume that as early as 125 there were a number of memoirs, reports, and monographs on the war which could have been used by Arrian, without prejudicing in the slightest his capacity to write on the basis of his own experience. On the other hand, there is the notice by Johannes Lydus (T14 Roos, P6 = F37), found after his discussion of the Caspian Gates (the Darial Pass): "Such is the account in the Roman writers concerning the Caspian Gates. Arrian in the *Alanike Historia* and especially in the eighth book of the *Parthica* describes them quite accurately, inasmuch as he himself was commander of the area, since he was in charge of that region under Trajan the Excellent."

The reference to the *History of the Alans* and a command in the area might naturally lead one to think of Arrian's governorship of Cappadocia under Hadrian. Arrian is said to have settled affairs in Iberia after warding off the Alans in 135,[40] and could have seen the Darial Pass at that time. If the reference is in fact to Arrian's governorship, then the name Trajan in Johannes Lydus is a mistake for Hadrian. However, the second reference, to *Parthica* Book VIII, places us firmly in Trajan's reign, since Arrian also referred to Elegeia in that book (P5 = F36), no doubt to describe Trajan's stay there in 114. If Arrian described the Darial Pass in the same book, the more probable conclusion is to trust Lydus' date and understand him to refer to a command in the area of the Darial Pass held by Arrian at the time of Trajan's expedition, when Trajan was at Elegeia and wanted to protect his northern flank from a surprise attack by the Alans through the pass. Such a mission beyond the frontiers of the empire into the territory of client kings was not uncommon; especially relevant is the presence of Roman garrisons in Iberia in the vicinity of Tbilisi and Baku under the Flavian emperors. Iberia supported Trajan's war; an Iberian prince died fighting at Nisibis. An early assignment to guard the Darial Pass, perhaps as military tribune, would have given Arrian experience in the area, a factor which would influence Hadrian when he later made him governor of the province.[41] There is no problem of age or rank; Arrian would have been in his late twenties, and depending on his career he could have served in various capacities with Trajan's army. In our fragments of the *Parthica* Arrian makes no statements of the sort "I have seen and know" found with reference to the Inn and Save (*Ind.* 4.15) or throughout the *Periplus*. Certain fragments, however, suggest autopsy without guaranteeing it: P46, the story of Trajan and the earring of Arbandes, quoted above; P77, the description of Sanatruces, also quoted above; and P85 (= F153), the description of native snowshoes. The weight of the evidence inclines towards Arrian's participation in the expedition.[42]

The time of composition of the *Parthica* remains a puzzle. Given his success in recording his years with Epictetus, Arrian may have begun taking notes for the Trajanic section of his history even during the course of the expedition. Lucian describes how the authors writing histories of Lucius Verus' Parthian war were writing as the war took place—and even described Verus' triumph before the war was over! Although it is thus possible that the *Parthica* was one of Arrian's early works, Arrian's presentation of Trajan as a great conqueror bound to die suggests a certain perspective on events, and Parthia and the wars with Parthia were of immediate interest in the Roman world throughout Arrian's lifetime. If Trajan's war was not the immediate occasion of the *Parthica*, Arrian might have been encouraged to write by his experience on the frontier in Cappadocia in the 130s, or even by the war led by Lucius Verus in 160–164.[43]

The *Parthica*, then, appears to have been an extensive review of Roman-Parthian relations, prefaced by a brief account of the rise of the Parthian nation and focusing especially on the recent campaign of Trajan. Trajan was portrayed as a successful general and emulator of Alexander, accomplishing his objective in humbling the Parthians despite the revolts of 116–17. Although Trajan's desire for conquest probably was viewed from a moralistic and philosophical standpoint, the overall presentation was laudatory. The general tone suits the policy of Hadrian, which was to honor the memory of Trajan and his operations against Parthia, while making no attempt to continue to hold Trajan's conquests.[44]

THE EVENTS AFTER ALEXANDER

The second major work, known as *Ta meta Alexandron* or the *Events after Alexander*,[45] narrated the first struggles among the successors of Alexander. This title is probably not Arrian's, although it is used by Photius and an anonymous Byzantine work on syntax. Photius refers to the *Anabasis* as *Ta kata Alexandron* (*The Events during Alexander's Lifetime*) and the anonymous Byzantine scholar cites the same work as *Ta peri Alexandrou* (*Concerning Alexander*). The title which we receive from the Byzantines, then, need not reflect the purpose or conception of Arrian, but the long summary of the whole work given by Photius (S1 = F9, 11) provides a basis from which Koehler, Reitzenstein, Roos, and Jacoby have been able to reconstruct its contents.[46]

When Alexander died in Babylon on 10 June 323, he left no clear successor to his empire; on his deathbed he is reported to have said that he was leaving his kingdom "to the strongest." Although he gave Perdiccas his ring, he was not able to give him his authority. The generals who had been held in check by Alexander's charm, ruthlessness, ability, and ascendancy over the soldiers each began to assert themselves in the power vacuum left by Alexander's death. It would take two generations before a stable pattern of power could be established, but the first and most important decisions were made by 320 B.C., when at the settlement of Triparadisus any real hope for keeping the empire a unity was given up. In the period between June 323 and Triparadisus the major events involve this wrestling for power: the first division of offices in Babylon immediately after Alexander's death; the quelling of revolts by various peoples, including the uprising in Greece called the Lamian War; and the attempt of Perdiccas by marriages and force to convert his regency for the two young kings, Alexander IV and Philip Arrhidaeus, into absolute rule over Alexander's empire. Perdiccas was supported by the Greek Eumenes, but opposed by Antipater, Craterus, and Ptolemy, and after an unsuccessful battle with the latter in Egypt, he was killed by his own troops in May 320. His death opened the way for the new accord of Triparadisus.[47] (Arrian's narrative of these events is presented in the table on pages 146–47.)

Considering the short period covered, the length of the work is surprising; Diodorus, our fullest extant account, treats the same period in half of Book XVIII. The history falls easily into the genre of the monograph on a specific period. Even as such, however, it stands out for its length—the general rule is that contemporary histories are long, but later monographs short. Some sense of the detailed narrative which is implied by ten books on three and a half years is discoverable in two fragments which preserve Arrian's own words for more than the few phrases usual in the citations of the *Suda*. Two palimpsest folios copied in the tenth century preserve part of Book VII (S24–25). The first begins at the end of Ptolemy's successful attempt to bring Alexander's body to Egypt despite Perdiccas' opposition. Perdiccas reacts to this by a series of moves: he marches from Asia Minor through

Year	Scene of Action	Events	Photius (S1 Roos)	Palimpsest and Papyrus Fragments
		Books I–V		
323	Babylon	The first struggles after Alexander's death; a compromise reached	1–3	
		Perdiccas' lustration of the army	4	
		Assignment of satrapies	5–8	
	Greece	Outbreak of Lamian War	9	
322		Leonnatus killed	9	
		Lysimachus in Thrace	10	
	Asia Minor	Perdiccas in Cappadocia	11	
	Greece	Craterus in Greece, wins battle of Crannon (Sept.)	12	
		Books VI–IX		
		Exile and death of anti-Macedonians in Athens	13	
		Fate of their opponents	14–15	
	Cyrene	Early history of Thibron	16	
		Thibron attempts to take over Cyrene	17–19	
321	Asia Minor	Perdiccas against Antigonus	20	
		Perdiccas' marriage alliances: Nicaea, Cleopatra, Cynane	21–23	
		Coalition of Antipater, Craterus and Antigonus against Perdiccas	24	
		Arrhidaeus takes Alexander's body to Egypt	25	S24
		Perdiccas in Cilicia		S24
		Perdiccas sends Docimus against Archon in Babylon		S24
		Troubles in Cyprus		S24
320		Eumenes in Sardis, Antipater and Craterus cross Hellespont	26	S25
		Eumenes fights Neoptolemus	27	PSI XII, 1284
		In a second battle Neoptolemus and Craterus are killed	27	
	Egypt	Perdiccas invades Egypt and is killed by his own officers	28	
		Ptolemy wins support of Perdiccas' troops; Peithon and Arrhidaeus take Perdiccas' place	29–30	

Year	Scene of Action	Events	Photius (S1 Roos)	Palimpsest and Papyrus Fragments
	Syria	Intrigues and troubles at Triparadisus; Antipater wins overall authority	31–33	
		New division of satrapies; Antipater starts back to Macedon	34–38	
		Book X		
	Asia Minor	Eumenes learns of Perdiccas' death; other leaders become outlaws	39	
		Antipater in Sardis	40	
		Eumenes establishes himself in interior	41	
		Quarrel of Cassander and Antigonus	42–43	
		Despite troubles with troops, Antipater crosses to Europe	44–45	

Cilicia toward Egypt, deposes on his way the satrap of Cilicia for being too friendly to Craterus, and sends Docimus to Babylon, with instructions to depose Archon the satrap of Babylon if possible. The narrative briefly follows Docimus as he confronts Archon and takes his place. Perdiccas meanwhile is engaged with dissident kings in Cyprus, against whom he gathers a fleet, marines, and cavalry under the combined command of Aristonous, once a bodyguard of Alexander. Here the first folio of the palimpsest ends. In these two pages Arrian describes with greater precision than any other author the feverish activity of Perdiccas as he is being challenged on all sides. The theft of Alexander's body is well known, but the removal of Philotas from Cilicia recurs only in a phrase of Justin (13.6.16: "Cilicia is taken from Philotas and given to Philoxenus"), and the events in Babylon and Cyprus are completely new to us. One notes also a delight in specifics: "He prepared many merchant ships, and had about 800 mercenaries and about 500 horses go on board. He appointed Sosigenes of Rhodes admiral, Medius the Thessalian commander of the mercenaries, and Amyntas commander of the cavalry, while Aristonous the bodyguard of Alexander was general of the whole force" (S24, lines 22–28).

The second folio of the palimpsest (S25) reveals Arrian's care in following the diplomatic maneuvering connected with Antigonus' crossing into Asia Minor, the ill-feeling of Menander, the satrap of Lydia, toward Eumenes, Cleopatra, and Perdiccas, and how Cleopatra's timely advice saved Eumenes from being ambushed by Menander. Again the narrative, insofar as it is legible, is particular and clear, explaining both the thoughts and the actions of the various actors.

A recently identified papyrus fragment from Oxyrhynchus (*PSI* XII, 1284)[48] preserves a passage from the battle of Eumenes against Neoptolemus. We know from Plutarch that Eumenes was defeated in the infantry battle, but routed Neoptolemus' cavalry and captured his baggage train. With this advantage, he was able to make the infantry surrender.[49] But this fragment reveals that Arrian knew much more. The papyrus preserves part of a unique account of Eumenes' parleying with the opposing Macedonian soldiers through a certain Xennias, a Greek who spoke the Macedonian dialect. Eumenes was able to persuade Neoptolemus' troops that although their phalanx could resist a frontal attack, his cavalry could harass them and keep them from food-gathering, so that it was best to surrender to him.

Such fragments are evidence of the generally high quality of Arrian's history, a quality due in no small degree here as in the *Anabasis* to a discriminating choice of sources. The general plan of the *Events after Alexander* is almost exactly that of the equivalent section of Diodorus;[50] the congruence with Diodorus suggests that they both used the same source, Hieronymus of Cardia.[51] But some caution is necessary, since Hieronymus' history spanned the period 323 to 272 (if not further), some fifty-two years, and although the number of books is not known, it appears extremely unlikely that he, despite his general reliability as a historian, provided anywhere as much detail as Arrian. Few other candidates present themselves as authors whom Arrian might have used to supplement Hieronymus. Nymphis of Heraclea's twenty-four books *On Alexander, the Successors, and Their Followers* (*FGrHist* 432 F17) and an anonymous History (*FGrHist* 155) are the only known historians of the period who precede Arrian; his only successor, Dexippus of Athens, seems to have used Arrian's account. I suggest that Arrian used together with Hieronymus an author he found invaluable in writing the *Anabasis*: Ptolemy. We know nothing of the scope of Ptolemy's narrative. All the extant fragments refer to Alexander, but it is in fact very likely that Ptolemy would have chosen to present not merely his view of Alexander, but also of the struggles

among the generals, especially the discreet and moderate role he had
played.[52] Arrian had used the narrative of Nearchus in the *Anabasis*
and then presented it more fully in the *Indike*; there may be a similar
use of Ptolemy in the *Anabasis* and the *Events after Alexander*. Errington, following Badian, has argued that Ptolemy published his book
not late in life, as regularly supposed, but quite early, soon after 320.[53]
He may therefore have taken as his stopping point the decisions at
Triparadisus and the return of Antipater to Europe, and thus set the
example for Arrian, who broke off his history at that point.

Alongside such reliable sources as Hieronymus and, if my hypothesis is accepted, Ptolemy, Arrian would have used less trustworthy
accounts. In the preface to the *Anabasis* he justifies using such material, which he qualifies as hearsay (*legomena*), if it is sufficiently interesting. An example of his use of *legomena* in the *Events after Alexander* occurs in the fragment describing the battle of Eumenes and
Craterus: "Eumenes *is said* to have found Craterus still alive. He
jumped down from his horse and lamented over him, testifying to
Craterus' courage, intelligence, excessive gentleness and unaffected
response to friendship . . ." (S26 = F177). The source of this anecdote
is unknown; Plutarch (*Eumenes* 7) reports the story with no allusion
to where he found it. Arrian clearly liked the picture of a general praising his fallen opponent on the battlefield but did not wish to treat it
as undoubtedly authentic, and so presented it as hearsay.

Arrian in this work, like Diodorus and Hieronymus, divides the action into campaign years, completing the account of one year before
beginning the next. On only two occasions does the Photian summary
suggest that this principle is violated: (1) after the deaths of Demosthenes and Hyperides in Book VI, Arrian follows the later history of
those responsible, recalling Demades' execution in 319 and Archias'
ultimate poverty and disgrace; and (2) before describing Thibron's
attempt to gain control of Cyrene, Arrian, like Diodorus (18.19.1),
finds it necessary to backtrack a bit to give the background of the
story. The transition from Demosthenes and the anti-Macedonians to
Thibron (Photius has one follow the other in his summary) may have
been facilitated by the fact that both Demosthenes and Thibron were
involved with Harpalus and the treasure stolen from Alexander. On
the other hand, even these exceptions may be distortions by Photius
of Arrian's narrative.[54]

Concerning the partition of books we know from Photius only the
divisions between Books V and VI and IX and X. Book X appears as

a neat unit, covering events in Asia Minor from Eumenes' discovery of Perdiccas' death to Antipater's return to Europe. At the end of Book IX, Antipater had completed the reorganization of the empire at Triparadisus and had set out for home. Book X backtracks to treat Eumenes' activity while the others were at Triparadisus and then follows Antipater on his way through Asia Minor, noting his troubles with his troops, with Cleopatra, and with Cassander and Antigonus, who insisted on quarreling. The noteworthy fact about the division of Books V and VI, on the other hand, is the continuity of action. Book V ends with the battle of Crannon and its immediate aftermath, the Greek acceptance of Macedonian terms. In Book VI, Arrian turns to the specific problem of Athens and the city's reaction to this final proof that its days of liberty were gone forever. Apparently the author wished to get maximum value from a dramatic moment by treating it in two halves, first the battle, then the Athenian aftermath. A somewhat similar technique is used in the *Anabasis*, where Alexander arrives at Gordion and receives new troops at the end of Book I, but cuts the Gordian knot at the beginning of Book II.

There are a number of omissions in Photius' summary, most notably the revolt of the Greeks whom Alexander settled in Bactria (Diodorus 18.7) and the two phases of the Macedonian-Aetolian war (Diodorus 18.24–25, 38). At least the Aetolian war would be an integral part of the struggle between Perdiccas and Antipater, so we may credit the omission to Photius rather than to Arrian. The papyrus and palimpsest fragments remind us how much Photius necessarily left out, and we must be on our guard not to limit Arrian only to what Photius reports.

Arrian's chief interest in writing the history, one gathers from the extant fragments, was to describe the military encounters which were so frequent in this period, and the diplomatic maneuvering which preceded them. No period in history was richer in important battles or boasted more illustrious generals. The team of brilliant and ruthless men whom Alexander by charm and force of will had kept under control had broken up, and each now had his own army and his own ambition and was ready to fight against native rebellions and his own ex-comrades to win a position for himself in the world Alexander had left. Some died quickly—Leonnatus, Neoptolemus, Craterus, Perdiccas—and new men took their places. The fragments show, as we have seen, a keen interest in troop movements and dispositions, siege works, and the tactics which meant victory for one side or the other.[55] Any biographical interest which Arrian might have had in these figures was secondary to their military activity, as we find time and again in the biographical notices which the *Suda* preserves from his history. The description of the impetuosity of Leosthenes ($S17 = F179$) or of the sense of superiority of Perdiccas ($S27 = F180$)[56] is directly linked to other reasons for their deaths, and not pure character portrayal. Leonnatus' long connection with Alexander and his own high opinion of himself would be an integral part of the narrative of his attempt to assert himself, with the support of the Macedonian cavalry, in the first days after Alexander's death, the apparent context of the characterization in $S12$ (= $F178$).[57] Nor do the two passages on Craterus preserved in the *Suda* biography follow the Xenophontic manner of recording brief notices and evaluations of a general after his death. The first ($S19 = F177a$) elaborates the contrast in character between Antipater and Craterus which was to play an important part in determining the outcome of the Lamian war and in all their relationships; the second ($S26 = F177b$) considers Craterus' death in the light of the Macedonians' respect for his outstanding qualities and of Eumenes' honorable treatment of his body.[58]

Diplomatic negotiations and secret intrigues were an important part of the struggle for power, and as such were described with care. Besides the account in the Vatican palimpsest of the activity of Antigonus, Menander, Eumenes, and Cleopatra ($S25 = F10B$), we may note Arrian's narrative of the various marriage alliances ($S1 = F9$, §§ 21–23, 26), the schemings of Eurydice ($S1 = F9$, §§ 31, 33) and Cleopatra ($S1 = F9$ and 11, §§ 21, 26, 40), and the quarrel and reconciliation of Cassander and Antipater ($S1 = F11$, §§ 42–43).

For a man with as abiding an interest in generalship as Arrian, the peculiar opportunities for military history in this period may be a sufficient explanation for his decision to write the *Events after Alexander*. We have no information either external or internal as to the time of composition of the work, so we cannot even say that it was composed as a continuation of the *Anabasis*. It is not an obvious or natural sequel, being different in scope and in the kind of material handled, as well as in size. Unlike the *Indike*, the *Events* is never mentioned or alluded to in the *Anabasis*, suggesting that Arrian had not even conceived it at the time of the *Anabasis*. It is possible, of course, for a historian to treat an earlier period after a later one, as we learn from the examples of Sallust and Tacitus. Nevertheless, it is more reasonable to assume that Arrian's interest in this period was first aroused by the figure of Alexander and that he turned to the *Events* sometime

after he completed the *Anabasis*. It is natural to connect this work
with Arrian's lifelong interest in Asia Minor. Asia Minor was the
major theater of action in the period covered by the *Events*, and
Eumenes, one of the leading figures of Hieronymus' account and apparently of Arrian's, remained there continuously. Finally, the subject
of the history, the problem of succession to imperial power, was not
without contemporary interest. Hadrian on his accession may not
have approved, but certainly found useful, the action of those in Rome
who ordered the immediate execution of four leading generals; if Perdiccas had been able to do the same, Alexander's empire might have
remained intact. The decision to end the history with Antipater's
return to Europe is not so arbitrary as some have argued. With the
deaths of Neoptolemus, Craterus, and Perdiccas, Ptolemy's successful
defense of Egypt as an independent unit, and Antipater's decision to
return to Macedonia as his home province, any immediate hopes for
a continuation of the empire of Alexander as a unit were crushed.
The separatist tendency had won out, and the way was open for the
establishment of the various Hellenistic kingdoms.[59] Thus Cappadocia
and Armenia could be independent, and Bithynia become the sovereign state whose history Arrian recorded in the *Bithyniaca*.

THE *BITHYNIACA*

The eight books of Arrian's *Bithyniaca*[60] represent local history, a different genre from his other writings. The historical sense of the Greeks
had been built especially by great works of "national" history—first
and foremost the poems of Homer, which for the Greeks preserved
a historical reality, though expressed in poetry; then the histories of
Herodotus, Thucydides, Xenophon, Ephorus, and Theopompus. In
these works the world of Greece was conceived as a unit, and the
author attempted to portray the events of the Greek world as a whole.
Yet this world was composed of individual city-states, each with its
own history, its own cults, and its own heroes, and by a natural reaction to the panhellenism of the monumental histories there arose the
genre of local history, which celebrated the past of city-states or regions.[61] These writings began at least as early as Herodotus and were
regularly composed by native sons—witness the *Chronicles of Lampsacus* by Charon (*FGrHist* 262) and the *Foundation of Chios* by Ion
(*FGrHist* 392). One of the main objects of these histories was to trace
the beginnings of their respective cities back to the earliest events of

prehistoric times, and to relate the tradition of the particular state to the larger Hellenic history recorded by Homer, Herodotus, and later writers. Genealogy, one of the formative elements of the Greek historical tradition, played an important part in this process of integrating the local history into the general Hellenic history.

In the second century A.D. there was a revival of interest in local history,[62] part of the general renewed confidence and self-assertion of the Greek world. Arrian, who in his writings and career was a major representative of this Greek renaissance, shared as well the desire to celebrate his native land and try his pen at the ancient genre of local history. The notice of Photius (B1 = T4, F14) gives us an idea of the purpose and content of the work:

He wrote the *Bithyniaca*, presenting as a gift to his native land its heritage [*tēi patridi dōron anapherōn ta patria*]. For in this work he specifies that he was Nicomedian by family, that he was born, raised, and educated in Nicomedia, and was a priest there of Demeter and Persephone, to whom the city is dedicated. . . . From the time when he began to have some capacity for writing, he had wanted to undertake to compose this work, but the preparation needed to remedy his deficiencies stretched out the time. He himself gives this explanation for his slowness in the matter. It begins, as has been said, from mythical times, and goes down to the death of the last Nicomedes. . . .

Photius certainly derived the above material, with the exception of the last sentence, from Arrian's preface, where the author would have placed himself in the series of those who narrated the traditions of their native land. The fact that Nicomedia had been founded relatively recently in Greek terms (ca. 265 B.C.), and by the king of Bithynia, would have led him to write the history of that region, rather than of his own city, which had no independent history.[63] This same emphasis on the history of a free state, a fundamental feature of Greek historiography, dictated that the work must end with the end of Bithynian independence, in 75 or 74 B.C., when Nicomedes IV left his kingdom in his will to the Roman people.[64]

Arrian's statement in his preface that his own deficiency delayed the work must refer not to literary weakness—the volume of his works suggests a facility with the pen from his youth—but lack of knowledge. The source problem for any local history, but especially for

Bithyniaca, was potentially much more complicated than for Arrian's other histories. The *Anabasis*, once Arrian made the decision to follow chiefly Aristobulus and Ptolemy, presented itself as a relatively straight-forward problem in historical narration, and apparently treatment of the *Events after Alexander* and the *Parthica* were similar. But to write *Bithyniaca*, a conscientious author would wish to become familiar with at least some of the writers who had attempted to relate Bithynian place and tribal names, cults, and migrations to Hellenic history. Moreover, Bithynia was a neighbor of Troy, and its history had to be integrated with the information found in Homer and other poets of the epic cycle. Not only local historians but Homeric scholars had been fighting for centuries over passages such as the catalogue of Troy's allies (*Iliad* 2.816–77): Demetrius of Scepsis (a city in the Troad) found it necessary to write thirty books to elucidate these sixty-two lines![65] Without pretending to suggest that Arrian tried to attain a scholar's knowledge of the problems,[66] it is clear that anyone who approached the task seriously would find he needed to do a lot of reading. Arrian's familiarity with Bithynia, its geography, cults, and customs, would no doubt have helped him, but the book in the nature of things is chiefly the product of reading and not original research and autopsy.

We do not know anything useful about earlier writers of *Bithyniaca*. Asclepiades of Myrleia (*FGrHist* 697), the earliest of whom any notice has been preserved, wrote in the first century B.C., apparently to satisfy the curiosity connected with Bithynia's change of status from kingdom to Roman province, composing perhaps ten books, of which we have six fragments. Parthenius borrowed from Asclepiades two love stories, of the kind which were common in the narration of the relations between Greek colonists and the indigenous population, for his *Amatory Narratives* (F1–2).[67] In the same period Alexander Polyhistor (*FGrHist* 273) devoted one of his many books to Bithynia and composed others on related subjects—the Black Sea, Paphlagonia, and Phrygia. Two centuries later a contemporary of Arrian, Nicander of Chalcedon, produced a book called *The Changes of Fortune of the Bithynian Kings* (*FGrHist* 700). Of four other authors who cannot be dated (*FGrHist* 698–99, 701–702) the most interesting is Demosthenes of Bithynia, who wrote an epic poem in ten books entitled *Bithyniaca*, which was used by Stephanus of Byzantium for information on place names.[68] These bits and pieces suggest a continuing interest in Bithynia but tell us little about how Arrian might have handled his material.

Nor do the extant fragments, of which only five record the book from which they are taken. Four of these are short geographical notices from Stephanus of Byzantium, giving no clue as to the contents of the respective books. The arrangement may have been topographical, chronological, or some combination. We would expect the history of the Bithynian kings to be treated chronologically, but the mythical and Homeric period could have been treated more freely. Only one fragment can be certainly fixed to a historical narrative,[69] and that is preserved not in Arrian's words but in the verse narrative of the Byzantine polymath Tzetzes:

> The Nicomedes who founded Nicomedia . . . had a very large dog, a Molossian and very faithful to him. Once, the queen, the wife of Nicomedes, whose name was Ditizele, a Phrygian by birth, was playing with the king, and the dog, thinking she was an enemy, closed his jaws over her right shoulder and pulled it away, grinding her flesh and bones with his teeth. She died in the arms of the king, and was buried at Nicomedia with great honor, in a gilded stone tomb. . . . The story has it that the dog, having fallen out of the king's favor, died from love of the king and grief for his wife. Arrian writes the story in the *Bithyniaca*. (B63 = F29)

The story is striking, and so was preserved. A love for unusual anecdotes such as this is a standard feature of Greek historiography, even in serious writers. Arrian may have been especially attracted to this story as a dog lover, for what it showed of this dog's faithfulness and affection. Nevertheless, it is disappointing that this is our sole fragment for the Hellenistic period. We could wish that we had some idea whether Arrian gave a serious account of the efforts of Nicomedes and his dynasty to maintain the independence of Bithynia among the conflicting pressures of the Hellenistic world.

Thanks to the twelfth-century Byzantine scholar Eustathius we are much better informed on Arrian's treatment of the earliest periods of Bithynian legendary history.[70] The *Bithyniaca* survived so long no doubt because since the foundation of Constantinople Bithynia had become one of the most flourishing and central parts of the empire, and Arrian's clarity of presentation and clear Attic style made it valuable for individual or school use. Eustathius quotes the *Bithyniaca* frequently in his commentaries on Homer and on the geographical work of Dionysius Periegetes, not only for historical information but even for grammatical points,[71] so that his most recent editor suggests that Eustathius may have taught the *Bithyniaca* in his school in Constantinople.[72] Eustathius' quotations are frequently verbatim[73] and thus provide a welcome occasion to evaluate, if only piecemeal, Arrian's work. Allowance must be made, of course, for Eustathius' own interests in considering the content and emphases of Arrian's history.

The material on the early period in the *Bithyniaca* was apparently usually introduced to explain names of places and tribes. This conclusion is undoubtedly influenced by Eustathius' selection, which was itself on this basis, but it fits into the general pattern of Hellenistic scholarship as well. Thus on the name Bosporus we find two explanations quoted by Eustathius (B36 = F20b):

Arrian states the following: "The crossing at Chalcedon and Byzantium was once called Mysian, because the Mysians once lived opposite Thrace, but was later called Bosporus [Cow-ford] on account of the misfortune of Io, who, the myths have it, was driven by a gadfly because of the anger of Hera and coming to these regions crossed at this point." But the same man [Arrian] says that according to some the Bosporus got its name not from this cow, but from another, "which when the Phrygians were attacking jumped fearlessly into the sea and crossed without injury the Chalcedon-Byzantium Bosporus. In this way she became a guide for those men, according to a prophecy which ordered them to make a cow their guide for the route. This they did, and crossed safely. A bronze cow is set up as a memorial of this crossing, erected at some later time by the Chalcedonians. Perhaps because of this cow a certain place there is called Damalis [Heifer] to this day."

In this story we find the standard aetiological explanation of the name Bosporus, referring to Io, cautiously ascribed to "the myths," and beside it a rationalized explanation connected with early tribal migrations and confirmed by a monument and another place name. Finally, even before Io, the crossing had been named Mysian because of their onetime location near it, although in later times Mysia was further south. Other fragments indicate this same desire to historicize mythological events.[74] The tendency is apparent also in the *Anabasis*, e.g., 2.16.5–6 on Heracles and the cattle of Geryon.

Not only god-driven mortals, but the gods themselves appear, as in the following explanation of why Ares was called Enyalios (B14 = F103): "On coming into Thrace, where Enyalios had his home, Ares wished to be entertained. But Enyalios did not wish to receive him, saying that he would not entertain anyone who was not stronger in war than himself. And he, 'It is time for you to entertain me, since I assert that I am stronger in war than you.' When Enyalios denied this, they fought and after a long battle Enyalios was killed by Ares, struck by his weapon, the broad Thracian sword. Therefore since Ares accomplished this great deed as a young man, he was called because of it Enyalios." Here, besides the unusual feature of calling Ares' opponent Enyalios rather than Enyos, we note the use of a brief direct quote to increase the vividness of the scene. Both this and the use of historical presents (*erchetai*, *piptei*) is typical of Arrian's narrative style in his other works. On another occasion—presumably while describing the laurel over the tomb of the Bebrycian king Amycus at Daphne near Byzantium—he mentions "the laurel [*daphnē*] which some say to have sprung from the ground because of Daphne, the daughter of Ladon, who while fleeing from her lover Apollo prayed that she might disappear under the earth, and received the answer to her prayer" (B40 = F87). This laurel is shown, Arrian tells us, at Daphne near Antioch, although we have no assurance that he actually saw it.

Two examples of Arrian's treatment of Homeric names will suffice for an idea of his technique in explaining them:

The Eneti, having been hard pressed in battle by the Assyrians, and having crossed into Europe, dwelt by the Po River and in the native language are called Veneti to this day instead of Eneti, and Venetia is the name of their land. (B46 = F63)

Those whom Homer in the Catalogue of Ships calls "Halizones, whom Hodius and Epistrophus ruled," were Bithynians. And Alybe, which he says was the "birthplace of silver" is [still] pointed out, and one can see an unfaded record [there], the works of the silver mines which are left. These men are called Halizones because they are closed in on all sides by the sea, on the north and east by the

Black Sea, on the south by the bay of Astacus, the one by Nicomedia, and on the west by the Propontis and the Bosporus, so that
the greater part of their territory is not far from being a peninsula,
and it is quite fair to say that they are embraced by the sea [*hali
zōnnysthai*]. (B22 = F97)

Both the Eneti and the Halizones in Homer's catalogue of Trojan allies
were problematic, because neither name was known in historical
times. The Eneti were early on associated with the Veneti at the head
of the Adriatic Sea, as here. Arrian's Assyrians, here and in B51
(= F74), must be taken to be the White Syrians, whom Strabo places
on the south coast of the Black Sea, in what was later called Pontus.
The question of the Halizones and Alybe, also unknown, was never
satisfactorily settled. An indication of the problems Arrian may have
encountered in the composition of the *Bithyniaca* is given by Strabo,
who devotes eight chapters (12.3.20–27) to the Halizones, reviewing
the opinions of Ephorus, Apollodorus, and others. Since Strabo argued particularly from the absence of silver mines anywhere east of the
territory of the Chalybes that Alybe was a corruption of Chalybe,
Arrian's comment (from autopsy?) on traces of silver mining in a
Bithynian Alybe is noteworthy. Strabo lists many alternate sugges-
tions, including Ephorus' emendation of Alizones to Amazones. Arrian's identification was not new (it is reported also by Pliny the Elder,
NH 5.143, and uses standard Greek etymological practices), but must
be seen as part of a long tradition of scholarship and speculation.

This is one of Arrian's more reasonable etymologies. In general he
is given to deriving geographical names—of cities, tribes, rivers—
from an eponymous hero, invented by Arrian or his source for this
purpose.[75] Occasionally the etymologies are more complicated, as in
B3 (= F16), where Deucalion establishes an altar to Zeus Aphesios
because he was saved (*apheithē*) from the flood, and the name Nemea
is derived from the word for pasture (*nemein*), because the animals
of Argos were pastured there, or in B36 (= F20), the passage on the
Bosporus quoted above. On some occasions he permits a name to be
taken over by another person, as in the case of Enyalios and Ares
(B14 = F103; cf. also B15 = F102) or notes a change in name (B22 =
F98).

Arrian, of course, as every local historian, gave special attention to
narratives of the foundation of a city. One apparently verbatim ac-

count shows that these stories could be quite short (B55 = F71): "Phanagoria, which Phanagoras the Teian founded, fleeing from the arrogance of the Persians. And again Hermonassa, named after Hermonassa the wife of a certain Semandros of Mytilene. When he led some men from the Aeolian cities to found a colony, and then died while founding the city, his wife became ruler of the city and gave her own name to it." Was there also a novelistic element in the story of the woman founder-queen? If so, the fragment does not suggest it. On the contrary, if Eustathius is quoting accurately, the fragment implies that Arrian gave a list of towns, with brief comments on each. The brevity may be explained by the distance from Bithynia of Phaenagoria and Hermonassa, which were on the straits of the Cimmerian Bosporus. Yet one gets the same impression from a notice on Zeleia in the Troad (B34 = F96): "Zeleia or Lycia: Apollo too [is called] Lycius because of this Lycia. For this reason also the father of Pandarus [is named] Lycaon, which name is not much different from that of this race." Perhaps Arrian did not attempt a narrative treatment of this kind of material but presented it in catalogue form, somewhat as he does the cities and rivers described in parts of his *Periplus*.

A trace of the familiar romantic foundation narrative, such as those told by Asclepiades of Myrleia or reported in Parthenius, can be found in the story of Crocodice, paraphrased by Eustathius (B39 = F61c): "[Arrian says] that Crocodice, an expert on drugs, while she was distributing wine group by group to her father's army, threw roots into the mixing bowls, drugs producing sleep and forgetfulness; so that they lay half-dead from the potion. Thus they were killed by the enemy because of love for the youth Prieneus." Crocodice presumably was the daughter of the native chieftain where Prieneus was attempting to found Priene. She fell in love with him, and weakened her father's troops so that the Greeks could found their city.[76]

With so many heroes, genealogy is an essential element of history, especially useful to correct erroneous stories which do not sufficiently show the importance of Bithynia in the heroic world. The family of the nymph Electra and her son Dardanus were preeminent, as one might expect in northwestern Asia Minor (B31 = F64, B32 = F95, B33 = F107), but others were considered as well.[77] Arrian distinguishes two Sarpedons (B29 = F58), knows the Amazons by name (B48 = F85), and can provide a nymph mother for every hero.[78]

A few fragments show that Arrian shared the local historian's interest in religion and customs, hardly surprising in one who also attempted more exclusively ethnographical works such as the *Indike* and the *Alanike*.[79]

The treatment of the early history, then, reflects the standard methodology of local history: use of mythological information, though rationalized to make a more "historical" account, explanation by etymology and aetiology, and in general a desire to fit Bithynia into the larger world of Hellenic saga. The vivid treatment of the death of the wife of Nicomedes I (if not completely due to Tzetzes) suggests that Arrian did not entirely avoid occasions to enliven his history with novelistic touches. Although he concentrated on Bithynia,[80] in his treatment of movements and migrations of peoples he was able to enlarge his focus, to touch Crete (B57 = F65), the Nile (B61 = F57), Babylon (B53 = F90), Gades (B62 = F64bis), Salamis (B59 = F66), Delos (B60 = F69), Melos (B58 = F70), and especially the Black Sea area—the cities of Phanagoria and Hermonassa on the Cimmerian Bosporus (B55 = F71), the Chalybes in Pontus (B52 = F73), the Iris River (B47 = F75), the Cappadocians of Pontus Polemoniacus (B51 = F74), the Cimmerians (B19 = F60, B43−44 = F76), Thracians (B14 = F103, B15 = F102, B16 = F68bis), and the nomadic Scythians (B47 = F75, B54 = F72). Arrian's description of the Scythians in the last mentioned fragment perhaps gives us the best example of stylistic craftmanship found in this work, an account of how the Scythians, under pressure from their enemies, abandoned a settled life in Thrace and became wanderers: "Once they ate bread and farmed, lived in houses and had cities, but when they received this blow from the Thracians, they changed their former ways and swore great oaths never to build a house or to break the ground with a plow or to build cities or to possess a treasured possession, but to make wagons their homes, wild game their food, milk their drink, to possess only animals which they could drive as they moved from one land to another. And thus from being farmers, they became nomads."

This larger view of the Bithynian past seems to confirm the observation of Rostovtzeff that in historical times Bithynia was deeply involved with the whole Black Sea area. Arrian related the early history of Bithynia to the movements of barbarian tribes like the Thracians and Scythians and to the progress of Greek colonization around the Black Sea. Bithynia was a crossroads in the migrations between Europe and Asia and between the Aegean and the Black Sea. All the peoples, Greek and barbarian, of the Black Sea littoral had their place in an account of the noble part that Bithynia had played in history before it had become a part of the Roman world-state.

DION, TIMOLEON, TILLOROBUS, AND THE ALANIKE

The three major works survived to Byzantine times, and thus some idea of their content has reached us. Of four other lesser works of a historical nature we know hardly more than the names. Photius tells us that Arrian wrote works on Timoleon and Dion which were mentioned in the preface to the *Bithyniaca* (B1 = T4): "[One work] narrates what was done by Timoleon of Corinth in Sicily; the other whatever deeds worth narrating were accomplished by Dion of Syracuse when he freed the Syracusans and all Sicily from Dionysius II, the son of Dionysius I, and from the barbarians, whom Dionysius had introduced so that he could more firmly rule as a tyrant." Dion of Syracuse (408–354 B.C.), the brother-in-law of Dionysius I and friend of Plato, was exiled by Dionysius II. In 357 B.C. he returned and drove the tyrant from Syracuse, then in the following years lost and regained control of the city, and was finally murdered in 354 B.C. His biography by Plutarch is built around his double role of philosopher and general, and as such he is set parallel to Brutus, with whom he compared favorably as general. It was presumably this double-faceted life which appealed also to Arrian, himself a philosopher-general. Photius' reference to deeds worth narrating (*axiaphēgēta erga*) recalls Arrian's preface to the *Anabasis*, where he promises to select whatever is more believable and more worth narrating (*axiaphēgētotera*) whenever Ptolemy and Aristobulus disagree. If the words which describe Dion's deeds reflect Arrian's own comments and are not Photius' addition, the narrative would have been favorable to Dion as liberator of Sicily from tyranny.

Much the same could be said of Timoleon. Timoleon was a Corinthian sent to Sicily in 345 to help the Syracusans against Dionysius II, who had installed himself once more as tyrant. Timoleon, a bold general and clever diplomat, was able to liberate Syracuse and began a crusade against tyrants in other cities, and in 341 won a great victory against the Carthaginians in Sicily. Although he had setbacks as well as successes, he was able to make peace with Carthage, crush the tyrants, and open a new period of prosperity for Greek Sicily. Timoleon as a successful general would naturally have appealed to Arrian. Moreover, the Stoic teaching against tyranny could make the tyrant-hater Timoleon into something of a philosopher.

Thus in some respects the studies of Dion and Timoleon form a pair and may in fact represent one book rather than two. These were the sole works in which Arrian turned his pen away from eastern affairs. Perhaps the composition of these works—whether monographs or biographies—may be connected with a tour of duty in Sicily. It is likely that he was still a young man, perhaps a quaestor, since the overt interest in philosophy (in the case of Dion) and the geographical theater so far removed from his mature works, as well as the context of Photius' statement, suggest that they were early works.

Lucian preserves our only notice of a third work. In defense of his decision to write on the false prophet Alexander, a contemporary figure whom he considered a charlatan, Lucian cites the case of Arrian: "For Arrian, the disciple of Epictetus, one of the most prominent of the Romans and one who lived with literature all his life, would defend us, since he suffered something similar; he thought it was worthwhile to write a life of Tillorobus the bandit. But we are writing of a much more fierce robber, who robs not in woods and mountains, but in the cities, not ravaging Mysia alone or Mount Ida, or pillaging a few of the more desert parts of the province of Asia, but filling the whole of the Roman empire, so to speak, with his robbing" (*Alex.* 2 = T24 Roos, F52 Jacoby). Tillorobus the bandit is otherwise unknown, although the name is found on inscriptions from Termessus and Apollonia in Pisidia. Lucian's last sentence, however, appears to contrast Alexander and Tillorobus and implies that the latter harried Mysia and the province of Asia, working from a base in the hills. As such his life could have been interesting to Arrian for two reasons: militarily, as a contemporary example of the tactics employed by mountain-based guerillas and the countertactics suitable against them; and also for the local interest of an episode in the contemporary history of Mysia, an area not far from Nicomedia and which he treated in his *Bithyniaca*.[81]

For none of these three works do we know the size or method of presentation. Presumably they were all short—twenty to thirty pages —and more likely historical monographs than lives in the Plutarchean manner.

Our notices of a book on the Alans, the *Alanike* or *Alanike historia*, are equally unsatisfactory. Photius mentions it (P1 = T2) as one of

Arrian's works ("He composed also the affairs of the Alans [*ta kata Alanous*], which he entitled *Alanike*") but probably it did not survive to his time. Johannes Lydus mentions it (P6 = F13) and it was perhaps used by Procopius (p. 286 Roos = F109), although Jacoby assigns that fragment to the *Bithyniaca*. The name implies a geographical and ethnographical work like the *Indike*, describing to the Romans this tribe which continued to invade their territory. It possibly contained an account of Arrian's confrontation with the tribe when it attacked Cappadocia in 135, although Jacoby is mistaken in ascribing to it the *Battle Formation against the Alans* (F12), which as we have seen is written in a style unsuitable for a history, preserving the imperatives and infinitives of a genuine order of battle. The *Alanike* was undoubtedly composed as a result of the Alan attack.

Despite the fact that they are preserved only in fragments and short notices, the lost works of Arrian serve to fill out the picture of their author. The *Anabasis*, in the light of these other works, is not a fluke of literature, the happy inspiration of a retired general, nor the wistful backward look of a Greek afraid to face the Roman present, but one of a series of intelligently conceived and smoothly executed histories by a man who was a professional both as soldier and as writer.

9

BETWEEN TWO CULTURES

IN the world of the second century A.D., a world which we are only beginning to understand, Arrian stands out as a complex and remarkable figure, representative of many aspects of his time, yet atypical in the way these aspects were combined in one person.

Despite the relative quiet prevalent within the Roman empire in these years, a series of wars and lesser conflicts, chiefly under Trajan, but continuing also in the reign which followed, kept the troops on the frontier in a state of tension. The empire felt the pressure of barbarian tribes in Britain, Europe, and the Caucasus, and of the Parthians in the East. A well-functioning army was essential to the defense of the empire, and an army could not function without commanders who could control their men and who understood how to use them in a campaign. In his career and in his writings Arrian practiced and described the activities of a good general. Of his career as a soldier we know little, except for his service at the Caspian Gates during the Parthian war of Trajan, until he assumed command of the two legions stationed in Cappadocia. There, however, we find him a conscientious commander during his inspection of the garrisons along the Black Sea and a successful general in his defense against the Alan attack of 135. His writings reveal better his fascination with all aspects of generalship, as well as his tendency toward didacticism when speaking of military matters. The *Dion* and the *Timoleon* without doubt narrated the battles of those two men against tyrants and Carthaginians; the *Tillorobus*, the outlaw raids of a Mysian bandit. In the section of the *Periplus* which describes his own visits of inspection and in the *Battle Formation against the Alans*, Arrian clearly intends that the various dispositions described be taken as examples to be imitated. The didactic aspect becomes explicit in the *Tactics* and the lost book *On Infantry Exercises*, written as manuals for officers of the Roman army by one who had himself partaken in the contemporary exercises which he describes.

As is the case with his namesake Xenophon, Arrian's historical works develop on a larger canvas the ideas on generalship found in the shorter treatises. We have seen that it was one of the major aims of the *Anabasis* to illuminate as explicitly as possible those features of each battle, siege, or other military action which would explain Alexander's genius as a general. Arrian's intention was not simply laudatory, but didactic, as is apparent from the restraint and the clarity of his presentation. The same desire to instruct in the art of warfare is apparent in his decision to treat the brief period from the death of Alexander to Triparadisus in an extraordinarily detailed ten books. Such length could be justified only by the many battles which took place in this period, which we may be sure were described with that same skill at creating a clear picture of the tactics used which is found in the *Anabasis*. In like manner the *Parthica*, with its concentration on the campaigns fought between the Romans and Parthians, must have been conceived in part as a casebook of battles, revealing the strengths and weaknesses of the tactics employed on either side, until Trajan's expedition asserted finally the superiority of Roman military genius.

Arrian shared with Xenophon his interest in the qualities of a good general, his experience in war, his didacticism, and as well his commitment to a moral philosophy which while not subtle, suited the world in which he lived. Epictetus, with his teaching on the freedom of the individual and the duty to assign values not on the basis of outside pressure but according to one's own judgment, found in Arrian a willing pupil, but one who did not allow his philosophy to hinder his progress in a senatorial career. As with Xenophon, philosophy was a facet, not the focus of Arrian's life. Nevertheless, the *Discourses* and the *Manual* are not simply the youthful expressions of esteem for a master forgotten in later years. The statues erected at Corinth and at Athens to Arrian the philosopher indicate that there was something in his life which distinguished him from his contemporaries, and in his nonphilosophical writings we find clear indications of the permanent effect of Epictetus' words. We have noted the Epictetian language of the epigram from Cordoba, and the gracious yet independent and far from sycophantic tribute paid to Hadrian in the *Periplus* and *Tactics*. Apparently even in the *Parthica*, as he narrated the conquests of Trajan, Arrian reminded his reader that human power had limits, that the conqueror would die despite his success, and that conquest could never be an absolute goal. The *Anabasis* is a moral as well as a military history, written by one aware of the insidious snares that enslave the powerful—flattery, the sense of being without limit in one's actions and desires, the notion that the power to kill is the power to rule. Alexander's inner development, the process by which he became worthy through superhuman labors and self-restraint of the glory that he had won, is as central to the *Anabasis* as the battles of Issus or Gaugamela and reveals the extent to which Arrian accepted Epictetus' system of values, even while adapting them for use in an active career. To him, what was accomplished was less important than the moral integrity of the men who accomplished. Nevertheless, how admirable and worthy of praise was one who could achieve great deeds with integrity!

Arrian expressed his thoughts on military tactics, generalship, and the manner in which a man could free himself from the tyranny by which he was threatened on every side through a revitalization of the literary tradition which he had inherited from classical Greece. This revitalization was possible because Arrian was confident in his own abilities and in his own age. An imitation which depends for its content and effect on a world five hundred years past must needs be slavish, weak, and inconsequential. Arrian on the contrary used the classical writers, especially Xenophon, Herodotus, and Thucydides, as models of style and clarity of expression, but not of the substance of his thought. This fact is remarkably clear in the case of his booklet on hunting, in which he treats the new and far superior techniques in use in his own day within a framework and by means of a vocabulary taken from Xenophon's work on the subject. The past and the present are combined in a harmonious whole, in which, however, there is a clear subordination of past to present.

The same subordination of a classical model to the needs of present expression is apparent in Arrian's use of the *koinē* Greek instead of literary Attic to record the diatribes of his master Epictetus. The conversations of Socrates reported in lucid and sometimes forceful Attic in Xenophon's *Memorabilia* provided a readily available model, and no doubt, as has been noted, Arrian took these conversations as a paradigm for his own work. Realizing, however, how much the effect of Epictetus' words depended upon their colloquial and unrhetorical directness, he chose to record the discourses in the popular language rather than falsely imitate the Attic of Xenophon. Or to express the matter differently, Arrian rejected the simple and servile imitation of Xenophon's dialect to achieve a more real imitation, following Xenophon in reporting the words of his master in the language in which he spoke them.

It has been said that Arrian, like some other writers of this period, turned to the history of the Hellenic past to flee an unhappy present in which Greece cowered under Roman rule.[1] Nothing could be farther from the truth. Arrian felt himself a part of Roman rule, not outside it—in this he differs from Plutarch, forty years his senior, despite the latter's close ties with powerful Romans. He held the highest offices open to the Roman elite and speaks with pride of Roman accomplishments. There is no trace of nostalgia or longing for better days in his historical works. It must be observed first that someone who writes ten books on a contemporary war—*Parthica* 8–17 on the three years of Trajan's Parthian campaign—can hardly be accused of hiding in the past. What little we know of the *Parthica*, in fact, indicates that it was the most detailed treatment ever made of Roman relations with Parthia, one of the foremost problems faced by the empire in Arrian's day. The *Parthica* alone should clear Arrian of any charge of flight from present reality. But even the *Anabasis*, if our analysis is correct, is not a rhetorical exaltation of Alexander as a representative of the glory of ancient Greece—in this it differs as much in substance as in style from a work such as Aelius Aristides' *On the Four [Great Men of Athens]*—but praises Alexander in contemporary terms for a military genius and personal greatness which were very relevant in Arrian's own world. The *Events after Alexander* indicates yet more clearly that Arrian's aim was not simple glorification of the past but instruction of the present. The rhetoricians of the Second Sophistic could find nothing to celebrate in the wars for power which followed the death of Alexander.[2] Arrian, on the other hand, found the topic congenial, for his purpose in writing was at least in part practical: to describe for the benefit of his contemporaries the battles fought by Alexander's captains. The *Bithyniaca* may represent a more nostalgic moment. The preface paraphrased by Photius suggests a certain sentimental desire to retrace the history of his native land, but the fragments which survive do not help us to decide whether the work would have had contemporary relevance as well, regarding the claims of preeminence of the various cities or of powerful families, or other factors of which we are ignorant. Finally, even in the case of the minor works, quite apart from the extraordinary *Cynegeticus*, Arrian reveals a re-

markable capacity to infuse traditional genres and models with contemporary relevance. The *Periplus* uses an ancient scheme to describe
the duties of a Roman governor and speaks with feeling of a man's
love for a friend. The *Indike* exploits Herodotus' Ionic dialect to supplement with ethnography and adventure the account of Alexander's
expedition. In the *Tactics*, Hellenistic military tactics are described for
their potential contemporary use and set side by side with the exercises of Hadrian's cavalry. Throughout Arrian appears as master, not
servant, of the classical form, an author who picks at will that part
of his heritage which he can use to profit and that which he will dis-
card or set aside for another occasion.

A concern with Asia Minor and the East is one of the unifying factors of Arrian's literary production. Several works deal with wars in
the area—the *Anabasis*, the *Events*, and the *Parthica*. Others describe
regions (the *Periplus*) or peoples (the *Alanike*, the *Indike*) there; the
Bithyniaca would have treated both. Arrian served once in Transcaucasia under Trajan, and again in Cappadocia under Hadrian, and
must have considered himself something of an expert on eastern affairs. Interestingly enough, his namesake Xenophon also shares this
continuing connection with the East, seen in the *Anabasis*, the *Hellenica*, and the *Cyropaedia*.

The overall picture that we form of Arrian is of a writer and man
of action completely at home in his own world, self-confident, proud
of his activity as a Roman senator and general and of his skill as a
man of letters. His Greek heritage and his philosophical training were
an integral part of his life, neither suppressed nor given undue pri-
macy. A book like the *Anabasis* was addressed to the elite of the
Roman empire—those administrators, senators, officers, and intellectuals who could appreciate the restrained classicism of his style, the
careful reconstructions of military operations, the interest in Alexander's moral development. Just as the statement of authorship in the
second preface of the *Anabasis* is much more subtle than that found in
Appian's *History*, the intended audience of the former work is much
more knowledgeable and refined. Far from presenting a useful précis
of history to help those in a hurry, Arrian intends to create a work of
historical art in the classical manner, to be appreciated both by prag-
matic senators and men of letters.

Arrian is frequently, and correctly, called the new Xenophon because of the many interests he and Xenophon had in common and because of their similar literary output. But among his contemporaries

Arrian appears most to resemble a man with an equal variety of interests, though less active as a writer, the emperor Hadrian. The two men both were intellectuals, lovers of Athens, philosophically minded, hunters. In a sense Hadrian seems to be the ideal audience of all that Arrian wrote, although only two works are known to have been dedicated to the emperor. Hadrian's philhellenism permitted him to appreciate the skill of Arrian's renewal of the classical historiographical tradition; his insistence on a well-trained army was echoed by Arrian's military manuals and tactical descriptions; his conscientious striving to be a good emperor was supported by the vision of the great ruler presented in the *Anabasis*; and his love for Antinous was sensitively understood in Arrian's words on Achilles and Patroclus and Alexander and Hephaestion. Hadrian possessed a restless, searching soul, but he may occasionally have found some peace in the work and in the friendship of this Greek from Nicomedia so at home in the Roman world, this huntsman-philosopher-general-writer who expressed in his life and work so many aspects of his own multifaceted character. It is doubtful, though, that he ever reached that calm and enviable state Arrian portrays in describing his own life at Athens with his dog Horme and friend Megillus. Whether this spirit was won by constant application of the lessons of Epictetus or was fruit of a highly successful career as senator and author, Arrian certainly speaks with a contentment and self-assurance that is difficult to find in any age.

ARRIAN'S WORKS

The names in English are followed by the abbreviations used in this book and the names in Greek and Latin. I have indicated the date when known, and the number of books if more than one.

EXTANT WORKS

The Discourses of Epictetus (Diss.). Diatribai; Dissertationes. Four books survive of at least eight written.
The Manual of Epictetus (Ench.). Encheiridion; Manuale.
Periplus of the Black Sea (Per.). Periplous Euxeinou Pontou; Periplus Ponti Euxini. A.D. 131/32.
Battle Formation against the Alans (Ect.). Ektaxis kata Alanon; Acies contra Alanos or Ectaxis contra Alanos. A.D. 135–37.
Tactics (Tact.). Techne taktike; Ars tactica. A.D. 136/37.
On Hunting (Cyn.). Kynegetikos; Cynegeticus.
The Anabasis of Alexander (Anab.). Alexandrou Anabasis; Alexandri Anabasis. Seven books.
On India (Ind.). Indike; Indica.

FRAGMENTARY AND LOST WORKS

Dion.
Timoleon.
Tillorobus.
Bithyniaca. Eight books.
Parthica. Seventeen books.
The Events after Alexander. Ta meta Alexandron; Historia successorum Alexandri.

On the Alans. Alanike; Alanica.

On the Nature, Composition, and Appearances of Comets. Peri kometon physeos te kai sustaseos kai phasmaton or *Peri meteorion; De rebus physicis.*

On Infantry Exercises. Cf. *Tact.* 32.3.

A CHRONOLOGY OF ARRIAN'S LIFE

Age	A.D.	
Age	*A.D.*	
0	ca. 89	A. born in Nicomedia
7	96	Domitian assassinated, succeeded by Nerva
9	98	Trajan succeeds Nerva
12–17	101–102 105–106	First and Second Dacian Wars
18–21	ca. 107–110	A. studies in Nicopolis with Epictetus; writing of *Discourses*
23	ca. 112	A. on Nigrinus' council at Delphi
25–28	114–117	Trajan's Parthian war
25	114	A. serving in Armenia and Iberia under Trajan?
28	117	Hadrian succeeds Trajan
37	ca. 126	A. praetorian proconsul of southern Spain (Baetica)
40	ca. 129	A. suffect consul at Rome
41	ca. 130	A. curator of public works?
42–48	ca. 131–137	A. governor of Cappadocia
42	131/32	Cotys king of Bosporus dies; A. writes the *Periplus*
46	135	Alan invasion beaten back, A. in Iberia; *Ectaxis*, and perhaps *Alanike*, written
47	136/37	The *Tactics* completed
49	138	Antoninus Pius succeeds Hadrian

56	145/46	A. eponymous archon of Athens
72	161	Marcus Aurelius succeeds Pius
75-77	164-166	Lucius Verus' Parthian campaigns

The date of A.'s death is unknown.

AN OUTLINE OF THE *ANABASIS*

Preface: Method
Book I: From Alexander's Accession to Gordion: Conquest of Asia
Minor
1. Preliminaries (1.1–11.2)
    a. Alexander's accession (1.1–1.3)
    b. Campaigns in Thrace and Illyria (1.4–6.11)
    c. Reduction of Thebes (7–10)
    d. Winter in Macedon (11.1–11.2)
2. The war with Darius (1.11.3–3.30)
    a. Crossing of the Hellespont (11.3–12.1)
    (The Second Preface, 12.2–12.5)
    b. The battle of the Granicus (13–16)
    c. Conquest of Aegean coast, including 20.2–23.4, siege of
        Halicarnassus (17–24.2)
    d. Lycian coast, inland to Gordion (24–29)
Book II. From Gordion to Gaza: The Mediterranean coast
    e. The war in the islands (1–2)
    f. The Gordian knot (3)
    g. The march to Mallus (4–5)
    h. The battle of Issus (6–11)
    i. Aftermath of victory (12–15.5)
    j. The siege of Tyre (15.6–25.3)
    k. The siege of Gaza (25.4–27)
Book III. From Egypt to the Iaxartes: final defeat of Darius
    l. Alexander in Egypt, including 3.4, the journey to Ammon's
        oracle (1–5)
    m. From Egypt to the Tigris (6–7)

APPENDIX 4

ARRIAN'S ACCOUNT OF THE BATTLE OF

GAUGAMELA, *ANABASIS* 3.7–15

I. Preliminaries to the battle (7–12)
    Framing story: the eclipse (7.6)
    The march from the Tigris until first contact (7.7)
    Macedonians capture prisoners for information (8.1–2)
        The composition of Darius' troops (8.3–6)
        The advantages of Darius' position (8.7)
    Rest; camp made for noncombatants (9.1)
    Advance; both forces in battle order (9.2)
        Council, decision to delay attack (9.3–4)
        Alexander goes scouting (9.5)
        Alexander's speech encouraging officers (indirect discourse)
        (9.5–8)
        Alexander rejects a surprise night attack (10.1–2)
            Arrian's approval of the decision (10.2–4)
        Darius' troops awake all night (11.1)
            Arrian's criticism (11.2)
        Persian order of battle (11.3–7)
        Macedonian order of battle (11.8–12.5)
II. The battle (13.1–15.4)
    Attack of Scythian and Bactrian cavalry (13.1–4)
    Attack of the scythe-chariots (13.5–6)
    Attack of the Persian line and Alexander's counterattack
    (14.1–2)
    Flight of Darius (14.3–4)
    Problems of the Macedonian center and left wing (14.4–15.3)

The attack on the camp (14.5–6)
The attack on the left wing; Parmenio calls for help
(14.6–15.1)
    Alexander's battle with the fleeing cavalry (15.2)
Alexander's pursuit of Darius (15.3–5)
Casualties (15.6)
Frame: date, eclipse recalled (15.7)

The preliminaries of the battle might be said to begin with Alexander's departure from Egypt in spring 331 (3.6.1), but the march as far as the Tigris was basically uneventful. Mazaeus threatened to hinder the crossing of the Euphrates but did not, and the report of Darius' decision to block the passage of the Tigris proved false. Both rivers were crossed without opposition, although the strong current of the Tigris made that ford more difficult (3.7.1–5). The true beginning of the battle narrative, therefore, is the omen of the lunar eclipse of 20 September 331, which took place while the troops were resting after crossing the Tigris, and which is used by Arrian as a frame for the battle. Alexander made a sacrifice and the seer Aristander predicted that there would be a battle in the course of the month and that Alexander would win (3.7.6). At the end of his account of the battle, Arrian recalls the prophecy (3.15.7).

    Arrian regularly frames his narrative of a battle with a pair of anecdotes. One such pair is provided by the figure of Arsites, who appears briefly before and after the battle of the Granicus. At the council of the Persians he is intransigent and insists on a confrontation with Alexander (1.12.10); afterwards he pays by his own suicide the price of his error (1.16.3). The frame is a conscious device of Arrian, for as a *legomenon* Arsites' suicide was probably not reported in Ptolemy or Aristobulus. Alexander's sacrifice to Heracles at Tyre (2.15.7–16.7 and 2.24.6) and Porus' position on the Hydaspes (5.8.4 and 5.19.3) function similarly for the siege of Tyre and the battle at the Hydaspes.

THE DATE OF COMPOSITION OF

ARRIAN'S WORKS

THE distressing fact is that the evidence for the time of composition of the most important works of Arrian is very slight. Most certain are the works from the Cappadocian period, discussed in chapter 3: the *Periplus* ca. 132, the *Ectaxis* ca. 135, the *Tactica* 136/137, the *Alanike* probably in the same period. The *Discourses* of Epictetus were completed after the master's death, since they refer to it, but there is no solid evidence fixing that event. Still, their composition may be thought to belong to Arrian's early years, between 108 and 138 A.D.[1]

The most difficult questions center around the major works: the *Anabasis* with its companion *Indike*, the *Parthica*, the *Events after Alexander*, and the *Bithyniaca*. Two recent studies, by Gerhard Wirth and A. B. Bosworth, have attempted to reconsider the question thoroughly, and come to opposite results.[2]

The essential argument of Wirth runs as follows.[3] The view of the ruler presented in the *Anabasis* seems to indicate that it was written for Marcus Aurelius, but before he became emperor (A.D. 161), and therefore after 136 when he entered into line for succession. Moreover, the reference to ἡ ἐμαυτοῦ in *Anab.* 1.12.5 must refer not to his *patria*, Nicomedia, but his chosen land, Athens, and ἀρχή in the same passage to his archonship in 146; therefore the *Anabasis* is after 146. Turning to Photius' summaries, Wirth notes first that in cod. 58 Photius lists the major works in the order *Parthica, Anabasis, Bithyniaca*; then he examines cod. 93, where he finds that the words τὰ περὶ Ἀλέξανδρον . . . μετὰ are an intrusive gloss. He thus can argue that when Photius calls the *Bithyniaca* τετάρτην, he is not referring to the series *Anabasis*, *Dion*, *Timoleon*, *Bithyniaca* but to one similar to that given in cod. 58, *Dion-Timoleon*, *Parthica*, *Anabasis*, *Bithyniaca*. Wirth considers this opinion, that the *Bithyniaca* was Arrian's fourth work, an inference of Photius, and doubts that the *Anabasis* was mentioned in the preface of the *Bithyniaca*. Other works (like the *Indike*), according to Wirth, would have appeared between these major works. The *Parthica*, on this understanding, would have been an early work, inspired by Arrian's participation in Trajan's Parthian campaigns, and the *Anabasis* a work of Arrian's maturity showing good use of sources and of Xenophon as a stylistic master. Since Lucian has Arrian in mind in writing *How to Write History*, the *Anabasis* was well known before 165.

Bosworth takes a different tack, establishing two fundamental facts, that Arrian was well known for his literary culture (*paideia*), and that it was possible to pursue a literary and a senatorial career simultaneously.[4] He then turns to the *Anabasis*, which he finds shows "no knowledge of the topography of Rome" and indicates no knowledge of or concern for Cappadocia. In *Anab.* 1.12.5 ἡ ἐμαυτοῦ must refer to Nicomedia, not Athens, and since there is no reference to Arrian's senatorial *cursus*, the *Anabasis* must have been written "before his senatorial career began," and of course before his consulship (ca. 129). Bosworth then turns to Photius cod. 93, which he accepts as it stands,[5] as an accurate summary of all that Arrian had to say about himself in the *Bithyniaca*. The statement that the works on Alexander, Dion, and Timoleon preceded the *Bithyniaca* would have been in Arrian's preface, and could not possibly be an interpolation in Photius. The *Bithyniaca*, therefore, was written shortly after the *Anabasis*, while its strong emphasis on Bithynia as his fatherland indicates that Arrian did not yet think of himself primarily as a Roman senator, and certainly not as an ex-consul.[6] Bosworth does not attempt to date the *Parthica* or the *Events after Alexander*, but supposes that they were written in the course of Arrian's adult life. His final timetable (pp. 184–85) suggests that the *Anabasis* appeared some time after 115, then the *Bithyniaca*; about 120 Hadrian would have adlected Arrian to the senate, and Arrian would have pursued his *cursus* until his retirement in 137. About the time of his archonship in Athens he wrote the *Cynegeticus*. The *Parthica* and *Events* could have been written any time after 120.

The whole attempt to establish a chronology of Arrian's major works may be vain, granted the lack of evidence and the subjective interpretations of what exists, especially Photius' summary of the *Bithyniaca* preface and *Anab.* 1.12.5. I have argued in chapter 5 against the interpretations of the latter passage by both Wirth and Bosworth: ἡ ἐμαυτοῦ probably refers to Rome, not Nicomedia or Athens, and Arrian is remaining purposely reticent about his own accomplishments. The pride in his own literary skill and his reference to his interests "from his youth" argue that he is not a young man and that the *Anabasis* is not his first major work. It would be reasonable, therefore, to place this passage, and the whole *Anabasis*, after his consulship.

The value of the summary of Photius is uncertain, because the text is possibly corrupt[7] and Photius' accuracy is questionable. The passage in Henry's edition runs as follows:

Μέμνηται δὲ ἐν ταύτῃ τῇ συγγραφῇ καὶ ἑτέρων πραγματειῶν ὧν ἡ μὲν ὅσα Τιμολέοντι τῷ Κορινθίῳ κατὰ Σικελίαν ἐπράχθη διαλαμβάνει, ἡ δὲ τὰ Δίωνι τῷ Συρακουσίῳ ὅσα ἀξιαφήγητα ἔργα ἐπετελέσθη, ἡνίκα τὰς Συρακούσας καὶ πᾶσαν Σικελίαν
5 ἀπὸ τοῦ δευτέρου Διονυσίου, ὃς ἦν παῖς τοῦ προτέρου, ἠλευθέρου, καὶ τῶν βαρβάρων, οὓς ὑπὲρ τοῦ βεβαίως τυραννεῖν Διονύσιος ἐπηγάγετο.

Φαίνεται δὲ τετάρτην γράφων τὴν τῆς πατρίδος ἀφήγησιν· μετά τε γὰρ τὰ περὶ 'Αλέξανδρον καὶ Τιμολέοντα καὶ Δίωνα,
10 μετὰ τὰς περὶ αὐτοὺς ἱστορίας ἤδε αὐτῷ ἡ συγγραφὴ ἐξεπονήθη, ἐξ ἀρχῆς μέν, ἀφ' οὗ γράφειν ἴσχυσε, ταύτην ἐνστήσασθαι καὶ συντάξαι τὴν ὑπόθεσιν βουληθέντι, τῆς δὲ παρασκευῆς τῷ ἐνδεῶς αὐτὸν ἔχειν παρατεινάσης τὸν χρόνον· ταύτην γὰρ αὐτὸς τῆς ἐπὶ τούτῳ βραδυτῆτος ἀποδίδωσιν αἰτίαν.

9 μετά τε—Δίωνα M: *om.* A   10 *post* μετὰ *add.* γὰρ A² *mg*

There is no doubt that the *Dion* and *Timoleon*, which are not otherwise known, were mentioned by Arrian, probably in words very close to lines 3–10 in Photius' text. He spoke of them, as we learn in the next paragraph, because he wished to explain why he had undertaken any work before the *Bithyniaca*. The difficulty lies in the phrase φαίνεται . . . Δίωνα, which introduces τὰ περὶ 'Αλέξανδρον without explanation and awkwardly overlaps the sense of μετὰ τὰς περὶ αὐτοὺς ἱστορίας. The probable solution, in my mind, is that the passage φαίνεται . . . Δίωνα, or even φαίνεται . . . ἱστορίας, represents Photius' own thoughts interjected into his paraphrase of Arrian's preface.

Henry in the notes to his edition and Bosworth (pp. 178–79) have observed how closely Photius follows autobiographical statements in Dionysius of Halicarnassus, Appian, Dio Cassius, and Diodorus (cod. 83, 57, 71, and 70). But even in these cases, where he was repeating his author almost verbatim, Photius makes significant additions or changes of his own. Thus, when Dionysius writes (*Ant. Rom.* 1.7.2) that he arrived in Rome at the end of the civil war, he gives the date, the middle of the 187th Olympiad. Photius (cod. 83) deletes this date and simply states, ". . . the civil war, *which was fought by Augustus himself and Antony*," substituting a nontechnical statement for the original, reflecting either his own recollection or a simplification for the benefit of his reader. In the same passage, he substitutes τὰ παρ' αὐτοῖς ἀρχαῖα ἐκμαθών for Dionysius' full account of his research in oral and written sources into the early history of Rome. The verb ἐκμαθών does appear in Dionysius, but in a different phrase. Again, Photius' attention wanders in reporting Appian pref. 15.62 in cod. 57, so that he changes ἐς τὰ πρῶτα ἥκων ἐν τῇ πατρίδι, καὶ δίκαις ἐν Ρώμῃ συναγορεύσας to ἐν Ρώμῃ δὲ τὰ πρῶτα δίκαις συνηγόρει, with a quite different sense.

In the *Bithyniaca* summary, φαίνεται indicates that Photius is inserting his own inference into the excerpted material. There would be no place for such a word in Arrian's preface. The notion that the *Bithyniaca* was fourth (τετάρτην) of Arrian's works would be part of that inference. Photius had just finished summaries of the *Anabasis* and the *Events after Alexander* in cods. 91 and 92, and had these works very much in mind. I suggest that in his desire to relate these works to the preface of the *Bithyniaca*, he concluded that they preceded the Bithynian history.[8] In this interpretation, despite the obvious difficulties, τὰ περὶ Ἀλέξανδρον would be Photius' phrase for the *Anabasis* and the *Events after Alexander* taken together as one large work.[9] Photius would have found no mention of works on Alexander in the preface of the *Bithyniaca*, which probably mentioned only the *Dion* and *Timoleon*. The implication is that the *Bithyniaca* was an early work, probably the earliest of the major writings.

The notion of the priority of the *Bithyniaca* runs counter to the common opinion but is not per se unreasonable.[10] The young writer would have tested his pen on two famous historical figures, Timoleon and Dion, while all the time thinking of his native region. We may wish to connect the two earlier works with a sojourn in Sicily, perhaps as quaestor or other official. Arrian's place in the Roman *cursus* might explain his special emphasis in the *Bithyniaca* preface on his ties to Nicomedia: despite his career in the imperial government, he has not forgotten his native city. The *Bithyniaca* by this hypothesis would not be a work of Arrian's retirement, but relatively early, perhaps during his twenties, and contemporaneous with the beginnings of his senatorial career.

A *caveat* is in order: the very number of interpretations warns the reader that this passage in Photius is an unreliable foundation for elaborate hypotheses. It is unfortunately the case that in the absence of any certain evidence for the relative chronology of the major works, our chief guide is the subjective sense of the inner relation among the various works. In my opinion, taking into account the above interpretation of Photius, the most satisfactory order, although hardly a compelling one, would be *Bithyniaca, Parthica, Anabasis* (with the *Indike*), and the *Events after Alexander*. The *Bithyniaca*, as we have seen, has some reason to be considered Arrian's first major work. In all probability, the *Parthica* was inspired by Arrian's own experiences during the Parthian war: his observation of Trajan and other commanders and his direct contact with the war moved him to set down his own account of the history of Parthian-Roman relations, and especially of the great war under Trajan. The time would have been in the first part of Hadrian's reign, perhaps before Arrian's consulship. With the publication of the *Parthica*, Arrian established himself as a gifted writer; his account of Epictetus' lectures was already in circulation among the philosophically inclined, his book on Bithynia had shown his mastery of local history, and now his Parthian history stood head and shoulders above the mass of memoirs, sterile imitations of Thucydides or Xenophon, and fatuous panegyrics of the emperor which followed upon the war. He was ready to attempt a literary-historical tour-de-force, a narrative history of Alexander the Great, which would put into perspective both Alexander's military genius and his triumph over his own personal weaknesses. The *Anabasis* would establish Arrian as one of the masters of Greek literature.

The *Anabasis* and its companion piece the *Indike* did not deceive the hopes of its author, in large measure because of the skill with which he was able to recreate for the contemporary reader the battles of Alexander. The battles of Alexander's successors were no less interesting as examples of extraordinary generalship, and the history of Ptolemy, which had proved so useful, probably was still available for basic narrative down to Triparadisus,[11] so Arrian determined to write, not a sequel to the *Anabasis*—no general or generals could bear comparison with Alexander—but a long monograph on the diplomatic and military struggle for power in the years immediately after Alexander's death. The *Events after Alexander* was Arrian's last work, a product of his leisure years in Athens.

On this hypothesis, Arrian would have written the *Anabasis* in his middle years, after his consulship, in Cappadocia or in Athens. In presenting my reconstruction of Arrian's literary career, I have relied on Bosworth's evidence that it was quite possible for a Roman senator to combine literary activity with imperial service. There is no need for the neat division established by Schwartz between Arrian's Roman career, to 137, and the composition of his histories, from 137 to his death. However, I find Bosworth's arguments for placing the *Anabasis* very early unconvincing. The proper interpretation of Arrian's refusal to boast at *Anab.* 1.12.5 has already been discussed. Let me now consider two other passages which Bosworth considers evidence for an early date for the *Anabasis*.

Arrian writes in *Anab.* 1.16.4 that twenty-five of the Macedonian *hetairoi* died in the battle of the Granicus and that bronze statues of these men were erected at Dium: τούτων χαλκαῖ εἰκόνες ἐν Δίῳ ἑστᾶσιν. The problem is the tense of ἑστᾶσιν. The perfect of ἵστημι, ἑστάναι, normally means "to stand," but in fact in Arrian's day the statues no longer stood at Dium, for they had been carried off in 148 B.C. by Metellus Macedonicus and for almost three centuries had graced the portico erected by him at Rome to celebrate his victory.[12] Such ignorance of Roman topography, Bosworth argues (p. 173), demonstrates that Arrian at the time of writing had never been in Rome, and therefore that the *Anabasis* belongs early in his life, before he began his senatorial *cursus*.

Arguments *ex silentio* are always suspect, but this is open to serious objections.

1. The perfect ἑστᾶσιν can mean not only "are standing," as translated by Bosworth, but "were set up." The perfect does not neces-

sarily imply the continuance of the action into the present time.[13]

2. The number of monuments in the Rome of Arrian's day would have boggled the mind of the most diligent tourist; silence on any one of them hardly argues total ignorance of the city. The Lysippean group may have been one of the sights of Rome, but mention of it survives only in Pliny—always indefatigable—and Velleius Paterculus.

3. Both Plutarch and Justin mention the monument to those fallen at the Granicus but neither comment on its transfer to Rome, although Plutarch at least was quite familiar with the city and frequently made allusions to its monuments.[14]

4. Arrian had every reason not to mention that the statues were moved to Rome, not, as Wirth argues,[15] because the Romans might find it embarrassing, but because it would diminish Alexander's triumph and could only weaken his presentation of his hero's first great victory.

In sum, *Anab*. 1.16.4 tells us nothing of Arrian's acquaintance with Rome or the date of the *Anabasis*.

The second passage (*Anab*. 2.4.2) narrates how, on leaving Gordion, Alexander marched first to Ankara, then into Cappadocia: "Alexander himself marched toward Cappadocia and brought into submission the whole territory to the west of the Halys River, and much beyond the Halys. After appointing Sabiktas satrap of the Cappadocians, he proceeded to the Cilician Gates." The notice of Alexander's march through Cappadocia is frustratingly short, and again Bosworth invokes an argument *ex silentio* (p. 174). "It is remarkable how little Arrian seems to know or care about Cappadocia," he states, suggesting that the *Anabasis* was composed before its author became governor of Cappadocia in 131. However, Curtius is equally laconic in describing Cappadocia's surrender,[16] Plutarch is yet more succinct,[17] and Diodorus and Justin omit Cappadocia altogether. The fact is that the sources did not report that Alexander did anything in Cappadocia, and Arrian did not permit himself digressions on subjects not relevant to his theme. If he had, he certainly would have said something more about Bithynia, his native country.[18] As it is, Arrian, brief as he is, is our fullest source for the submission of the satrapy of Cappadocia.[19]

There is no evidence that the *Anabasis* was written before Arrian's consulship and command in Cappadocia.

NOTES

1. See the discussion in chapter 2 of the *Discourses* and the other philosophical works.

2. Gerhard Wirth, "Anmerkungen zur Arrianbiographie: Appian-Arrian-Lukian," *Historia* 13 (1964) 209–45; A. B. Bosworth, "Arrian's Literary Development," *CQ*, n.s. 22 (1972) 163–85, with some further arguments in "Arrian in Baetica," *GRBS* 17 (1976) 55–64 at 62–64. Important earlier discussions of the chronology of Arrian's works are *RE* s.v. Arrianus, 1231–36; Friedrich Reuss, "Arrian und Appian," *RhM* 54 (1899) 446–65; Felix Jacoby, *FGrHist* II B, comm., 552. See also E. L. Bowie, "Greeks and Their Past in the Second Sophistic," *Past and Present* 46 (1970) 3–41 at 24–27.

3. "Anmerkungen," 223–31.

4. "Arrian's Literary Development," 163–72.

5. He explicitly rejects Wirth's characterization of τὰ περὶ ᾽Αλέξανδρον . . . μετὰ as an intrusive gloss, although he accepts the possibility that περὶ αὐτοὺς ἱστορίας might be an interpretation.

6. Bosworth's argument on this point seems weak: Roman senators with prestigious careers could still recall and honor their birthplace as *patria*. Cf C. P. Jones, "The Plancii of Perge and Diana Planciana," *HSCP* 80 (1976) 231–37, esp. 236–37.

7. Jacoby, *FGrHist* II B, comm., 552, also has doubts about the strange wording of the crucial phrases in Photius.

8. Jacoby, *FGrHist* II B, comm., 552, rightly remarks that Arrian would not have mentioned such disparate works as the *Anabasis* and the short pieces on Dion and Timoleon in one breath. Wirth, "Anmerkungen," interprets the phrase μετὰ . . . Δίωνα as an interpolation, which is possible (the scribe remembering the preceding works on Alexander), but less likely. Photius regularly inserts names to clarify references in his excerpts; on occasion he can be shown to make mistakes in the process: see Tomas Hägg, *Photios als Vermittler antiker Literatur* ("Acta Universitatis Upsaliensis, Studia Graeca Upsaliensia," 8; Uppsala 1975) 108–09.

9. The same usage is probably found in the summary of the *Parthica*, cod. 58, where Photius lists among the major works τὰ κατὰ ᾽Αλέξανδρον and the *Bithyniaca*, but does not explicitly name the *Events after Alexander*. Jacoby, *FGrHist* II B, comm., 552, notes that from cod. 91 and 92 it is apparent that Photius knows that the two works are separate; he may still have thought of them together, however. In cod. 91 τὰ κατὰ ᾽Αλέξανδρον refers to the *Anabasis*, but includes the *Indike* as well, as is apparent from the last paragraph of the codex.

10. Of the authors cited in n. 2 above, for example, Schwartz argues for the order *Anabasis, Bithyniaca, Parthica, Events*; Jacoby (following Photius with some hesitation) for *Anabasis, Bithyniaca, Events, Parthica*; Wirth for *Parthica, Anabasis, Bithyniaca*; and Bosworth for *Anabasis, Bithyniaca*, followed by the other two in uncertain order.

11. See the treatment of the *Events after Alexander* in chapter 8.

12. See Vell. 1.11.4, Pliny *NH* 34.64. Pliny is listing the works of Lysippus, who designed the group; Velleius, praising Metellus and his portico.

13. See William Watson Goodwin, *Syntax of the Moods and Tenses of the Greek Verb* (Boston 1900) § 46, citing Plato *Theaet.* 144 B, ἀκήκοα μὲν τοὔνομα, μνημονεύω δ᾽ οὔ. On the general tendency to use the perfect for an aorist in later prose, see Jules

Albert de Foucault, *Recherches sur la langue et le style de Polybe* (Paris 1972) 134–37, and Pierre Chantraine, *Histoire du parfait grec* ("Collection Linguistique," 21; Paris 1927) 228. The same sort of freedom in the choice of the proper tense to describe monuments may be found in Plutarch's references to the statue of Valeria/Cloelia, *Publ.* 19.8 and *Mor.* 250F; cf. Philip A. Stadter, *Plutarch's Historical Methods* (Cambridge, Mass. 1965) 84.

14. See C. Theander, "Plutarch und die Geschichte," *Bulletin de la société royale des lettres de Lund* 1950–51, I, 1–86, at 12–15, and Lawrence Joseph Simms, *Plutarch's Knowledge of Rome* (Diss. Univ. of North Carolina, 1974) 116–17 (summary in *Dissertation Abstracts* 35 [1974] 3709A–3710A).

15. "Anmerkungen," 231.

16. Curt. 3.1.24 and 3.4.1 (Bosworth also notes his silence).

17. Plut. *Alex.* 18.5 ἐντεῦθεν Παφλάγονά τε καὶ Καππαδόκας προσαγαγόμενος . . .

18. He only mentions his native region at *Anab.* 1.29.5, where in describing the course of the river Sangarius, he notes that it flowed through the land of the Bithynian Thracians.

19. Bosworth also criticizes Arrian's uncertainty in stating that the Araxes flowed into the Caspian Sea (*Anab.* 7.16.3; Arrian writes ὁ πλείων λόγος κατέχει). The passage, however, seems to be a statement of knowledge in Alexander's day, not Arrian's, a regular practice of our author. Moreover, the river's course in the level plain between the mountains and the sea has changed frequently. In the last century the Araxes did not flow into the sea, but into the Kur River, and thence to the sea; it has since been diverted directly to the sea by a canal. Plutarch *Pomp.* 34.4 and Appian *Mithr.* 103 (cited by Bosworth) firmly state that the Araxes flowed into the Kur. Arrian may well have used the phrase ὁ πλείων λόγος because he knew that the Araxes did not in fact flow directly into the Caspian in his day.

Bosworth's argument in "Arrian in Baetica," 62–64, that Arrian's reference in *Anab.* 2.16.4 demonstrates his ignorance of Spanish topography, has been discussed in chapter 1 in connection with his proconsulate of Baetica. Bosworth in his argument does not appreciate Arrian's love of archaic terminology, even when not strictly correct.

NOTES

CHAPTER I[*]

1. See the treatment of Arrian's *Cynegeticus* in chapter 4, of the *Discourses of Epictetus* in chapter 2, and of the *Tactica* and *Ectaxis* in chapter 3.

2. Xenophon's *Cyropaedia*, although it is concerned with the reign of Cyrus the Great almost two centuries before his own time, is not a history but a historical novel. Although it may have influenced Arrian, there is no parallel to it among Arrian's works.

3. On the tradition of Roman senatorial history see Ronald Syme, "The Senator as Historian," in *Histoire et historiens dans l'antiquité* ("Entretiens Hardt," 4; Geneva 1956) 185–201.

4. See the section on the *Bithyniaca* in chapter 8.

5. The name, Lucius, appears on a statue-base found in Athens: Dina Peppas-Delmousou, "Basis andriantos tou Arrianou," *AAA* 3 (1970) 377–80. The original reading of A(ulus) was corrected to L(ucius) by James H. Oliver, "Arrian and the Gellii of Corinth," *GRBS* 11 (1970) 335–38. Although from the photo A(ulus) appears possible, Aulus is extremely rare with Flavius; a rough count in *CIL* gives 93 examples of L. Flavius to 2 of A. Flavius. See also Eugene N. Borza, "Some Notes on Arrian's Name," *AAA* 5 (1972), with a new photograph, 100–102, and Elias Kapetanopoulos, "Arrian's Praenomen Again," *AAA* 6 (1973) 301–4, who emends an inscription long known from Nicomedia (*SEG* I, 446) to read Lucius Flavius Arrianus.

6. See, e.g., H. F. Pelham, "Arrian as Legate of Cappadocia," *EHR* 11 (1896) 625–40, at 626 = *Essays* (Oxford 1911) 212–33, at 213. Arrian of course would have been too young to have received a grant of citizenship directly from the Flavians, since Domitian, the last of the dynasty, was assassinated in 96.

7. Henri Doulcet, *Quid Xenophonti debuerit Flavius Arrianus* (Paris 1882) 2–3.

8. A Greek or other non-Roman upon assuming Roman citizenship would take the praenomen and nomen of the emperor who made the grant, or of the patron who had urged his case: see René Cagnat, *Cours d'Épigraphie*

Latine[4] (Paris 1914) 77; John Edwin Sandys, *Latin Epigraphy*[2] (Cambridge 1927) 217–18. Since all the Flavian emperors bore the praenomen Titus, if Arrian's family received its citizenship from one of them, the praenomen in the family would be Titus. Cf. Eric Birley, *Roman Britain and the Roman Army* (Kendal 1953) 159, and on Flavian names, Gavin Townsend, "Some Flavian Connections," *JRS* 51 (1961) 54–62. Members of the family were distinguished by using their Greek names as *cognomina* (as Arrian did Xenophon). See, e.g., the family of T. Flavius Clitosthenes, *PIR*[2] F 243. Note that the family of another prominent Bithynian, Dio Cocceianus of Prusa, had been Roman citizens for two generations (Dio Chrys. *Or.* 41.6). His grandfather may have been made a citizen by Claudius (thus H. von Arnim, *Leben und Werke des Dio von Prusa* [Berlin 1898] 123). C. S. Walton argues that we should calculate that Roman citizenship had been in the family of any second-century senator from the East for a hundred years: "Oriental Senators in the Service of Rome: A Study of Imperial Policy to the Death of Marcus Aurelius," *JHS* 19 (1929) 38–66, at 61–62. Eduard Schwartz in his extensive article on Arrian cautiously avoided a precise statement, saying only that Arrian's father must already have possessed Roman citizenship (*RE* s.v. Arrianus, 1230).

9. We may note L. Flavius, suffect consul in 33 B.C., who was with Antony in Armenia and possibly elsewhere in Asia Minor (*PIR*[2] F 188), L. Flavius Fimbria, cos. A.D. 71 (*PIR*[2] F 269), and L. Flavius Silva Nonius Bassus, cos. A.D. 81 (*PIR*[2] F 368). The well-known family of writers, the Philostrati of Lemnos, were L. Flavii (*PIR*[2] F 332, 333), but are much later. Occasionally *praenomina* do change in families: the Cretan T. Flavius Sulpicianus Dorio had a son and grandson named Lucius (*IGRR* I, 964, 1015–18; *PIR*[2] F 374–75). A friend of Plutarch was named L. Flavius Pollianus Aristio (*PIR*[2] F 339), although a son of T. Flavius Soclarus. Perhaps Soclarus' wife was a daughter of a L. Pollio, or Pollianus was adopted by one. By analogy, Arrian could derive his praenomen from a L. Arrius, but the only notable men of this name known in this period are restricted to the town of Pisauri (modern Pesaro): *PIR*[2] A 1091, 1103–4.

10. Pelham, "Arrian as Legate," *EHR* 11 (1896) 626 = *Essays*, 214, suggests that it might indicate a connection with that branch of the *gens Arria* which was closely connected with Roman Stoicism, especially through Arria, the wife of Thrasea Paetus.

11. Philip A. Stadter, "Flavius Arrianus: The New Xenophon," *GRBS* 8 (1967) 155–61. The reader should note that not all scholars have accepted this argument, remarking that the name Xenophon does not appear on inscriptions, and considering it a kind of honorary title such as was common in the period. I continue to hold my opinion. If Xenophon was indeed an honorary title, it is all the more surprising that it does not appear on inscriptions, which are our chief source for the practice.

12. *SIG*³ 829.

13. Thus *SEG* I, 446; *AE* 1905, 175; *IGRR* III, 111; *IG* II², 2055; Peppas-Delmousou, "Basis," 377–80; *ArchDelt* 25 (1970) pt. 1, p. 29; A. Plassart, *Fouilles de Delphes* III: *Epigraphie*, fasc. IV, *Inscriptions de la terrasse du temple*, pt. II (Paris 1970) nos. 290, 294. Arrian did not use Xenophon as part of his official nomenclature, even on the Athenian inscription honoring him as a philosopher: Peppas-Delmousou, "Basis," 377–80. Although the stone is broken and the last part of the name is not preserved, there appears to be no room for Xenophon. The honorary inscription from Corinth (below, n. 88) preserves no part of Arrian's name. In the Cordoba dedication (see n. 61) he is simply Arrianos.

14. Even in the epistolary salutation which serves as title to the *Periplus*, although he writes Xenophon in the text.

15. See the references in Stadter, "The New Xenophon."

16. Karl Münscher, *Xenophon in der griechisch-römischen Literatur, Philologus*, Supplementband 13, 2 (Leipzig 1920). Although in modern times Xenophon is best known for his *Anabasis*, recounting the march of the 10,000, his many writings on Socrates (*Memorabilia* in four books, *Apology of Socrates*, *Symposium*, and *Oeconomicus*) established his ancient reputation as a philosopher.

17. Theo Wirth, "Arrians Erinnerungen an Epiktet," *MusHelv* 24 (1967) 149–89 and 197–216, at 204–8.

18. The discussion of this date is set forth below, p. 11.

19. See John Morris, "*Leges Annales* under the Principate," *Listy Filologické* 87 (1964) 316–37; Eric Birley, "Senators in the Emperor's Service," *ProcBritAc* 39 (1953) 197–214; Ronald Syme, *Tacitus* (Oxford 1958) II, 653–56.

20. If his consulate was in 125 (see below) or his career delayed for some reason.

21. If his consulate was in 130 (see below) and he reached it as early as 38 (see the career of C. Julius Quadratus Bassus, as reconstructed by Christian Habicht, *Altertümer von Pergamon* VIII, 3: *Die Inscriften des Asklepieions* [Berlin 1969] 52).

22. On the province of Bithynia see A. H. M. Jones, *Cities of the Eastern Roman Provinces*² (Oxford 1971) 147–52; David Magie, *Roman Rule in Asia Minor to the End of the Third Century after Christ* (Princeton 1950) 302–30, 588–90, 596–605, 626–27 and notes; T. Robert S. Broughton, "Roman Asia Minor," in *Economic Survey of the Roman Empire*, ed. Tenney Frank (Baltimore 1938) IV, 499–918, at 773–78 and index; *CAH* XI (Cambridge 1936) 575–80; Brandis, *RE* s.v. Bithynia, III (1899) 507–39. On Nicomedia see Broughton, "Roman Asia Minor," 773–74; W. Ruge, *RE* s.v. Nikomedeia, XVII (1936) 486–92; and Louis Robert, "La Titulature de Nicée et de Nicomedie: la gloire et la haine," *HSCP* 81 (1977) 1–39.

23. See E. Gren, *Kleinasien und der Ostbalkan in der wirtschaftlichen Entwicklung der römischen Kaiserzeit* ("Uppsala Universitets Arsskrift," 9; Uppsala 1941); Sir John Linton Myres, *Geographical History in Greek Lands* (Oxford 1953) 246–50; and Magie, *Roman Rule*, 1185 n. 11.

24. On relations with the Bosporus, see M. Rostovtsef (Rostovtzeff), "Pontus, Bithynia and the Bosporus," *ABSA* 22 (1916–17, 1917–18) 1–22, and Louis Robert, *Studii clasice* 16 (1974) 54 and n. 6.

25. Pliny *Ep.* 10.15–121.

26. See A. N. Sherwin-White, *The Letters of Pliny, A Historical and Social Commentary* (Oxford 1966) 527. On Pliny's Bithynian letters see especially Ladislav Vidman, *Étude sur la Correspondance de Pline le Jeune avec Trajan* (Prague 1960 = Rozpravy Ceskoslovenske Akademie VED, Rada spolecenskych ved, Rocnik 70, sesit 14).

27. Bithynian speeches: Dio Chrys. *Or.* 38–51; the case before Pliny, *Ep.* 10.81–82. On Dio and the political climate in Bithynia in his day see now C. P. Jones, *The Roman World of Dio Chrysostom* (Cambridge, Mass. and London 1978). Bruce Fairgray Harris, *Bithynia under Trajan* (Auckland 1964), compares the views of Dio and Pliny on the role of the emperor in Bithynia.

28. For the gradual increase in Roman citizens among the upper classes of the Greek cities, see the observations of Habicht, *Inschriften* 163–64.

29. Photius, *Bibliotheca* cod. 93 = *Bithyniaca* F1: "In this work (the *Bithyniaca*) he states that he was Nicomedian by family, and that he was born, raised, and educated there, and had the title of priest of Demeter and her daughter, to whom, he says, the city was dedicated." An inscription from Nicomedia reported in *Hellenikos philologikos syllogos* 2 (1864) 253 n. 5 (see Roos, note to T17) mentions the priesthood, but apparently is false; Arrian is called *toparchēs* of Cappadocia, although *toparchēs* is never used of a *legatus Augusti pro praetore*, and the form of the name, Arrianus Flavius, is in inverse order to all other preserved examples. For other references to the cult of Demeter at Nicomedia, see Ruge, *RE* s.v. Nikomedeia, 485–86.

30. Cf. Henri-Irénée Marrou, *A History of Education in Antiquity* (London and New York 1956) 103, 160. Some began their higher studies as early as sixteen: see M. L. Clarke, *Higher Education in the Ancient World* (London 1971) 6.

31. On Nicopolis see F. Schober in *RE* s.v. Nikopolis 2, XVII (1936) 511–18; Ulrich Kahrstedt, "Die Territorien von Patrai und Nikopolis in der Kaiserzeit," *Historia* 1 (1950) 549–61; G. W. Bowersock, *Augustus and the Greek World* (Oxford 1965) 93–94.

32. See the *Discourses*, prefatory letter to Lucius Gellius, and chapter 2.

33. Simplicius, in the preface to his commentary on Arrian's *Encheiridion*, says that Arrian described the life and death of Epictetus. Apparently this means that an account of Epictetus' last words with his students was included

in the lost books of the *Discourses*. We have no certain evidence for the time of Epictetus' death.

34. For a full collection of the evidence on Epictetus' teaching career, see Heinrich Schenkl, *Epicteti Dissertationes* (Leipzig 1916) I−XXXIII, who, however, incorrectly argues that Arrian studied with Epictetus in the first years of Hadrian's reign (ca. 117−120). Epictetus mentions the Dacian War at *Diss.* 2.22.22. Cf. on this question also Karl Hartmann, "Arrian und Epiktet," *NJbb* 15 (1905) 248−75; and Théodore Colardeau, *Étude sur Épictète* (Paris 1903). Arrian's experience with Epictetus is described fully in the following chapter.

35. On the equestrian career under the principate, see Hans Georg Pflaum, *Les Procurateurs équestres sous le haut-empire romain* (Paris 1950) and *Les Carrières procuratoriennes équestres sous le haut-empire romain* (Paris 1960).

36. An equestrian could be raised to senatorial rank by the grant of the *latus clavus*, the broad purple stripe on the toga which was the mark of the senatorial order, making it possible for one to stand for the quaestorship, the office which admitted one to the senate. At any stage of one's career, the emperor could *adlect* a man to the senate, granting the person the rank of those who had held a particular office, and skipping over the preceding posts: *adlectio inter quaestorios, inter aedilicios*, etc. On adlection to the senate see Bruno Stech, *Senatores qui fuerint inde a Vespasiano usque ad Traiani exitum*, *Klio* Beiheft 10 (1912, repr. 1963); D. McAlindon, "Entry to the Senate in the Early Empire," *JRS* 47 (1957) 191−95; Hans Georg Pflaum, "Principes de l'administration romaine impériale," *Bulletin de la Faculté de Lettres de Strasbourg* 37 (1958−59) 179−95, esp. 184, 193; André Chastagnol, "Les modes d'accès au Sénat romain au début de l'Empire, remarques à propos de la table claudienne de Lyon," *Bulletin de la Société Nationale des Antiquaires de France* (1971) 282−310.

37. See above, n. 5.

38. On the movement of provincials first to Roman citizenship, then to equestrian, and finally senatorial rank, see Arthur Stein, "Zur sozialen Stellung der provinzialen Oberpriester," *Epitymbion Heinrich Swoboda dargebracht* (Reichenberg 1927) 300−311.

39. See Pflaum, "Principes," 182, and the frequent letters of Pliny recommending men to Trajan's attention, *Ep.* 10.4, 26, 85, 86, 87, and Pliny's reference in 10.2 to a recommendation on his behalf by Servianus.

40. The evidence is collected and analyzed by Birley, "Senators." This view has been challenged, however, by Brian Campbell, "Who were the 'viri militares'?" *JRS* 65 (1975) 11−31, esp. 17−18.

41. Birley, *Roman Britain*, 135.

42. See the case of C. Julius Quadratus Bassus, first military tribune, then vigintivir (as triumvir monetalis), then quaestor, a sequence which implies that his father was of equestrian rank. See Habicht, *Inschriften*, 47 n. 10. Other

examples are collected by George W. Houston, "Vespasian's Adlection of Men *in senatum*," *AJP* 98 (1977) 35−63, at pp. 53−54.

43. Birley, "Senators," 201−2 and 213.

44. For Nigrinus' career, see *PIR*[2] A 1408; Ronald Syme, *Danubian Papers* (Bucharest 1971) 95−96, 106−7, 162−63, and *Tacitus*, 244−45, 599−600; and Habicht, *Inschriften*, 50. On the family and its connections with Greece, see C. P. Jones, *Plutarch and Rome* (Oxford 1971) 32−33, 51−54.

45. Pliny *Ep.* 9.13.13, 15.

46. *Historia Augusta*, Hadr. 7.1. The execution of the four consulars remains a puzzle: Syme, *Tacitus*, 244−45, suggests that Nigrinus was a friend of Hadrian but talked too much of his own qualifications for rule; others see Nigrinus as a real conspirator, or an innocent victim of Hadrian's ruthlessness.

47. The dossier of the decision made by Nigrinus was engraved in a series of inscriptions in Greek and Latin recently reedited with a commentary by Plassart, *Inscriptions*, 38−46, nos. 290−96. Arrian appears in no. 290 on p. 43 (= *SIG*[3] 827): "in consilio adfuerunt Q. Eppius, Fl. Arrianus, C. Papius Habitus, T. Liv[ius?]." This punctuation is confirmed by a second inscription, no. 294, p. 57: "[in consilio adfuerunt . . .]us Pollio (leaf) Q. Eppius (leaf) Fl. [Arrianus]", where the leaves used as punctuation are lightly engraved but visible, ridding us of the ghost Q. Eppius Flavius Arrianus alternately identified with or distinguished from Arrian. See Plassart, p. 46. The date of Nigrinus' presence in Achaea is put by Plassart, p. 41, in fall 114 because Trajan is called Optimus Princeps, but the title had been in unofficial use since 103; see F. A. Lepper, *Trajan's Parthian War* (London 1948) 34−39. Syme, *Danubian Papers*, 107, thinks "there is a strong temptation to assume the post [of Nigrinus in Greece] consular: perhaps from 111 or 112 to 114"; but Groag, *PIR*[2] A 1408 seems to think the post praetorian, therefore held by Nigrinus before 110. Nigrinus also appears judging a dispute in an Athenian inscription, *Hesperia* 32 (1963) 24−25, likewise undated. The appearance of Arrian on the council is an argument for dating the correctorship after 110, since before he would have been rather young. The objections sometimes advanced against identifying Nigrinus' councilor with our Nicomedian arise from the identification of Arrian with the Athenian *prytanis* of 167/68 and 172/73, which no longer seems possible (see below).

48. On councils of magistrates, see Mason Hammond, *The Antonine Monarchy* (Rome 1959) 371−73. The most famous was the *consilium principis*, or imperial privy council, on which see John A. Crook, *Consilium Principis* (Cambridge 1955).

49. See on the progressive opening of the senate to Greeks, and the reasons for it, Stech, *Senatores*, 171−84; Walton, "Oriental Senators"; Pierre Lambrechts, *La Composition du Sénat romain, de l'accession au trône d'Hadrien à la mort de Commode (117−92)* (Rijksuniversitet te Gent, *Werken vitgegeven door de Faculteit van Wijsbegeerte en Letteren*, 79e Aflevering; Ant-

werp 1936), and "Trajan et le recrutement du sénat," *AntCl* 5 (1936) 105–14; Mason Hammond, "The Composition of the Senate, A.D. 68–235," *JRS* 47 (1957) 74–81.

50. Most eastern senators in this period came from Roman colonies or cities with a large Roman population: Christian Habicht, "Zwei neue Inschriften aus Pergamon," *IstMitt* 9/10 (1959–60) 109–27, esp. 122–25; and Barbara Levick, *Roman Colonies in Southern Asia Minor* (Oxford 1967) 103–20. For Trajan's more open policy, see Lambrechts, *La Composition du Sénat*, and Hammond, "Composition of the Senate."

51. Cf. A. N. Sherwin-White, *The Roman Citizenship*[2] (Oxford 1973) 260–63, 397–98, 409–11. In Arrian's day there was only one Roman colony in Bithynia, Apamea Myrleia. The important cities preferred Greek ways.

52. On Plutarch's views see Jones, *Plutarch and Rome*, 110–21.

53. For a presentation of the evidence, see the discussion of the *Parthica* in chapter 8.

54. Arrian (P36; cf. *FGrHist* II D, p. 575) records the epigram by Hadrian for Trajan's dedications to Zeus Kasios (also in *Anth. Pal.* 6.332), but otherwise does not name him in the extant fragments of the *Parthica*. Hadrian was left in charge of Syria during Trajan's last campaign into Mesopotamia in 117.

55. See Pliny *Panegyric* 81.1–3 and Jacques Aymard, *Essai sur les chasses romaines* (Paris 1951) 492–502. On Arrian's interest in the chase, see chapter 4.

56. Cf. his address to the soldiers at Lambaesis, preserved on an inscription, *ILS* 2487 and 9133–35 = E. Mary Smallwood, *Documents Illustrating the Principates of Nerva, Trajan and Hadrian* (Cambridge 1966) no. 328.

57. *Tact.* 44.1–2.

58. Hadrian's treatment of Athens as spiritual center of the Greek East is especially well documented: see Paul Graindor, *Athènes sous Hadrien* (Cairo 1934); John Day, *An Economic History of Athens under Roman Domination* (New York 1942) 183–251; Anna S. Benjamin, "The Altars of Hadrian in Athens and Hadrian's Panhellenic Program," *Hesperia* 32 (1963) 57–86; and J. H. Oliver, "The Athens of Hadrian," in *Les Empereurs romains d'Espagne* (Paris 1965) 123–133.

59. See Ronald Syme, "Hadrian the Intellectual," in *Les Empereurs romains d'Espagne*, 243–253; Willem den Boer, "Religion and Literature in Hadrian's Policy," *Mnemosyne* ser. 4, 8 (1955) 123–44; L. W. Daly and W. Suchier, *Altercatio Hadriani Augusti et Epicteti Philosophi* (Urbana 1939).

60. *Historia Augusta*, Hadr. 25.9.

61. Antonio Tovar, "Un nuevo epigrama griego de Córdoba: Arriano de Nicomedia, proconsul de Betica?" in *Estudios sobre la obra de Americo Castro*, ed. P. Lain Entralgo (Madrid 1971) 403–12; Manuel F. Galiano, "Sobre la nueva inscripción griega de Córdoba," *Emerita* 40 (1972) 47–50;

Miroslav Marcovich, "The Epigram of Proconsul Arrian from Cordoba," *ZPE* 12 (1973) 207–9; Jeanne and Louis Robert, *Bulletin Epigraphique* 1973, no. 539; Giuseppe Giangrande, "El epigrama de Arriano a Artemis," *Emerita* 44 (1976) 349–55; A. B. Bosworth, "Arrian in Baetica," *GRBS* 17 (1976) 55–64; W. Eck, *RE* s.v. Flavius 44, suppl. 14 (1974) 120; W. Burkert, "Nochmals das Arrian-Epigramm von Cordoba," *ZPE* 17 (1975) 167–69; Miroslav Marcovich, "Nochmals Cordoba, Wiederum Arrian," *ZPE* 20 (1976) 41–43; W. Peek, "Zum Arrian-Epigramm von Cordoba," *ZPE* 20 (1976) 87–88; Ludwig Koenen, "Cordoba and No End," *ZPE* 24 (1977) 35–40. See also below, chapter 4.

62. Although Greek senators usually held posts in the East, positions in the western provinces were not unknown. Cf., e.g., Claudius Charax, legionary legate in Britain: Habicht, "Zwei Neue Inschriften," 109–27, esp. 115.

63. *Pace* Bosworth, "Arrian in Baetica," 62–63, who argues that *Anab.* 2.16.4 gives no indication of autopsy.

64. We know only a few names and no specific dates for the proconsuls of Baetica under Hadrian: see Werner Eck, *Senatoren von Vespasian bis Hadrian* (Munich 1970) 238; and Bosworth, "Arrian in Baetica," 61.

65. The consulship itself is well attested on stone and by later authors (Photius *Bibl.* 58.4; *Suda* s.v. Arrianos). The legate of Cappadocia, moreover, had from the time of Vespasian been an ex-consul.

66. *CIL* XV, 244 and 552; Renato Bartoccini, *Le Terme di Lepcis (Leptis Magna)* ("Africa Italiana," 4; Bergamo 1929) 77 n. 2: "Severo et Arrian(o) cos."

67. Herbert Bloch, *I Bolli laterizi e la storia edilizia romana* (Rome 1938) 328–29, with the chart on p. 242 (= *Bulletino della commissione archeologica comunale del governatorato di Roma* 66 [1938] 196–97, 110).

68. The inscription of Priscus, Bartoccini, *Le Terme di Lepcis*, 76–77, *IRT* 361; of Praesens, Bartoccini, 91–92, *IRT* 545. The proconsulship of Priscus, once thought to be in 127, has been redated by Syme, *REA* 67 (1965) 347–50; cf. Eck, *Senatoren*, 212. The date must be reconsidered, however, in the light of the discovery that Q. Pomponius Marcellus was proconsul of Asia, not Africa: cf. *AJA* 78 (1974) 132.

69. Attilio Degrassi, *I Fasti consolari dell'impero romano* (Rome 1952) 37.

70. H. Bloch, "*Consules suffecti* on Roman Brick-stamps," *CP* 39 (1944) 254–55, esp. n. 7.

71. He was in Dioscurias when the Bosporan King Cotys died in that year: *Per.* 17.3 and *PIR*² J 276 (Tib. Iulius Cotys).

72. Eck, *Senatoren*, 204 and n. 373. Arrian's immediate predecessor was T. Prifernius Paetus Geminus, who is attested for 128/29: see David French, "Latin Inscriptions from Aksaray (Colonia Archelais in Cappadocia)," *ZPE* 27 (1977) 247–49.

73. *PIR*² B 174.

74. The office is attested for Bruttius by *IRT* 541, but its exact position in his *cursus* is uncertain: see Syme, *Historia* 17 (1968) 90–91 and Eck, *Senatoren*, 191 n. 328. Arrian should perhaps be connected with an undated inscription from Rome, *CIL* VI, 31132, "[locus datus a . . .]o Arriano / [curatore operum publicorum et aedium sa]crarum."

75. Willy Hüttl, *Antoninus Pius* (Prague 1933) II, 155–57 attempted to establish the date by other criteria, which are unfortunately unreliable. Beginning from the possible but quite unproven assumption that Arrian was governor of Syria immediately upon leaving Cappadocia (e.g., A.D. 138–40), he sets his consulship between those of his predecessor Cn. Minucius Faustinus Sex. Iulius Severus (cos. 127) and Sex. Iulius Maior, legate in the early 140s, who was then thought to have been consul in 132. Now Maior's consulship is dated ca. 126 (see *PIR*² J 397) or perhaps 129 (Eric Birley, *JRS* 52 [1962] 222 and 225) and this rather tenuous argument loses all force.

76. The post is attested by various inscriptions: *IGRR* III, 111 (= Roos T17), found at Sebastopolis in Cappadocia, ἐπὶ Φλ(αουίου) ᾿Αρριανοῦ / πρεσβευτοῦ καὶ ἀντιστρατήγου τοῦ Σεβαστοῦ; *Corinth* VIII, no. 124 (see below, n. 88); and *AE* 1905, no. 175 (= Roos T11) as reasonably restored, "Had[rianus . . .] / per Fl. A[rrianum] / leg[(atum) Augusti pr(o) pr(aetore) Cappadociae]". Arrian's name cannot be restored in *CIG* II, 2108f = *Corpus Inscriptionum Regni Bosporani* no. 47, as suggested by Doulcet, *Quid Xenophonti*, 25. The Nicomedian inscription mentioning Arrianus Flavius as *toparch* of Cappadocia is false; see above n. 29.

77. Pelham, "Arrian as Legate," *EHR* 625–40 = *Essays*, 212–33. On Cappadocia, see Magie, *Roman Rule*, 200–202, 491–95, 605–8, 621–22; Broughton, "Roman Asia Minor," 650–51; *CAH* XI, 606–13. Particular problems encountered by Arrian as governor are discussed in chapter 3.

78. On the difficulties posed by this frontier, see the excellent popular account by Freya Stark, *Rome on the Euphrates* (London 1966), with numerous photos of the landscape, as well as Lepper, *Trajan's Parthian War*, and Karl-Heinz Ziegler, *Die Beziehungen zwischen Rom und dem Partherreich* (Wiesbaden 1964).

79. The dates of this tour are in dispute, but it is probably in 129–31: Magie, *Roman Rule*, 621–22.

80. *AE* 1905 no. 175, quoted in n. 76. Originally published by M. Rostowzew (Rostovtzeff), *Mémoires de la Société archéologique et historique d'Odessa* (1904), it has been republished with a speculative restoration by Lev Andreevich Elnickij, *VDI* 88 (1964) 138–40.

81. On the Alans, see M. Rostovtzeff, in *CAH* XI, 94–97; A. B. Bosworth, "Arrian and the Alani," *HSCP* 81 (1977) 217–55. They had made earlier invasions in A.D. 35 and 72–73 (ibid. 95, 143); on the latter occasion Vespasian

had refused to aid the Parthian king. The collaboration between Arrian and Vologases on this occasion seems an indication of Hadrian's policy of *détente* with Parthia.

82. Dio Cass. 69.15.1. See also Themistius *Orat.* 34.8 and Iohannes Lydus *De magistratibus* 3.53.1 (= Roos T12–14).

83. *IGRR* III, 111 (see n. 76).

84. See Eck, *Senatoren*, 215 and n. 418.

85. See especially G. A. Harrer, "Was Arrian Governor of Syria?" *CP* 11 (1916) 338–39; Hüttl, *Antoninus Pius*, 155–57; and Géza Alföldy, *Konsulat und Senatorenstand unter den Antoninen* ("Antiquitas," Reihe 1, Bd. 27; Bonn 1977) 238–39. Lucian could be referring to Arrian in *De morte Peregrini* 14, when he speaks of "the governor of Syria at that time, a man who took delight in philosophy." The capstone of an outstanding senatorial career would have been the proconsulship of Africa or Asia, normally held some fifteen years after the consulship. There is no evidence that Arrian held either post. However, the gaps in our lists of governors for these two provinces in the years 140–150 do not permit us to exclude the possibility that Antoninus Pius honored him in this fashion. See in general Bengt E. Thomasson, *Die Statthalter der römischen Provinzen Nordafrikas von Augustus bis Diocletianus* ("Skrifter Utgivna av Svenska Institutet i Rom," 8vo, IX, 1–2; Lund 1960).

86. *Suda* s.v. Arrianos; cf. Photius *Bibl.* cod. 58.

87. Contrast the view of A. B. Bosworth, "Arrian's Literary Development," *CQ* n.s. 22 (1972) 163–85.

88. John H. Kent, *Corinth*, VIII, 3: *The Inscriptions, 1926–1950* (Princeton 1966) 55–56, no. 124, connected with Arrian by G. W. Bowersock, "A New Inscription of Arrian," *GRBS* 8 (1967) 279–80, with restorations by Jeanne and Louis Robert, *Bulletin Épigraphique* 1968, no. 253: [φιλ] ὁσοφ[ον?——] / [πρεσ]βευτὴν [αὐτοκράτορος] / Καί[σα]ρος Τραια[νοῦ ʼΑδρ]ι[ανοῦ] / [Σ]εβα[σ]τοῦ ἀντιστ[ράτηγ]ον [τῆς] / ἐπαρχ[είας τῆς Καππαδ]οκ[ίας Λ.] / [Γ]έλλιος Μ[ένανδρος καὶ Λ. Γέλλιος] / [Ιο]ῦστος υ(ἱὸς) τὸ[ν φίλον καὶ] / εὐεργ[έτην]. The family seems to have made a hobby of erecting statues to their friends, especially to the procurators of Achaea: see Kent, p. 58, and the inscriptions listed in *PIR*² G 128 and 132. In Arrian's day the active members of the family were L. Gellius Menander, his son L. Gellius Menandri f. Iustus, and his two grandsons L. Gellius Menander (II) and L. Gellius Iustus *filius*. On this stemma, and the use of *filius* = junior, see Oliver, "Arrian and the Gellii," who argues that L. Gellius Menandri f. Iustus is "much more likely" to be Arrian's friend.

89. Peppas-Delmousou, "Basis," emended by Oliver, "Arrian and the Gellii," 338: Λ. φλ. ʼΑρριανὸ[ν] / ὑπατικὸν φιλό[σο]/φο[ν]. See also Borza, "Arrian's Name," and Kapetanopoulos, "Arrian's *Praenomen* Again."

90. Géza Alföldy, *Noricum* (London 1974) 57 and 60. For the heavy river traffic on the Inn, see p. 58; on the Save, p. 60. These are the only two water routes discussed by Alföldy for this province. Bosworth, "Arrian's Literary Development," 172, questions the accuracy of Arrian's statement, noting Pliny's assertion that the Danube had sixty tributaries, of which half were navigable (*NH* 4.79). But Pliny's statement, apart from the relativity of the term "navigable," is a vague generalization, whereas Arrian's is precise and conforms to our other evidence. The Dravus and the Savus are the only tributaries which Pliny in his description of the Danube expressly states are navigable (*NH* 3.147). In all Pliny names eleven tributaries in 3.147−149. Arrian is discussing major tributaries, comparable to the major rivers of India, and not minor streams; his intent is undoubtedly to correct Herodotus' account of the tributaries of the Danube at 4.48−50. The statement that the Save enters the Danube at Taurunus, challenged by Bosworth, is supported in Pliny (*NH* 3.148). Noricum would not have been a normal station for a senator.

91. *IG* II², 2055 (= Roos T21); M. Mitsos, *ArchDelt* 25 (1970) pt. A, 29−33; and Simone Follet, *Athènes au IIe et au IIIe siècle* (Paris 1976), 211−12. For the date, see Kolbe, *AthMitt* 46 (1921) 131−32, 148; J. H. Oliver, *Hesperia* 11 (1942) 85.

92. See in general Daniel J. Geagan, *The Athenian Constitution after Sulla*, *Hesperia* Suppl. 12 (1967). On the wealth required of an archon see Geagan, "Hadrian and the Athenian Dionysiac Technita," *TAPA* 103 (1972) 133−160 at 153, and Day, *Economic History*, 239−41. Sophists, as among the wealthiest men of their day, are frequently recorded as donating very heavily with such liturgies: see G. W. Bowersock, *Greek Sophists in the Roman Empire* (Oxford 1969) 17−42. The burdens of the office were heavy enough that on several occasions the Athenians could not find anyone, native or stranger, willing and able to be archon, so that the post had to be left empty, the year being named "the year after N. was archon."

93. See Michael Woloch, *Roman Citizenship and the Athenian Elite: A Prosopographical Survey, A.D. 96−161* (Toronto 1973). The emperor Domitian was archon but not a citizen: ibid., p. 215.

94. On the Areopagus in Roman times, see most recently Daniel J. Geagan, "Ordo Areopagitarum Atheniensium," in *Phoros: Tribute to Benjamin Dean Meritt* (Locust Valley 1974) 51−56.

95. The ephebe: M. Mitsos, *Archeologike Ephemeris* 1950−51, p. 40, line 150 = *IG* II², 2045, line 9, on which see Elias Kapetanopoulos, "Herakleides' Archonship and Abaskantos' *Paidotribia*," *CP* 65 (1970) 96−98, and "Some Observations on 'Roman Athens,'" *Historia* 19 (1970) 561−64 at 561. Member of boule: *IG* II², 1773, line 10 [Φλ. Ἀρρ]ιανός (A.D. 166/67) and 1776, line 10 Φλ. Ἀρριανός (A.D. 169/70). Follet, *Athènes*, 35 seems to think that this *prytanis* is our Arrian.

96. Cf. Bosworth, "Arrian's Literary Development," 181 and n. 6.

97. *IG* II², 4251−53 (= Roos T25), on which see Paul Graindor, "L'Historien Arrien et ses descendants," *Marbes et textes antiques d'époque impériale* (Univ. de Gand, "Recueil de travaux publ. par la Faculté de philosophie et lettres," fasc. 50, 1922) 49−52. Other consuls named Arrianus listed by Degrassi, *Fasti Consolari*, are L. Claudius Arrianus (saec. II?), Arrianus Aper Veturius Severus (saec. II), and L. Annius Arrianus, cos. 243 (pp. 117, 113, and 67).

98. Marguerite Yourcenar, *Memoirs of Hadrian* (New York 1954) 162−63, 221, 277−79.

99. *RE* s.v. Arrianus, 1234−36.

100. I do not agree with the conclusion of Georg Wirth, "Anmerkungen zur Arrianbiographie," *Historia* 13 (1964) 209−45, that the *Anabasis* must be dated after Arrian's archonship at Athens.

101. Bosworth, "Arrian's Literary Development," 169−70. I am not convinced by his efforts to prove that the *Anabasis* was written before Arrian's consulship. See appendix 5 for a more detailed treatment of this difficult question.

102. Galen *De usu partium*, vol. II, p. 151 ed. Helmreich. This part of the work was written between 169 and 175 A.D., when Arrian would have been quite old. It is possible, however, that Galen refers to one of the other consuls named Arrian, who were mentioned in note 97.

103. Galen *De libris propriis* 11.

104. Gellius *Noctes Atticae* 1.2.

105. Marcus Aurelius *Ad se ipsum* 1.7.

106. Lucian *Alexander seu Pseudopropheta* 2.

CHAPTER 2

1. On the life of Epictetus, see P. A. Brunt, "From Epictetus to Arrian," *Athenaeum* 50 (1977) 19−48; Fergus Millar, "Epictetus and the Imperial Court" *JRS* 55 (1965) 140−48, esp. 141−42; and Joseph Souilhé in *Épictète, Entretiens* (Paris 1943) I, I−IX.

2. On the content of Epictetus' teaching see Adolf Friedrich Bonhöffer, *Epiktet und die Stoa* (Stuttgart 1890); Théodore Colardeau, *Étude sur Épictète* (Paris 1903); Paul Elmer More, *Hellenistic Philosophies* (Princeton 1923) 94−171; Phillip De Lacy, "The Logical Structure of the Ethics of Epictetus," *CP* 38 (1943) 112−25; Max Pohlenz, *Die Stoa*³ (Göttingen 1964) I, 327−41, II, 161−67; F. H. Sandbach, *The Stoics* (New York 1975) 164−70.

3. On similarities and differences between the calls to conversion of Epictetus and Christian preachers, see A. D. Nock, *Conversion* (Oxford 1933) 176−86.

4. For an overview of Stoic attitudes toward civil life, especially at Rome, see Sandbach, *The Stoics*, 140–48. On Arrian and Alexander, see chapter 6. Brunt, "From Epictetus," 36–48, in emphasizing the Stoic rejection of fame as a value, neglects the role of duty in their scheme, and so somewhat misrepresents Epictetus' influence on Arrian's presentation of Alexander.

5. Cf. *Diss.* 1.6.30: "My nose is running. . . . Is it reasonable that there be runny noses in the world?" as a complaint of one who does not understand God's providence.

6. On Epictetus as a teacher, see Colardeau, *Étude*, 71–113; Otto Halbauer, *De diatribis Epicteti* (Leipzig 1911); B. L. Hijmans, Jr., *Askēsis: Notes on Epictetus' Educational System* (Utrecht 1959); Souilhé, *Épictète* I, xxx–xlii. The exact relation between Epictetus' teaching and Arrian's *Discourses* is not known, though a theory is offered below.

7. See especially De Lacy, "Logical Structure."

8. On the diatribe see Donald R. Dudley, *A History of Cynicism* (London 1937) 62–63, 85–86; Souilhé, *Épictète* I, xxii–xxx.

9. Epictetus himself sketches a typical occasion: "'We are passing through, and while we are hiring our ship, we have a chance to take a look at Epictetus; let's see what in the world he has to say.' Then you leave with the remark, 'Epictetus was nothing at all, his language was full of solecisms and barbarisms'" (*Diss.* 3.9.14). There is a list of visitors in Brunt, "From Epictetus," 20–21. Theo Wirth, "Arrians Erinnerungen an Epiktet," *MusHelv* 24 (1967) 149–189 and 197–216 argues that such interviews were almost always private (see esp. pp. 162–63); wrongly, in my opinion: see below.

10. T. Wirth, "Arrians Erinnerungen," 176, notes that this *corrector* should not be identified with the Maximus named by Epictetus at sections 3 and 10 of this chapter, as is frequently done, despite the fact that there was a *corrector* of Achaea named Maximus about this time: see Pliny, *Ep.* 8.24; cf. A. N. Sherwin White, *The Letters of Pliny, A Historical and Social Commentary* (Oxford 1966) ad loc.; and C. P. Jones, *Phoenix* 22 (1968) 111–12. It seems strange, moreover, to identify Pliny's Maximus with the *corrector* with the Sex. Quinctilius Valerius Maximus of *CIL* III, 384: Pliny's advice that the *corrector* recall that he is dealing with the Greeks, the heirs of a noble heritage, does not seem appropriate to one who is a native of Alexandria in the Troad. It is possible that the Maximus referred to by Epictetus at 3.7.3 and 10 was the *corrector* preceding the one whom he was addressing, and identical with the *corrector* named by Pliny.

11. In general on Epictetus' unsympathetic attitude toward political life at Rome, see Millar, "Epictetus," and Chester G. Starr, Jr., "Epictetus and the Tyrant," *CP* 44 (1949) 20–29.

12. The work is cited in antiquity by a number of names, which has led some to think that Arrian wrote several works reporting Epictetus' teaching,

but it seems most likely that all the names refer to the same work. See for a review of the arguments Souilhé, *Épictète* I, xii–xix. The *Discourses* and *Manual* are available in the Loeb Library edition by W. A. Oldfather, as well as in other English translations.

13. Karl Hartmann, "Arrian und Epiktet," *NJbb* 95 (1905) 257, 274–75. Brunt, "From Epictetus," 19, speaks of "verbatim notes" but does not discuss the problems involved.

14. T. Wirth, "Arrians Erinnerungen," 149–89 and 197–216, and on the letter to Gellius, 148–61. De Lacy, in analyzing the coherent development of the first book of the *Discourses*, suggests that Arrian has substantially rewritten Epictetus' lectures, although he leaves Arrian's exact contribution imprecise. See De Lacy, "Logical Structure," 113 and n. 15.

15. The theory of H. W. Stallwag, *Het Eerste Boek der Diatriben* (Amsterdam 1933) 7–14, that the *Discourses* were actually edited and published by Epictetus himself, and that the letter of Arrian was mistakenly affixed to them, does not take sufficient account of the evidence for Arrian's authorship.

16. T. Wirth, "Arrians Erinnerungen," 162–63.

17. T. Wirth, "Arrians Erinnerungen," 207–212.

18. See above, chapter 1, n. 88.

19. The most important articles on this work are by Wilhelm Capelle, "Der Physiker Arrian und Poseidonios," *Hermes* 40 (1905) 614–35, who compared the theories expressed to those of Posidonius, but through a misunderstanding of Photius' text assigned this Arrian to the second century B.C.; U. v. Wilamowitz-Moellendorff, "Der Physiker Arrian," *Hermes* 41 (1906) 157–58, who corrected Capelle and reassigned the writer to the second century A.D.; and finally August Brinkmann, "Die Meteorologie Arrians," *RhM* 73 (1924) 373–401 and 74 (1925) 25–63, who demonstrated, on the basis of style and general interests, that the author was in fact Arrian of Nicomedia. The fragments (three from Stobaeus, one each from Philoponus, Priscianus Lydus, and Photius) are edited by Roos, *Arrianus* II, 186–95, under the title *Fragmenta de rebus physicis* (here, C).

20. Photius *Bibl.* cod. 250 (460b 17) = C5.

21. See J. M. Rist, *Stoic Philosophy* (Cambridge 1969) 174, and Pohlenz, *Die Stoa* I, 33, 64–110, 295–98.

22. See the fragments in L. Edelstein and I. G. Kidd, *Posidonius* I (Cambridge 1972).

23. See Gundel, *RE* s.v. Kometen, XI, 1 (1921) 1188, and Ludwig Friedländer's commentary to Juvenal 6.407 (Leipzig 1895), with the introduction, pp. 8–10.

24. Aristotle, followed by Posidonius and some other Stoics, argued that comets were atmospheric manifestations, like thunder and lightning. See Gundel, *RE* s.v. Kometen, 1164–67; Edelstein and Kidd, *Posidonius* I,

122−26; Eduard Zeller, *The Stoics, Epicureans, and Sceptics* (repr. New York 1962) 206−7 and notes.

25. We might notice that thunder, lightning, and rainbows discouraged the Roman troops on the Parthian campaign at the siege of Hatra (reported in Dio Cass. 63.31.4, and no doubt in Arrian's *Parthica* as well).

26. *Arrianus* II, xxvii−xxviii. He was no doubt influenced by the fact that John Philoponus (C1) and Priscianus Lydus (C2) cite the work as *On Atmospheric Phenomena* (*Peri Meteōrōn*).

27. Brinkmann, "Meteorologie," 56.

28. The title is not infrequently found on inscriptions: see Marcus N. Tod, "Sidelights on Greek Philosophers," *JHS* 77 (1957) 132−41; Jeanne and Louis Robert, *Bulletin Épigraphique* 1958, 84; L. Robert, *Hellenica* 11−12 (1960) 108 n. 1, and 485; Christian Habicht, *Altertümer von Pergamon* XIII, 3: *Die Inschriften des Asklepieions* (Berlin 1969) 162−63.

29. See Karl Münscher, *Xenophon in der griechisch-römischen Literatur*, *Philologus* Suppl. 13, 2 (1920) 90−91, 121−27.

30. Gerhard Wirth, "*Arrianos ho philosophos*," *Klio* 41 (1963) 221−33, traces the notices of Photius and the *Suda* calling Arrian a philosopher to the life written by Dio Cassius, but errs in thinking that Dio was the first to call him so.

CHAPTER 3

1. Arrian's *Periplus* has recently appeared in two new editions, each with translation and commentary: Gerardo Marenghi, *Arriano, Periplo del Ponto Eusino* ("Collana di Studi greci," 29; Naples 1958); and Nathela Kečagmadze (Tbilisi 1961), in Georgian, with Russian summary. It also appears in Roos II, 103−28. There is an English translation by Thomas Falconer, *Arrian's Voyage round the Euxine Sea . . .* (Oxford 1805). See also the two articles by Margenghi, "Sulle fonti del *Periplo* di Arriano," *StItal* 29 (1957) 217−23, and "Carattere e intenti del *Periplo* di Arriano," *Athenaeum* n.s. 35 (1957) 177−92. On the date of the *Periplus*, see below, n. 25.

2. See in general Rudolph Güngerich, *Die Küstenbeschreibung in der griechischen Literatur* ("Orbis Antiquus," 4; Munster 1950). Much has been written about Arrian's relation to other lost or preserved guides to the Black Sea. Arrian is frequently thought to have used Menippus of Pergamon (see Gisinger, *RE* s.v. Menippus 9, XV, 1 (1931) 862−88, especially the tables of parallels at 869−82), but the question is not vital. Certainly Arrian made use of an earlier *periplus*, or several, but he felt free to add, subtract, or correct at will. See in general Aubrey Diller, *The Tradition of the Minor Greek Geographers* (n.p. 1952) 147−64 on Menippus and 102−46 on the anonymous Byzantine *periplus* which uses Arrian among others. Cf. also Marenghi, "Sulle

fonti," and Tuomo Pekkanen, "Procopius and the Periplus of Arrian," *Eranos* 62 (1964) 40–51.

3. See Güngerich, *Küstenbeschreibung*, 12 and 19–21.

4. The exact chronology of the journeys of Hadrian in the East remains problematic, but the most probable date for the visit to the Euphrates frontier and Trapezus appears to be 131: see David Magie, *Roman Rule in Asia Minor* (Princeton 1950) I, 621–22, and Wilhelm Weber, *Untersuchungen zur Geschichte des Kaisers Hadrianus* (Leipzig 1907 and Hildesheim 1973) 264–66. Weber is wrong, however, in arguing that Hadrian went East from Trapezus to Sebastopolis (266–67).

5. This first part, from Trapezus to Sebastopolis (Dioscurias) may be outlined:

  1. Trapezus (1–2)
  2. First stop: Hyssou Limen (3)
  3. Second stop: Athens (4–5)
  4. Third stop: Apsaros (6)
  5. Rivers passed, from Trapezus to the Phasis (7)
  6. Fourth stop: the Phasis River (8–9)
  7. Fifth stop: the Chobos River (10.1)
  8. Sixth stop: Sebastopolis (10.2–4)
  9. Nations passed, from Trapezus to Sebastopolis (11.1–3)
  10. Orientation of coastline, from Trapezus to Sebastopolis (11.4–5).

6. See in general on the problems of the northeast frontier of the empire A. B. Bosworth, "Arrian and the Alani," *HSCP* 81 (1977) 217–55 and "Vespasian's Reorganization of the North-East Frontier," *Antichthon* 10 (1976) 63–78.

7. The presence of Roman troops in Transcaucasia is attested by inscriptions: see *IGRR* III, 133, Roman troops in Iberia in A.D. 75; *AE* 1951, no. 263, a member of the Legio XII Fulminata, which was based in Cappadocia, near Baku under Domitian; *AE* 1947, no. 125, and 1950, no. 96, a Publicius Agrippa *pitiax* in Iberia. See also Statius *Silvae* 1.4, Moses of Chorene 2.54, with Z. Iampolskii, *VDI* 31 (1950) 177–82 and Lev Andreevich Elinitzkii, ibid., 193–94.

8. For a discussion of this aspect of Arrian's journey, see H. F. Pelham, "Arrian as Legate of Cappadocia," *EHR* 11 (1896) 625–40 = *Essays* (Oxford 1911) 212–33. Cf. also Karl Hartmann, *Flavius Arrianus und Kaiser Hadrian* (Augsburg 1907) 15–24, and Bosworth, "Alani."

9. On the relation of the *Periplus* to these dispatches, see Marenghi, "Carattere." The dispatches, despite Arrian's use of the present and future tense in referring to them, apparently preceded the *Periplus*. Pliny's correspondence demonstrates how often a conscientious governor would write to the emperor.

10. Dio Cass. 69.15.1. Pharasmanes is mentioned at *Per.* 11.2. The Alans

were repulsed by Arrian: see below on the *Battle Formation against the Alans*.

11. Arrian states that he would like to have the inscription to Hadrian recut. The new version may have survived in the very handsome monumental inscription preserved in the church of Panagios Chrysokephalos in Trebizond: see T. B. Mitford, "Some Inscriptions from the Cappadocian *Limes*," *JRS* 64 (1974) 160−75 at 160−62, and Selina Ballance, "The Byzantine Churches of Trebizond," *AnatSt* 10 (1960) 141−75, esp. 146−51.

12. The heights of the Alps and the Caucasus are indeed roughly equivalent, though Mount Elbrus in the Caucasus at 18,483 feet is substantially higher than the tallest Alpine peak, Mount Blanc (15,781 feet). The Alps would be the highest mountains Hadrian had seen in his travels. The reference to the Prometheus story is probably meant to recall Aeschylus' *Prometheus Bound*. Arrian quotes *Prometheus Unbound* at *Per*. 19.2.

13. On Arrian's description of this part of the coast, see N. I. Lomouri, *VDI* 62 (1957) 96−110, and O. D. Lordkipanidze, "La Géorgie et le monde grec: quelques résultats des recherches archéologiques récentes en Géorgie," *BCH* 98 (1974) 897−948. Arrian erected a dedication to Hadrian at Sebastopolis: *AE* 1905, no. 175 (quoted in chapter 1, n. 76).

14. The second part of the *Periplus*, from the Thracian Bosporus to Trapezus, is divided into sections by the major harbors and rivers:

   1. From Byzantium to Kalpes Limen (12)
   2. From Kalpes Limen to the Parthenios River and the border of Bithynia (13)
   3. From the Parthenios to the Halys (14)
   4. From the Halys to Trapezus (15−16).

There follows a transitional paragraph (17), reiterating the distance from Trapezus to Sebastopolis and explaining his decision to continue the *periplus* to the Cimmerian Bosporus.

15. After Trapezus, he is thought to have visited Nicopolis, Neocaesareia, Amaseia, and Sebastopolis. See Magie, *Roman Rule*, 622; Albino Garzetti, *From Tiberius to the Antonines* (London 1974) 400.

16. *Per*. 1.1 and Xen. *Anab*. 4.8.22.

17. *Per*. 2.3 and Xen. *Anab*. 6.4.25.

18. *Per*. 11.1 and Xen. *Anab*. 5.2.1.

19. *Per*. 25.1 is a loose summary of Xen. *Anab*. 7.5.12.

20. Named citations: *Per*. 12.4 and Xen. *Anab*. 6.4.3−6 (Kalpes Limen); *Per*. 13.6 and Xen. *Anab*. 6.3 (the Bithynian Thracians); *Per*. 14.4 and Xen. *Anab*. 6.1.15 (Armene); *Per*. 16.3 and Xen. *Anab*. 5.5.3 (Kotyora). Arrian notes concerning Kotyora that Xenophon called it a *polis*, but now it is just a village, and not a very big one at that. Anonymous echoes: *Per*. 13.3 and Xen. *Anab*. 6.2.1 (Heraclea); *Per*. 14.5 and Xen. *Anab*. 6.1.15 (Sinope); *Per*. 16.4 and Xen. *Anab*. 5.3.2 (Kerasus).

21. Cf. 14.3 on the harbor of Abonos, 13.6 on the Bithynian Thracians and Xenophon, and the comment on Kotyora mentioned in n. 20.

22. The major divisions of the third part, from Sebastopolis to the Cimmerian Bosporus and Byzantium, are:

1. From Sebastopolis to the Bosporus and the Tanais River (18–19.3)
2. From Pantacapeum to the Psilon mouth of the Danube (19.3–20.3)
3. The island of Achilles (21–23)
4. From the Danube to Byzantium (24–25).

23. Cf. also his reference to the problem at *Anab*. 3.30.7–9.

24. On the isle of Achilles and its cult see E. Diehl, *RE* s.v. Pontarches 2, XXII, 1 (1953) 1–18, with the bibliography cited; Eugène Belin de Ballu, *Olbia, cité antique du littoral nord de la mer noire* (Leiden 1972) 77–82. There is a quite different account of Achilles and Helen on Leuke by Philostratus, *Heroicus* 211,17–214,10 ed. Kayser.

25. This reference to the death of King Cotys, which took place in A.D. 131/32 (see *PIR*² I 276) gives us our best indication of the date of the *Periplus*. If the work was to fulfill the purpose which Arrian gives it in chapter 17, it would have to have been sent to Hadrian only a short time after Cotys' death.

26. *Per*. 23.3: "I write these things about the island of Achilles having heard either from those who have landed there or who have heard from others."

27. On Theodosia, see V. F. Gajdukevič, *Das bosporanische Reich*² (Berlin 1971) 205, 394–95; A. Hermann, *RE* s.v. Theodosia 2, V, 2A (1934) 1921–22; Ellis H. Minns, *Scythians and Greeks* (Cambridge 1913) 555–60. On Tyras see E. Diehl, *RE* s.v. Tyras 2, VII, 2A (1943) 1850–63; M. Rostovtzeff, *The Social and Economic History of the Roman Empire*² (Oxford 1957) 659; Minns, 445–49. The entry in the *pridianum* discovered by Hunt, which was thought to show the presence of a Roman garrison in Tyras under Trajan, has been shown to be irrelevant, since the name Tyras cannot be read: see Robert O. Fink, *Roman Military Records on Papyrus* (n.p. 1971) 224–25 on no. 63, line 21. For a bibliography of Russian archaeological work 1940–1960 see Eugène Belin de Ballu, *L'Histoire des colonies grecques du littoral nord de la mer noire*² (Leiden 1965).

The problem with Tyras may not be real, since the text of Arrian is corrupt at this point, and there clearly is a lacuna of at least one word and perhaps more. Tyras could conceivably have been lost in the lacuna.

28. The most effective exponent of this theory was C. G. Brandis, "Arrians Periplus Ponti Euxini," *RhM* 51 (1896) 109–26. Many others accepted Brandis's argument, notably Minns, "Scythians." See also Victor Chapot, "Arrien et le Périple du Pont-Euxin," *REG* 34 (1921) 129–54.

29. Friedrich Reuss, "Zu Arrians *Periplous Pontou Euxeinou*," *RhM* 56 (1901) 369–91; Carl Patsch, "Arrians Periplus Ponti Euxini," *Klio* 4 (1904) 68–75; and especially A. G. Roos, "Ad Ursulum Philippum Boissevain sep-

tuagenarium epistula de Arriani Periplo Ponti Euxini," *Mnemosyne* n.s. 54 (1926) 101–17. The question is discussed and bibliography reviewed by Marenghi, *Periplo*, 9–23. Unfortunately, he does not treat the archaeological evidence: see the review by D. M. Pippidi, *Athenaeum* 36 (1958) 264–68.

30. M. Rostowzew (Rostovtzeff), *Skythien und der Bosporus* (Berlin 1931) I, 60–62; cf. his *Iranians and Greeks in South Russia* (Oxford 1922, repr. New York 1969) 154–55.

31. Rostowzew, *Skythien* 60–61; cf. *Per.* 19.4–5.

32. Basilius Latyshcev, *Inscriptiones antiquiores orae septentrionalis Ponti Euxini Graecae et Latinae* (Hildeshem 1965) II, 33; *IGRR* I, 877. There is no justification for restoring Arrian's name on the stone, as was suggested by Doulcet. For Rhoemetalces, see *PIR*² I 516.

33. The Greek text of the *Tactics* is in Roos II, 129–76. There is no English translation. On this work see most recently Franz Kiechle, "Die 'Taktik' des Flavius Arrians," *Bericht der römisch-germanischen Kommission des Deutschen Archäologischen Instituts*, 45 (1964) 87–129; Philip A. Stadter, "The *Ars Tactica* of Arrian: Tradition and Originality," *CP* 73 (1978) 117–28; and Everett L. Wheeler, "The Occasion of Arrian's *Tactica*," *GRBS* 19 (1978) 351–65.

34. For a more detailed analysis of the relation between Arrian's work and earlier manuals, see Stadter, "*Ars Tactica*."

35. Kiechle, "Taktik," 108–14, argues that this first portion of the *Tactics* marks a revival under Hadrian of Hellenistic phalanx tactics to combat the armored cavalry of the Parthians and Sarmatians. Bosworth, however, has shown the weakness of the evidence for such a revival and demonstrated that Arrian's use of the phalanx against cavalry as described in the *Ectaxis* is quite different from Hellenistic practice ("Alani," 242–45). This does not mean, however, that Arrian did not think it of practical use to understand how the Macedonian system worked.

36. *CIL* VIII, 2532 = E. Mary Smallwood, *Documents Illustrating the Principates of Nerva, Trajan, and Hadrian* (Cambridge 1966) no. 328. See the translation in Michael Grant, *The Army of the Caesars* (New York 1974) 239–40.

37. Kiechle, "Taktik," gives a full commentary and discussion of this section of the treatise. R. W. Davies, "Fronto, Hadrian and the Roman Army," *Latomus* 27 (1968) 75–95, esp. 88–89, explains the use of the training weapons described by Arrian. Wheeler, "Occasion," believes that this half of the *Tactica* describes a special *armatura* given in honor of Hadrian's twentieth year as emperor.

38. The folio which held the last lines of the *Ectaxis* has been torn out of our unique manuscript. Fortunately not a great deal of text was lost. The following work in this manuscript, Onosander, began at the top of the verso

of the lost folio. Since pages were apparently removed from this manuscript for their blank parchment, there must have been some blank space on the recto of the folio, after the end of the *Ectaxis*. One side of the folio equals about forty Teubner lines, so we may suppose that no more than twenty lines are missing. The work as it now stands is 162 lines long.

39. This work, and the invasion of the Alans which provoked it, are the subject of an excellent study by Bosworth, in "Alani." I am heavily indebted to this article in the following paragraphs, although I have disagreed with Bosworth on some points. The Greek text is in Roos II, 177–85. The recent English translation by Bernard S. Bachrach, *A History of the Alans in the West* (Minnesota 1973) 126–32, contains a number of errors; that by Anthony Dent, "Arrian's Array," *History Today* 24 (August 1974) 570–74, has various editorial additions and omissions.

40. The regulation of Philip V from Amphipolis: see *Revue archéologique* 3 (1934) 40.

41. See the treatment of the *Alanike* at the end of chapter 8.

42. See Bosworth, "Alani," 249.

43. See especially Josephus, *Bell. Jud.* 5.47–50, 3.115–20.

44. Bosworth notes the unusual concentration of archers in Arrian's army, "Alani," 237 and n. 80.

45. See Bosworth, "Alani," 229–30, citing especially Themistius *Orat.* 34.8 (= Roos T13). The ancient Caspian or Caucasian Gates, the modern Darial or Krestory Pass, leads from Ordzhonikze across the Caucasus to Tbilisi. The territory of Iberia was the upper valley of the Kur, in Soviet Georgia and Azerbajdzan.

46. *Per.* 6.1–2, 10.1; cf. the discussion of the *Periplus*.

47. See n. 7 above.

48. Arrian intends to use this guard, together with the customary cavalry guard, *equites singulares*, as a mobile striking force during the battle: "[They should be assigned to him] so that he can go up and down the whole phalanx and learn where there is a difficulty, remedy it, and care for it" (*Ect.* 23).

49. *PSI* XII, 1284, from the *Events after Alexander*. See the discussion of the *Events* in chapter 8.

CHAPTER 4

1. The Greek text is in Roos II, 76–102. There is a translation into English and commentary by William Dansey, *Arrian on Coursing: The Cynegeticus of the Younger Xenophon* (London 1831), and a translation by Denison B. Hull in *Hounds and Hunting in Ancient Greece* (Chicago and London 1964). The latter explains a number of statements in Arrian and other writers by analogy with modern experience but occasionally has difficulty with Arrian's Greek text.

2. See especially his statement at *Cyn.* 1.4 that he had had since his youth the same pursuits as Xenophon, "hunting, generalship, and wisdom."

3. For an excellent general introduction to hunting in Arrian's day, see Jacques Aymard, *Essai sur les chasses romaines, des origines à la fin du siècle des Antonins (Cynegetica)* (BEFAR 171, Paris 1951), especially 173-82 on Hadrian's hunts, and 469-537 on the meaning of hunting to the Romans and Hadrian in particular.

4. On Hadrian as hunter, see also Bernard W. Henderson, *The Life and Principate of the Emperor Hadrian* (London 1923) 15-18.

5. The text was found on a single manuscript page now lost, and on an inscription, perhaps false, found near Avignon in France but also lost: see *CIL* XII, 1122. In some way which we cannot explain, a version of the text was known to Uguccione da Pisa (d. 1210): see Giancarlo Schizzerotto, "Uguccione e l'epigrafe per il cavallo di Adriano," *Maia* 20 (1968) 276-83. Such a poem by Hadrian for Borysthenes is mentioned by Dio Cassius, 69.10.

6. On this series of reliefs see Aymard, *Chasses* 527-37 (with excellent photographs, plates 35, 37-39), and Irmgard Maull, "Hadrian's Jagddenkmal," *Jahreshefte des Oesterreichischen archäologischen Instituts* 42 (1955) 53-67 and the bibliography cited there.

7. *CIL* II, 2660.

8. This translation is based upon the interpretation of Giuseppe Giangrande, "El Epigrama de Arriano a Artemis," *Emerita* 44 (1976) 349-55, which seems the most sastisfactory of the many offered; see also the comments on this inscription by A. B. Bosworth, "Arrian in Baetica," *GRBS* 17 (1976) 55-64. For further bibliography on this unusual epigram, see chapter 1, n. 61.

9. Cf. *Cyn.* 33-34 on offerings to Artemis and other woodland gods.

10. See on this work Hans Rudolf Breitenbach, *RE* s.v. Xenophon 6, IX, 2A (1967) 1910-21; Aymard, *Chasses*, 364-72; and Hull, *Hounds and Hunting*, passim. Breitenbach argues strongly that the work is not genuine; Aymard considers it Xenophontic. Since Arrian undoubtedly attributed the whole work to Xenophon, it can be treated as genuine for our purpose.

11. On the *vertragus*, with a number of pictures and a discussion of Arrian's description, see Gerhart Rodenwaldt, "Vertragus," *Jahrbuch des deutschen archäologischen Instituts* 48 (1933) 202-25. Arrian is our chief source for the use of this dog.

12. On the interrelationship between Arrian and Xenophon, see the more detailed treatment in Philip A. Stadter, "Xenophon in Arrian's *Cynegeticus*," *GRBS* 17 (1976) 157-67.

13. Arrian probably refers again to Horme at chapter 32, where he states that a good male is better than a bitch, but hard to find, "so that a truly noble male hound seems to me an important possession, which comes to a hunter only through the goodwill of some god."

14. Note also that Arrian self-confidently presumes that inclusion in this

minor piece will insure the hound's immortality. He clearly expected his work to be a permanent addition to the literature on hunting and to survive as Xenophon's had.

15. For a more detailed analysis of this point, see Stadter, *"Cynegeticus"* 159–61.

CHAPTER 5

1. See the recent review of ancient historical proems by Tore Janson, *Latin Prose Prefaces* (Stockholm 1964) 16, 64–83, with bibliography. H. Lieberich, *Studien zu den Proemien in der griechischen und byzantinischen Geschichtschreibung* ("Program des kgl. Realgymnasiums München," 1897/ 1898 and 1899/1900; Munich 1898, 1900) provides a list and brief analysis of surviving proems, from Hecataeus to Zonaras. See also the particular studies on Thucydides by Max Pohlenz, "Thukydidesstudien," *NachGöttingen*, 1920, 56–82, and Fritz Bizer, *Untersuchung zur Archäologie des Thukydides* (Tübingen 1937); and on Ephorus by R. Laqueur, "Ephorus," *Hermes* 46 (1911) 161–206. D. C. Earl has examined *topoi* in historical proems, and their unusual treatment by Sallust, in his article, "Prologue-form in Ancient Historiography," *ANRW* I, 2 (1972) 842–56.

2. Lists of *topoi* common in prefaces may be found in the works cited in the previous note. See also Georgios Engel, *De antiquorum epicorum didacticorum historicorum prooemiis* (Marburg 1910), who collects prefaces and analyzes them very generally under eight headings: *indicatio, dispositio, recordatio, causa, dedicatio, commendatio, scriptor de se ipse loquens,* and *invocatio numinum.*

3. On the proems of Herodotus, see Henry R. Immerwahr, *Form and Thought in Herodotus* (Cleveland 1966) 80–81. Note that Herodotus does not discuss the subject of his work as such (ibid., 18–19).

4. On Arrian's proemial statements see especially Guido Schepens, "Arrian's View of his Task as Alexander-Historian," *Ancient Society* 2 (1971) 254–68, and Abraham Benjamin Breebaart, *Enige historiografische aspecten van Arrianus' Anabasis Alexandri* (Leiden 1960) 23–27 et passim.

5. Pref. 1, "concerning Alexander the son of Philip"; pref. 2, "concerning Alexander"; pref. 3, "concerning Alexander."

6. The fragments of the lost Alexander historians are collected by Jacoby, *FGrHist* 117–153; they are translated by C. A. Robinson, *The History of Alexander the Great* I (Providence 1953). A general account is given by Lionel Pearson, *The Lost Histories of Alexander the Great* (n.p. 1960). Our extant continuous accounts besides Arrian are Diodorus Siculus Book XVII, *The History of Alexander* by Quintus Curtius Rufus, Plutarch's *Alexander,* and Justin's epitome of Books XI–XII of Trogus' *Philippicae Historiae.*

7. One contrasts the assumed diffidence expressed by Livy in his preface: "I do not know whether it will be worth the effort. . . ."

8. Note that Herodotus inserted a second preface at the beginning of Xerxes' expedition against Greece (7.20–21).

9. The reference to Homer as herald of Achilles is also in Plutarch (*Alex.* 15.8), but note that Arrian has deleted the mention of Patroclus to make more smooth the transition to his own comments.

10. The anecdote of Alexander's words on Achilles and Homer appears frequently as part of the *topos* of the praise of history (see Janson, *Latin Prose Prefaces*, 149–50) but is here integrated into a larger picture of the relation of author to subject.

11. See Immerwahr, *Form and Thought*, 80.

12. Although some favor a date for Curtius subsequent to Arrian, most critics place his history in the first century A.D., in the time of Caligula or, more likely, Vespasian. In the reign of Marcus Aurelius (and therefore almost certainly after Arrian) a certain Amyntianus wrote a history of Alexander (*FGrHist* 150). Photius says that he boasted (like Arrian) that he would narrate Alexander's deeds worthily, but that in fact he wrote very badly (T1).

13. See L. Cracco Ruggini, "Sulla cristianizzazione della cultura pagana: il mito greco e latino di Alessandro dall'età antonina al medioevo," *Athenaeum* n.s. 43 (1965) 3–80.

14. On the influence of Alexander in the Hellenistic and Roman world, see R. M. Errington, "Alexander in the Hellenistic World," in *Alexandre le grand: image et réalité* ("Entretiens Hardt," 22; Geneva 1976) 137–79; Gerhard Wirth, "Alexander und Rom," ibid., 181–210 (with discussion, 211–21); P. Ceausescu, "La Double Image d'Alexandre le Grand à Rome" *Studii Clasice* 16 (1974) 153–68; Dorothea Michel, *Alexander als Vorbild für Pompeius, Caesar, und Marcus Antonius* ("Collection Latomus," 94; Brussels 1967); Dietmar Kienast, "Augustus und Alexander," *Gymnasium* 76 (1969) 430–56; Friederich Pfister, "Alexander der Grosse: die Geschichte seines Ruhmes im Lichte seiner Beinamen," *Historia* 13 (1964) 37–79; Alfred Heuss, "Alexander der Grosse und die politische Ideologie des Altertums," *Antike und Abendland* 4 (1954) 65–104; Piero Treves, *Il Mito di Alessandro e la Roma di Augusto* (Milan and Naples 1953); F. Weber, *Alexander im Urteil der Griechen und Romen bis in die konstantinischen Zeit* (Diss. Giessen 1909); and W. Hoffman, *Das literarische Porträt Alexanders des Grossen im griechischen und römischen Altertum* (Leipzig 1907). On the variety of viewpoints expressed by Stoic writers, see J. Rufus Fears, "The Stoic View of the Career and Character of Alexander the Great," *Philologus* 118 (1974) 113–30, correcting Johannes Stroux, "Die stoische Beurteilung Alexanders des Grossen," *Philologus* 88 (1933) 222–40. See also the bibliography in Jakob Seibert, *Alexander der Grosse* (Darmstadt 1972) 217–19.

15. This recognition of the need for literary excellence in an Alexander historian does not imply that Arrian is a practitioner of "rhetorical" historiography, as implied by Eduard Schwartz, "Tyrtaeos," *Hermes* 34 (1899) 455, and *RE* s.v. Arrianus, 1235. Arrian is in no way comparable to writers like Dionysius of Halicarnassus or Curtius, although he was strongly influenced by classical models. Cf. Schepens, "Arrian's Task," 259, n. 14.

16. For the strictly philological problems of this passage see the commentaries of K. W. Krüger (Berlin 1851) and C. Sintenis (Leipzig 1849) ad loc. The passage has been discussed recently by Schepens, "Arrian's Task"; Breebaart, "Aspecten," 23–27; Gerhard Wirth, "Anmerkungen zur Arrianbiographie," *Historia* 13 (1964) 223–29; A. B. Bosworth, "Arrian's Literary Development," *CQ* n.s. 22 (1972) 163–85, esp. 167–68, 174–75. Cf. also E. Meyer, "Arrians Geschichte Alexanders des Grossens," *Hermes* 33 (1898) 648–52, and Schwartz, "Tyrtaeos," 455.

17. Cf. also Herodian 1.2.5. For some ridiculous examples, roughly contemporary with Arrian, see Lucian, *Hist. conscr.* 14–17, 30, 32.

18. See, e.g., *Diss.* 1.22.10, 2.17.24; *Ench.* 1.1. At *Diss.* 2.6.24 Epictetus advises, "Never lay claim to anything that is not your own."

19. The point in this sentence is not that he has held no office worth mentioning (thus Bosworth, "Development," 174–75), but that no office is worth mentioning. The tone implies that he had held major ones, of which some might be proud, but concerning which he prefers to keep silent. This is hardly a defensive passage. In this regard, note that *patrias* here must mean "native city," that is Nicomedia (see Bosworth, "Development," 174 and n. 6), but the expression *en tēi emautou*, "in my country," is general. Although it could refer to Nicomedia, it is better taken in this context as meaning the Roman Empire.

20. A secondary motive, of course, might be to reject the ridiculous pomposity of contemporary writers such as those attacked by Lucian, *Hist. Conscr.* 14–17. Arrian's complete silence on his name is quite different, it seems to me, from the haughty simplicity of the famous sophists P. Aelius Aristides Theodorus and M. Antonius Polemo, who wrote their names on dedicatory inscriptions as Aristides and Polemo: see Louis Robert, *Études anatoliennes* (Amsterdam 1970) 216–17.

21. I take *logoi* to be Arrian's writings in general, not solely the Alexander history. The *logoi*, like his native city, family, and offices, preexist the Alexander history, for they are what justify his decision to undertake it. Arrian has provided a sample of these writings in his account of Alexander's European campaigns, *Anab.* 1.1–11, immediately preceding this statement.

22. The expression "from my youth" seems to support the general impression that Arrian is writing as a mature man, almost certainly after his consulship.

23. The concept here developed recalls, but is really quite different from,

that attributed to Callisthenes at *Anab.* 4.10.2, that "Alexander and his deeds" would be made known by Callisthenes' history and that the writer came to Alexander's court not to receive glory from the king but to bestow it upon him. This is the typical rhetorical *topos* (well developed by Plutarch in *De fama Atheniensium*) of the superiority of the writer to the general or statesman, criticized by Arrian at 4.10.2. Here Arrian modifies it to a balance of two different spheres. The Callisthenes story, which is reported nowhere else in this form, was purposely introduced by Arrian as a *legomenon*, and phrased with verbal echoes of 1.12.2–5, no doubt to permit this comparison between Callisthenes and himself.

The conditional clause in the last statement ("if indeed Alexander was in arms") allows no doubt: Alexander was best, and Arrian will be also. For that use of *eiper oun kai* in this way, cf. *Anab.* 7.2.3 (the Brahmin replied that "he too was the son of Zeus, if indeed Alexander was," equivalent to "just as much as Alexander was").

24. Compare "whoever wonders . . . let him wonder" in pref. 3 with "whoever finds fault . . . let him find fault, but let him consider" in 7.30.1.

25. See the works cited in n. 14, especially Fears's on the Stoic portrait of Alexander.

26. Arrian further justifies his criticism "for the sake of his own truthfulness and the benefit of mankind." "Truthfulness" here recalls the preface, returning to the theme of truth and reliability developed there. "Benefit" is an allusion to the theme of the usefulness of history, which had a long and honorable tradition beginning with Thucydides 1.22, but here it is not developed. The phrase "benefit of mankind" serves as a rhetorical counterpoise to the preceding phrase but reflects also the influence of Epictetus (*Diss.* 1.19.13; cf. above p. 23).

27. Judgment: cf. *epilexamenos* ("selecting"), *moi edoxe* ("I decided"); credibility: cf. *pistotera* and *pistoteroi* ("more trustworthy"), *ou pantēi apista* ("not entirely incredible"); narrative interest: cf. *axiaphēgētotera* ("more worthy of narration"), *axiaphēgēta* ("worthy of narration"). The interest in *axiaphēgēta* is traditional: see Herodotus 1.16.2, 1.77; Josephus *AJ* 15.11.5, and the notion in Thucydides and Xenophon of *to axiologon* (e.g., *Hell.* 5.1.4, 2.3.56, 4.8.1; Thuc. 1.1.1, 1.17, 3.90.1). See Hans Rudolf Breitenbach, *Historiographische Anschauungsformen Xenophons* (Diss. Basel; Freiburg, Switzerland 1950).

28. Cf. the remarks on Arrian's style by A. B. Bosworth, "Arrian and the Alexander Vulgate," in *Alexandre le grand: image et réalité* ("Entretiens Hardt," 22; Geneva 1976) 1–33, esp. 6–7.

29. Cf., e.g., on the second point, Lucian *Hist. Conscr.* 40.

30. See the recent study of Ptolemy by Jakob Seibert, *Untersuchungen zur Geschichte Ptolemaios I* (Munich 1969), as well as the standard histories. On Ptolemy's history see especially Hermann Strasburger, *Ptolemaios und*

Alexander (Leipzig 1934); G. Wirth, *RE* s.v. "Ptolemaios I als Schriftsteller und Historiker," XXIII, 2 (1959) 2467–85; Pearson, *Histories*, 188–211; R. M. Errington, "Bias in Ptolemy's History of Alexander," *CQ* n.s. 19 (1969) 233–42; and the commentary by Jacoby, *FGrHist* 138. The argument developed in this section, I hope, will adequately demonstrate why I find completely without foundation the argument occasionally advanced that Arrian did not actually use either Ptolemy or Aristobulus directly, but a source now lost which had already combined the two (e.g., Mario Attilio Levi, *Introduzione ad Alessandro Magno* [Milan 1977] 277–330).

31. Cf. Errington, "Ptolemy's History," expanding on the observation in E. Badian's review of Pearson's *Histories*, *Gnomon* 33 (1961) 660–67 at 666, and for further signs of Ptolemaic bias, Bosworth, "Alexander Vulgate."

32. Parallel citations: F26b, F28a, F28c (ascribed); F2, F4 (unascribed). Dubious: F5, on the legendary foundation of Anchialos, perhaps from another Ptolemy, Euergetes II (Jacoby also prints it as *FGrHist* 234 F12); F31–33. Incredible: F11, the story that the Macedonians were able to win at Gaugamela only after Alexander sounded a retreat and had their beards shaved!

33. Badian has noted in his review of Pearson, *Gnomon* 33 (1961) 664, that Arrian had been very selective in using Aristobulus (as we know from Strabo) and that it is probable that he was equally selective in using Ptolemy. We would never guess from Arrian, for example, that Ptolemy might be an authority on trees, although he is cited on this subject by Pliny the Elder (T2).

34. See F3, 4, 6, 14, 15, 18, 20, 24, 26; cf. Pearson, *Histories*, 196–206.

35. F8. On F8 and 9, and what they suggest about Ptolemy as a historian, see C. Bradford Welles, "The Reliability of Ptolemy as a Historian," in *Miscellanea di studi alessandrini in memoria di A. Rostagni* (Turin 1963) 101–16.

36. The fragments of Aristobulus are collected in *FGrHist* 139. For discussions of his work, see Jacoby, comm. to *FGrHist* 139; Pearson, *Histories*, 150–87; Hermann Strasburger, *BibO* 9 (1952) 205–8; J. R. Hamilton, "Cleitarchus and Aristobulus," *Historia* 10 (1961) 448–58; P. A. Brunt, "Notes on Aristobulus of Cassandria," *CQ* n.s. 24 (1974) 65–69, and "Alexander, Barsine, and Heracles," *Rivista di filologia e di istruzione classica* 103 (1975) 22–34.

37. E.g., W. W. Tarn, *Alexander the Great* (Cambridge 1949) II, 38–42. We cannot cavalierly define the mission mentioned in F35 (Strabo 15.1.19, "having been sent on some business") as flood control, rather than, say, a diplomatic mission, an ethnographic survey, or tax-gathering. The job of restoring Cyrus' tomb (F51) had of course nothing to do with engineering.

38. Note that the historian Callisthenes is described as the secretary (*epistolographos*) of Alexander in a newly discovered painted list at Taormina: see Giacomo Manganaro, "Una biblioteca storica nel ginnasio di Tauromenion e il P. Oxy. 1241," *La Parola del Passato* (1974) 389–409, esp.

391–94. Before this we had no indication of his official capacity or whether he had any at all.

39. F9b, 19, 20, 28a, 35–39, 41–42, 48, 49b, 51b, 56–57. Other geographical material can be found in F6, 12, 40.

40. There are brief notices cited from Aristobulus on the Caucasus (F23 = 3.28.5–7), the Tanais (F25 = 3.30.7), the Gedrosian desert (F49 = 6.22.4–8), and the island of Icarus (F55 = 7.20.5). Pearson discusses many other geographical passages which can reasonably be attributed to Aristobulus in his chapter on him in *Histories*.

41. Note the conscious omission of the epigram on the ship Alexander dedicated to Heracles at Tyre, as "not worth remembering," *Anab.* 2.24.6.

42. Agreement: *Anab.* 2.12.5, 3.26.1, 4.14.1, 5.7.1, 6.11.5, 6.28.2, 7.13.3, 7.15.6, 7.26.3. Disagreement on details: *Anab.* 3.3.5–6, 3.4.4, 4.3.5, 4.14.3, 5.20.2. The fundamental study of Arrian's citations of his sources is still that of Eduard Schwartz, *RE* s.v. Arrianus, 1237–44. See also, for a different point of view, P. A. Brunt in *Arrian* ("Loeb Classical Library"; London and Cambridge, Mass. 1976) I, xxix–xxxii.

43. See especially A. B. Bosworth, "Errors in Arrian," *CQ* n.s. 26 (1976) 117–39.

44. The debate continues over the relative dates of Aristobulus and Ptolemy. Although I believe Ptolemy to be earlier, the fact that the accounts of both were fused by Arrian makes it impossible to say whether Aristobulus used Ptolemy. He certainly disagreed with Ptolemy regularly. There is no reason to think that Ptolemy was attempting to correct Aristobulus in accounts such as that of Alexander's battle with the son of Porus (*Anab.* 5.14.3–6).

45. On this remarkable statement, see Lionel Pearson, "The Diary and the Letters of Alexander the Great," *Historia* 3 (1955) 429–55 at 430 n. 4, and C. Gorteman, "*Basileus philalēthēs,*" *Chronique d'Egypte* 33 (1958) 256–67. Arrian at the end of his book quotes Alexander as saying that a king should always tell the truth to his subjects and that they should always expect the truth from him (*Anab.* 7.5.2).

46. See Strasburger, *Ptolemaios*, 9, "Mit Recht ist in neurerer Zeit von Niemanden mehr bezweifelt worden, dass es das Werk des Ptolemaios war und nicht das des Aristobul, das den Grundstock der Anabasis bildet," with bibliography. The thesis was carried *ad absurdum* by E. Kornemann, *Die Alexandergeschichte des Königs Ptolemaios I. von Aegypten: Versuch einer Rekonstruktion* (Leipzig and Berlin 1935). The relevant passages are misunderstood by Strasburger, 9.

47. It is wrong to assume that this sentence is part of the quotation of Ptolemy, as is done by Jacoby (*FGrHist* 138 F20 and commentary) and Pearson (*Histories*, 172). The quotation begins only after Arrian's analysis of the action, at 5.14.6, with the resumptive *alla . . . gar legei* ("But he [Ptolemy]

says . . .”). Cf. also Hugo Montgomery, *Gedanke und Tat* (Lund 1965) 172 n. 8.

48. See also 7.15.6, “nor the Alexander historians with whom I especially agree, Ptolemy the son of Lagus and Aristobulus.”

49. See, e.g., Schwartz, *RE* s.v. Arrianus, 1238; Strasburger, *Ptolemaios*, 23; and Pearson, *Histories*, 196–206. Contrast the useful corrective by Badian, in his review of Pearson, *Gnomon* 33 (1961) 664, and the conclusion of N. G. L. Hammond, “Alexander’s Campaign in Illyria,” *JHS* 94 (1974) 66–87 at 77 for the Illyrian campaign.

50. See note 34.

51. It is not possible to be absolutely sure that citations that are apparently *legomena* are not in fact from Aristobulus or Ptolemy. That is, Arrian occasionally uses the formulae “it is said” or “some say” to report information from his two major sources. A clear instance is the visit of Alexander to the tent of the captured Persian women, which begins at 2.12.3 with “some say” and ends at 2.12.5 with “that is what Ptolemy and Aristobulus say.” Some historians use “it is said” or similar expressions to imply disbelief or wonder at a story, separating themselves from the tale. Arrian occasionally does this, as for example with the Nysa narrative in Book V, but such stories generally seem to represent matter added to the accounts of Ptolemy and Aristobulus. See in general on the problem of *legomena* in the *Anabasis*, Schwartz, *RE* s.v. Arrianus, 1239–43.

52. See the list of omens interpreted by Aristander in Helmut Berve, *Das Alexanderreich* (Munich 1926) II, 62–63, no. 117, and the general discussion in I, 90–92. Arrian is the most consistent Alexander historian in reporting Aristander’s activity, listing eight occasions when the seer interpreted omens for Alexander, all correctly. Curtius is next with four, one of which he tells us was mistaken. Omens and other similar items are also listed by Robinson, *History* II, 101–2.

53. On the nexus of stories associated with Alexander’s crossing of the Hellespont see especially H. U. Instinsky, *Alexander der Grosse am Hellespont* (Godesberg 1949).

54. The pattern, although natural, is not necessary. Such works as Xenophon’s *Agesilaus*, Theopompus’ *Philippica* or—to take a modern example—J. F. C. Fuller’s *The Generalship of Alexander the Great* (New Brunswick 1960) use widely differing methods to praise their subject and his deeds.

55. For Herodotus’ use of the march as an element of organization, see Immerwahr, *Form and Thought*, 130–33 and index s.v. March sections. Immerwahr notes that Herodotus follows the principle of accounting for the whereabouts of the king whenever possible in describing Eastern campaigns. The march format of Xenophon’s *Anabasis* is well known. The commentaries of Caesar also follow the same basic pattern.

56. The one fragment we possess of Trajan’s own history of his Dacian wars (Hermann Peter, *Historicorum Romanorum Reliquiae*² [Stuttgart 1964]

II, 117) seems to indicate that he also used a march sequence as the base of his account: "inde Berzobim, deinde Aizi processimus" ("Then we went on to Berzobis, and then on to Aizisis").

57. A convenient list of the places on the march listed by Arrian and the parallel notices of the other Alexander historians may be found in C. A. Robinson, *The Ephemerides of Alexander's Expedition* (Providence 1932) 14-62.

58. Arrian regularly reports Persian decisions to resist Alexander just before a battle or other engagement. See, for example, in this passage (1.12-24), 1.12.8-10 (the Persian council before the Granicus), 1.18.4 (Miletus), 1.20.2-3 (Halicarnassus). Parallel to this are the embassies from cities or Persian commanders which decided to surrender: 1.12.7 (Priapus), 1.17.3 (Sardis), 1.18.1 (Magnesia and Tralles), etc. The flight of the troops garrisoning Ephesus immediately precedes the march to that city (1.17.9).

59. More normally the case is that the enemy is making moves which only become known to Alexander at their conclusion: e.g., 1.2.2-3, the movements of the Triballi; 1.7.1-3, the revolt of Thebes; 1.12.8-10, the Persian council before the Granicus; 2.6.3-7, Darius' movement from Assyria to Issus, etc.

60. See the outline of the *Anabasis* in appendix 3.

61. On the ancient historian's conscious use of books as units for his history, see Philip A. Stadter, "The Structure of Livy's History," *Historia* 21 (1972) 287-307. Note also the practice of Curtius, who ended his books with major events: the battle of Issus (III), the battle of Gaugamela (IV), Darius' death (V), the conspiracy of Philotas (VI), the capture of the Sogdian rock (VII), the battle with Porus (VIII), the Gedrosian desert and the Carmanian bacchanal (IX).

62. Polybius followed a fixed schedule of two years per book through most of his history: see 9.1.1, 14.1a.5 and F. W. Walbank, *Polybius* (Berkeley 1972) 108-10. The lack of any purely mechanical balance of years, books, and pages in Arrian's *Anabasis* is apparent from this table:

	Years	Number of years	Pages*	Pages per year
Book I	336-334	2.5	53.5	21.4
Book II	333-332	2	44	22
Book III	331-330	2	48.25	24.1
Book IV	329-327 (?)	3	51.25	17.1
Book V	326	1	43.25	43.25
Book VI	325-spring 324	1.5	44.5	29.6
Book VII	324/23	1	46.75	46.75
Average		1.85	47.4	29.2

*Roos, ed. min. (1910), and counting two pages for the lacuna at 7.12.

63. Hdt. 2.5, quoted by Arrian at *Anab.* 5.6.5.

64. On the notion in the Alexander historians that Alexander reaches the corners of the continent of Asia, see Pearson, *Histories,* 13–16. Alexander's crossing of the Danube, a fourth great river and boundary, is recorded by Arrian at the beginning of Book I (1.3.1).

65. Note that instead the manuscripts of Diodorus divide Diodorus' Alexander-book into two halves at 17.63.4, after Alexander's victory at Gaugamela and the defeat of Agis by Antipater. Curtius apparently ended the fifth of his ten books with the death of Darius and began the sixth with Antipater's defeat of Agis (some pages are missing in our manuscripts).

66. We should also perhaps include in this list the reflections on the fall of Thebes, since the ultimate course of its destruction is traced to the anger of the gods towards Thebes for having supported the Persians in the Persian wars and otherwise shown themselves hostile to other Greeks (1.9.7).

67. The second preface continues this theme and develops the additional notion that only Arrian can celebrate Alexander's achievements fittingly.

68. The *gar* at 2.6.7 shows that this sentence is Arrian's own explanation of events.

69. Gaza was considered impregnable by its defender: see 2.25.4, 2.26.3. Arrian appears to have exaggerated the difficulty of attacking the city to magnify Alexander: see Bosworth, "Alexander Vulgate," 23–25.

70. *Anab.* 4.4.3: "Alexander replied that it would be better to face the worse dangers than for the conqueror of nearly all Asia to make himself ridiculous to Scythians, as Darius the father of Xerxes had been long ago." Darius, according to Hdt. 4.122–24, had pursued the Scythians beyond the Tanais (in this case, the Don) without ever meeting them in battle. Arrian may also be thinking of the fate of Cyrus the Great, who pursued the nomad Massegetai beyond the Araxes but was killed by them (Hdt. 1.201–16).

71. Arrian prefers to treat the Indus rather than the Hindu Kush as the boundary of India: cf. his statement at the beginning of the *Indike,* 1.1 and 2.1, "All the territory that lies west of the Indus up to the river Cophen is inhabited by Astacenians and Assacenians, Indian tribes. . . . But the parts from the Indus eastward, these I shall call India, and its inhabitants Indians."

72. See the ascription of the story to Clitarchus, 137 F17. Jacoby (*FGrHist,* comm. ad loc.) has no basis for saying that it was found in Aristobulus. The real question, however, is not that of sources, but why Arrian chose to present so fully this incredible episode.

73. Heracles had been surpassed at Aornus (4.30.4); Dionysus had founded only one city, Nysa, as a monument to his deeds, but Alexander many (5.1.5). Cf. also Alexander's speech at the Hyphasis, 5.26.5.

74. As far as the march notices are concerned, Alexander had set out for the Indus at 4.30.7, reached it at 5.3.5, and crossed it at 5.8.2.

75. Hermann Strasburger, "Alexanders Zug durch die Gedrosische Wüste,"

Hermes 80 (1952) 470–77, notes that Arrian does not emphasize other dangerous marches, as do our other sources, and suggests that his use of Nearchus is responsible for the detailed account of the army's difficulties we find here. Apart from other difficulties with this theory, our analysis of the structure of the *Anabasis* sufficiently explains why Arrian reserves the major descriptions of the dangers encountered by Alexander and his men for the fifth and sixth books.

76. Arrian had described as well the monument of Sardanapalus at Anchialos, *Anab.* 2.5.2–4. That inscription read, "Sardanapalus the son of Anakyndaraxes built Anchialos and Tarsus in one day; you, stranger, eat, drink, and be merry, since other human things are not worth *this* [a hand-clap]." Sardanapalus' words contrast with the epic desire for glory of Cyrus, but both tombs warn of the final fate of a king.

77. Note also Alexander's new sense of regret at burning the palace of Persepolis (6.30.1).

78. At 6.30.1 Alexander is at the Persian palace (Persepolis). He then went to Susa (7.4.1), along the river Eulaeus to the Persian Gulf (7.7.1–2), over to the Tigris, up the Tigris to Hephaestion's camp (7.7.6), and on to Opis (7.8.1). After the lacuna of 7.12 we find Alexander at the Nysaean plain (7.13.1) and Ecbatana (7.14.2). From there he marched through the Cossaeans (7.15.1) toward Babylon, crossing the Tigris at 7.16.5. He entered Babylon (7.19.1), took a brief excursion down the Euphrates to the Pallakopas canal (7.21.1), and returned to Babylon (7.23.1), there to die.

79. *Anab.* 7.3.6: "These and other such things have been recorded by various writers, all useful for men, for whoever cares to know how strong and unconquerable is the human spirit in accomplishing whatever it wishes." For useful observations on the structure of 7.1–3, see E. Badian, "A King's Notebooks," *HSCP* 72 (1967) 183–204 at 192–93.

80. That Alexander's premature death was a sign of heaven's favor seems to be implied also by another device of Arrian. Twice in the *Anabasis* Alexander sacrifices "for good fortune" (*epi xumphorais agathais*). The first time (7.14.1) the sacrifice is immediately followed by Hephaestion's death; the second time (7.24.4) by the beginning of Alexander's sickness. There seems to be a clever parallel with the story of Cleobis and Biton, part of Solon's advice to Croesus (Hdt. 1.31). The story of Calanus had already established that death was not evil in itself but might even be welcome at the proper time.

81. Epictetus also frequently reminded his audience that the emperor would ·die: *Diss.* 1.24.15–18, 25; 1.25.22; 2.5.29; 2.6.22; 3.22.30; 4.1.95.

CHAPTER 6

1. Compare Arrian's own practice in his orders for the formation against the Alans, *Ect.* 12–31. In general on Arrian's presentation of Alexander's

thought process in battles, see Hugo Montgomery, *Gedanke und Tat* (Lund 1965) 164–73.

2. These words (*xunebē hopōs eikasen*) recur regularly in Arrian's account: *Anab.* 1.1.9, 1.27.7 (*eikazen*), 2.10.3, 4.2.5, 5.23.5; cf. also 3.18.9, 4.29.6.

3. Plutarch and Justin subordinate the description of the battle (*Alex.* 11.9–10, Just. 11.3.7) to other incidents: Timocleia's bravery in Plutarch (*Alex.* 12), the council on the fate of Thebes in Justin (11.3.8–4.6).

4. In general, one should note that most of the observations on Alexander's tactics in J. F. C. Fuller, *The Generalship of Alexander the Great* (New Brunswick 1960) are based on notices in Arrian. Mario Attilio Levi, *Introduzione ad Alessandro Magno* (Milan 1977) 301, notes that the first two books of the *Anabasis* give the impression that "one is dealing with a manual of military history in the form of a monograph."

5. See William Kendrick Pritchett, *Ancient Greek Military Practices*, Pt. I ("University of California Publications in Classical Studies," 7; Berkeley 1971) 127–33. Xenophon imagines their use by his fictional ideal general, Cyrus, in the *Cyropaedia*. Arrian intended to use scout cavalry to spy out the position of the enemy in his march against the Alans (*Ect.* 1 and 11).

6. The *diplen phalanga* of 1.13.1 is presumably the same as the *diphalangia* of *Tact.* 29, although Arrian does not specify which kind of double formation Alexander used.

7. Diodorus, following a quite different tradition, writes that Alexander fought the next day (i.e., accepted Parmenio's advice as given in Arrian), and not on the bank of the river, but on the plain after crossing. For various discussions, see Fuller, *Generalship*, 147–54; E. W. Davis, "The Persian Battle Plan at the Granicus," *Laudatores Temporis Acti: Studies in Honor of W. E. Caldwell* ("Sprunt Studies in History and Political Science," 46; Chapel Hill 1964) 34–44; Peter Green, *Alexander of Macedon 356–323 B.C.* (Harmondsworth 1974) 489–512; Nikos Th. Nikolitsis, *The Battle of the Granicus* ("Skrifter Utgivna av Svenska Institutet i Athen," 4to, 21; Stockholm 1974), as well as the standard histories of Alexander. Arrian's description of the Macedonian battle formation, with two separate contingents led respectively by a Craterus and by Craterus the son of Alexander (see Helmut Berve, *Das Alexanderreich* [Munich 1926] II, 220 n. 3), appears to present an irresolvable problem: we cannot be certain whether there is an error in Arrian, his source, or our manuscripts, or whether there were in fact two men named Craterus.

8. Apparently Arrian considered that the Persian defensive stance was reasonable, and saw no difficulty in having Alexander agree. But Arrian is impressed that Alexander saw a larger aspect of the battle situation, the psychological factor.

9. Arrian is very aware of the importance of the Macedonian lances in this cavalry battle, both in single combat (1.15.6–8) and in massed formation

(1.16.1). In his *Tactics* (4.3), Arrian had mentioned lance-cavalry, noted that the Romans used them as well (4.7), and described exercises for them (43.2). His own troops carried lances into battle against the Alans (*Ect.* 25 ff.).

10. Again Arrian blends history and the present: Alexander's battle cry to Enyalios, the god of battles (1.14.7), is prescribed also in his own order to his troops (*Ect.* 25). Cf. also the battle against Porus, 5.10.3.

11. The basic accounts of the battle are *Anab.* 3.13–15, Diod. 17.58–61, Curt. 4.15–16, Plutarch *Alex.* 32–33. The notice of Justin 11.14.1–2 is too short to be useful. For modern accounts see W. W. Tarn, *Alexander the Great* II: *Sources and Studies* (Cambridge 1948) 182–90; G. T. Griffith, "Alexander's Generalship at Gaugamela," *JHS* 67 (1947) 77–89; Fuller, *Generalship*, 163–80; A. R. Burn, "Notes on Alexander's Campaigns," *JHS* 72 (1952) 85–91; Eric William Marsden, *The Campaign of Gaugamela* (Liverpool 1964). Griffith, Fuller, and Marsden furnish plans of the battle. For an overview of the content and arrangement of Arrian's account of the battle, see the outline in appendix 4.

12. Arrian may have recalled that Xenophon's ideal general, Cyrus the Great, also had had an advance scout squadron before his main army and had dispatched a special force to collect prisoners to obtain better information (*Cyr.* 6.3.2–6).

13. This seems to be the only recorded occasion on which Alexander accepted the advice of Parmenio. The incident is not reported in any other author; Arrian recorded it for its exemplary value. The problem of the treatment of Parmenio in the Alexander historians has frequently been discussed: see most recently A. B. Bosworth, "Arrian and the Alexander Vulgate," in *Alexandre le grand: image et réalité* ("Entretiens Hardt," 22; Geneva 1976) 30–32.

14. Note that in other accounts both Alexander and his men are presented as terrified by Darius' army.

15. The notion of a leader or an army being "enslaved in mind" also appears at Issus, 2.10.1 (Darius) and may be contrasted with the attitude of Porus at 5.19.1. Cf. the same expression in Thucydides 7.71.3.

16. Perhaps for this very reason Arrian made an error in saying that Amyntas, one of the commanders of the phalanx, was son of Philip, not of Andromenes. See Bosworth, "Alexander Vulgate," 9–14.

17. The term is explained in *Tact.* 29.1–2 to mean two groups of men with their backs to one another; here, however, Arrian apparently means a second phalanx which is prepared to turn if attacked from behind.

18. Alexander's plan for Gaugamela as presented by Arrian is similar to Xenophon's description of the fictional battle of Thymbrara (*Cyr.* 7.1), in which Cyrus also must face an army which proposes to outflank him on both sides. See the analysis and battle plan in John Kinloch Anderson, *Military Theory and Practice in the Age of Xenophon* (Berkeley 1970) 165–91.

19. Arrian here apparently is thinking of the success with which the phalanx parted before the wagons of the Thracians (*Anab.* 1.1.10) and of the Greek action at Cunaxa (Xenophon *Anab.* 1.8.20). In other authors the scythe-chariots are either completely successful in their mission (Curt. 4.15.3−4) or partly so (Curt. 4.15.14−17, Diod. 17.58.2−5).

20. Arrian is the only author to say that Alexander in this battle used this formation, which he describes with some care in *Tact.* 16.6−14, 17.3.

21. This close combat around Alexander is imaginatively described by Curtius (4.15.21−30) and Diodorus (17.60.1−4). On aiming spears at the face, compare Arrian's account of the Granicus (1.16.1) and the remark of Caesar at Pharsalia (Plutarch *Caesar* 45.2−3).

22. Cf. Burn, "Notes," 87−88.

23. On the varying accounts of this force, see Burn, "Notes," 86−87.

24. Note that Arrian does not say that Alexander had begun full pursuit of Darius: Alexander when last seen was in the close hand-to-hand combat with the pick of the Persians and had just put Darius to flight. The pursuit mentioned in 3.14.4 would be the driving attack on a very large force which had just turned, designed to prevent them from regrouping, not a headlong chase. Arrian's Alexander is not one to pursue without thought for other parts of the battle: at the Granicus he turned back to deal with the mercenaries (1.16.2); at Issus he had waited till the phalanx had driven the mercenaries and cavalry back from the river (2.11.7); and at the Hydaspes what pursuit there was, was made by the fresh soldiers of Craterus (5.18.1). Arrian in his own plans shows himself equally cautious in pursuit: see *Ect.* 27−29. Griffith ("Alexander's Generalship," 82−84) points out that Alexander in fact could hardly have been called back from a true pursuit of Darius. See also N. G. L. Hammond, "A Note on 'Pursuit' in Arrian," *CQ* 28 (1978) 136−40.

25. Xenophon *Hell.* 4.3.19.

26. The following paragraphs are based upon the excellent analysis of the differences between the vulgate and Arrian's account by Bosworth, "Alexander Vulgate," 16−23. Bosworth believes that the omissions and exaggerations originate in Ptolemy; but they agree exactly with Arrian's purpose as expressed in *Anab.* 1.12.2−5, and I would ascribe them in large part to Arrian's own treatment.

27. See Bosworth, "Alexander Vulgate," 22−23, who also notes that the size of the siege mound built at Gaza is enormously exaggerated in Arrian. On the other hand, Bosworth's difficulty with the size of the stones forming the breakwater at the base of the Tyrian walls is based on a misunderstanding. These stones were not catapulted into deep water, but simply dropped (*Anab.* 2.21.7).

28. For a brief account, see J. R. Hamilton, *Plutarch: Alexander: A Commentary* (Oxford 1969) lx−lxii. See also the bibliography found in chapter 5, n. 14.

29. Arrian refers to the story as a *legomenon* at 7.14.5, criticizing the action as not at all suitable to Alexander, but barbaric and parallel to Xerxes' famous insolence in desiring to fetter the Hellespont.

30. For special treatments of these events, see F. Cauer, "Philotas, Kleitos, Kallisthenes," *NJbb*, suppl. 20 (1894) 1–79; Truesdell S. Brown, "Callisthenes and Alexander," *AJP* 70 (1949) 225–48; and Ernst Badian, "Alexander the Great and the Loneliness of Power," in *Studies in Greek and Roman History* (Oxford 1964) 192–205.

31. 4.8.2, 8.9, 9.2, 9.3, 9.7, 9.9, 10.1, 10.3, 10.5, 12.3, 13.2, 13.5, 14.1, 14.2.

32. Cf. in general on this phenomenon Guy L. Cooper III, "Intrusive Oblique Infinitives in Herodotus," *TAPA* 104 (1974) 23–76. Arrian was no doubt strongly influenced by Herodotus in his use of this technique.

33. Arrian's statements of his personal opinion are found at 4.8.3, 8.5, 9.1, 9.2, 9.6, 9.8, 10.1–2, 12.6–7, and 14.3–4.

34. Compare the advice of Epictetus at *Diss.* 4.1.40, 139.

35. Plutarch *Alex.* 50.2 also is sympathetic to Alexander, calling the incident a misfortune for Alexander. But Arrian's words reflect Epictetus' ideas: cf. *Diss.* 1.18.3, 9.

36. From Plutarch *Alex.* 54.4–6 we know the source is Chares, the royal chamberlain.

37. Note that it is not the questions concerning Alexander which are new, but Arrian's attempt to suggest answers through his interpretation of incident. For different approaches, cf. Dio Chrys. *Or.* 4 or Plutarch *Alex.* The latter's technique in using a variety of anecdotal material to build up a favorable picture of Alexander is particularly noteworthy.

38. Plutarch *Alex.* 24–5 and Curt. 4.2.17 also repeat this dream, but not the interpretation given here.

39. Homer *Iliad* 22.304–5: "I will not die without effort or glory, but after accomplishing something great for those coming after to hear of."

40. Darius' last rites: 3.22.5. The Persian women: 2.12.3–8, 4.19.6–20.3; cf. 3.17.6. Other leaders: 3.23.7, 4.21.7–8, 6.15.7. Cities: 1.22.7, 4.27.2–3. Ephesus: 1.17.12. The comment of Arrian on the story of Alexander and Hephaestion's visit to the women's tent is characteristic of his desire to see the best in Alexander: "This I have included not as necessarily true, nor as wholly incredible. If it happened in this way, I praise Alexander for his compassion toward the women and his trust and regard for his companion. If on the other hand it is the kind of thing that writers thought credible that Alexander would have said and done, I praise him for that as well" (2.12.8).

41. The problem of Arrian's presentation of Alexander's attitude toward the gods and his own divinity is a large one, which I have not tried to examine here. See most recently E. Badian, "The Deification of Alexander the Great," in *Protocol of the Twenty-first Colloquy* ("Center for Hermeneutical Studies

in Hellenistic and Modern Culture, Protocol Series," no. 22; Berkeley 1967); and Lowell Edmunds, "The Religiosity of Alexander," *GRBS* 12 (1971) 363–91. The evidence used by Edmunds for Alexander's religiosity is, interestingly enough, chiefly drawn from Arrian, whereas Arrian makes no mention of the divine honors voted Alexander by the Greeks.

CHAPTER 7

1. See Hdt. 3.102–105, 3.38. For Ctesias, see F. Jacoby, *RE* s.v. Ktesias 1, XI 2 (1925) 2033–73, and *FGrHist* 688. The accounts of India before Alexander are collected by Wilhelm Reese, *Die griechischen Nachrichten über Indien bis zum Feldzuge Alexanders des Grossen* (Leipzig 1914). Translations are available in the series edited by John Watson McCrindle, *Ancient India as Described in Classical Literature* (Westminster 1901).

2. The gold-guarding griffins were associated by Herodotus with the far north, not India: see Hdt. 3.116, 4.13. He refers his account to Aristeas of Proconnesus, who apparently introduced the Greeks—and the West—to griffins: see J. D. P. Bolton, *Aristeas of Proconnesus* (Oxford 1962).

3. Arrian's sense of structure was of course quite different from that of a writer like Herodotus, for whom the length of a *logos* was not a major criterion: see Henry R. Immerwahr, *Form and Thought in Herodotus* (Cleveland 1966) 15. Note that Arrian gives us no ethnographic account of Egypt or other countries conquered by Alexander in the *Anabasis*.

4. The name *Indike* (*Indikē xyggraphē*; see *Anab.* 5.6.8, 6.16.5) recalls Thucydides' reference to Hellanicus' book on Athens as *hē Attikē xyggraphē*, 1.97.2. Most titles of books on peoples are neuter plural adjectives: *Persica*, *Aegyptiaca*, even Arrian's own *Bithyniaca* and *Parthica*. Arrian's books on India and on the Alans (*Alanike*) are exceptions. The *Indike* is not an ethnographical work in the usual sense, and Arrian may have preferred a different title for this reason. We may ask whether the *Alanike* was also unusual in some way. On the use of the feminine singular adjective as a title in early works, see Felix Jacoby, *Atthis* (Oxford 1949) 79–80. Arrian also called his *Anabasis* a *xyggraphē*: *Ind.* 19.8, 21.8, 23.6, 26.1, 40.1 (in 32.1 it is a *logos*). The feminine titles of the individual books of Appian's *Romaika* (*Basilike*, etc.) agree with *biblos* understood: see Appian pref. 14. The *Indike* has been edited and translated frequently; the most available editions are Roos II, 1–73 (Greek only); E. Iliff Robson, *Arrian* ("Loeb Classical Library"; Cambridge, Mass. 1967) II, 306–435 (Greek and English); Arrien, *L'Inde* ("L'Association Guillaume Budé"; Paris 1927) by Pierre Chantraine (Greek and French, with a useful introduction).

5. *Anab.* 5.6.8, 6.16.5, 6.28.6.

6. Cf. also *Ind.* 43.14.

7. *Ind.* 19.8, 21.8, 23.6, 32.1, 40.1, 43.14. On these cross-references, see F. F. Schwarz, "Arrian's *Indike* on India: Intention and Reality," *East and West* n.s. 25 (1975) 193—94, 200.

8. For a list of other ethnographic *logoi* in Herodotus and a discussion of their purpose, see Immerwahr, *Form and Thought*, 317—23. For ethnographical accounts in general, see Felix Jacoby, "Über die Entwicklung der griechischen Historiographie und den Plan einer neuen Sammlung der griechischen Historikerfragmente," *Klio* 9 (1909) 80—123, esp. 88—96 = *Abhandlungen zur griechischen Geschichtschreibung* (Leiden 1956) 16—64, esp. 26—34; and Karl Trüdinger, *Studien zur Geschichte der griechisch-romischen Ethnographie* (Diss. Basel 1918).

9. See A. G. Roos, "De Arriani *Indicae* dialecto Ionica," *Mnemosyne* 55 (1927) 23—43. There is no reason to think that Arrian's Ionic derives from his sources, Megasthenes and Nearchus. There is no evidence that Megasthenes wrote in Ionic: see E. A. Schwanbeck, ed., *Megasthenis Indica* (Bonn 1846, repr. 1966) 25. Lionel Pearson's suggestion (*The Lost Histories of Alexander the Great* [n.p. 1960] 112) that Nearchus wrote in Ionic has little to recommend it. See below, p. 125. Lucian (*Hist. conscr.* 18) criticizes a historian for slavishly imitating Herodotus in both phrasing and dialect. However, Lucian's own work *De dea Syria*, written in Ionic, shows that the Ionic dialect was considered appropriate if handled well.

10. See especially Julien Guey, *Essai sur la guerre parthique de Trajan (114—117)* ("Bibliothèque d'Istros," 2; Bucharest 1937).

11. Dio Cass. 68.29.1—2.

12. Much has been written on this trade. Our principal evidence is the anonymous *Periplus Maris Erythraei* and the finds of Roman coins and artifacts in India. See R. E. M. Wheeler, "Roman Contacts with India, Pakistan and Afghanistan," in *Aspects in Archaeology in Britain and Beyond: Essays Presented to O. G. S. Crawford*, ed. W. Grimes (London 1951) 345—73; James Innes Miller, *The Spice Trade of the Roman Empire, 29 B.C. to A.D. 641* (Oxford 1969); H. Schiwek, "Der persische Golf als Schiffarts- und Seehandelsroute in Achämenidischer Zeit und in der Zeit Alexanders des Grossen," *Bonner Jahrbücher* 162 (1962) 4—97; Schwarz, "Arrian's *Indike*," 181—92; and Albrecht Dihle, "Der Seeweg nach Indien," *Dies Philologicae Aenipontanae* IV (Institut für Sprachwissenschaften; Innsbruck 1974), and his forthcoming article, "Die entdeckungsgeschichtlichen Voraussetzungen des Indienhandels der römischen Kaiserzeit," in ANRW II, 9, 2 (1976) 546—80. See also the comments and bibliography by Schwarz, "Neue Perspektiven in den griechisch-indischen Beziehungen," *Orientalistische Literaturzeitung* 67 (1972) 5—26 at 19—20. The date of the *Periplus* has been disputed between the early third century and the first century A.D.; David W. Macdowall, "The Early Western Satraps and the Date of the Periplus," *Numismatic*

Chronicle ser. 7, 4 (1964) 271–80 (not cited by Schwarz) argues for ca. A.D. 120–130.

13. Pearls bought by Romans, *Ind.* 8.9; parrots and apes in Rome, *Ind.* 15.9–10. The elephants which Arrian saw dancing (*Ind.* 14.5–6) were probably African.

14. See in general on the continuity of the Western literary tradition on India, quite independent of actual contacts, Albrecht Dihle, "The Conception of India in Hellenistic and Roman Literature," *Proceedings of the Cambridge Philological Society* 10 (1964) 15–23. On the *Indike* in particular see Schwarz, "Arrian's *Indike*," 192–200. Schwarz stresses the fact that Arrian intended to describe India "only with a view of Alexander's campaign and the time immediately following Alexander" (194–95).

15. Cf. the *Tactica* and *Periplus of the Black Sea*. Perhaps even the *Parthica* fell into two parts, one past history (Books I–VII), and the other on Trajan's campaign (VIII–XVII).

16. See Arrian's comment at *Ind.* 17.6–7, *Anab.* 6.28.6. It is not correct to say that the *Indike* "lacks literary form" (as does Pearson, *Histories*, 123), but it is true that Arrian has an unusual habit of combining disparate forms to make a new whole.

17. Cf. the schemes in J. Meunier, "Les sources de la monographie d'Arrien sur l'Inde," *Musée Belge* 26 (1922) 5–24 at 8, and B. C. J. Timmer, *Megasthenes en de Indische Maatschappij* (Amsterdam 1930) 22–25.

18. Actually only a few kings are mentioned: Dionysus, Spatembas, Bouduas, Kradeuas, Heracles, and Sandrakottos (Chandragupta), but they are considered part of a sequence; see *Ind.* 8.1–9.9. The period before Dionysus, who apparently was the first of the kings, is treated ahistorically in *Ind.* 7.2–4.

19. See Immerwahr, *Form and Thought*, 67–68, 96–97.

20. The fragments of Megasthenes are collected in *FGrHist* 715. The epitome in Diodorus is F4. His work is discussed by Schwanbeck, *Indica*; Timmer, *Megasthenes*; O. Stein, *RE* s.v. Megasthenes 2, XV, 1 (1931) 230–326; J. Duncan M. Derrett, *Die kleine Pauly* s.v. Megasthenes, 3 (1969) 1150–54; and Truesdell S. Brown, *The Greek Historians* (Lexington, Toronto, and London 1973) 141–51. See also E. R. Bevan, "India in Early Greek and Latin Literature," *Cambridge History of India* (1922) I, 391–425, on India in early Greek and Roman literature, especially Megasthenes, who was by far the most influential writer of *Indica*. His basic veracity has been confirmed by modern study: see Derrett and Schwarz, "Neue Perspektiven," 12–13. The hypothesis that Arrian used Megasthenes indirectly through Eratosthenes (Friedrich Reuss, "Zur Überlieferung der Geschichte Alexanders des Grossen," *RhM* 57 [1902] 578–81) has been refuted by Timmer, *Megasthenes*, 25–28.

21. Timmer, *Megasthenes*, 30, 304.

22. For the accuracy of Megasthenes' description of Indian society, see the bibliography cited by Derrett, "Megasthenes."

23. Cf. Strabo 15.1.7 = Eratosthenes fragment *I B*, 23, in H. Berger, *Die geographische Fragmente des Eratosthenes* (Leipzig 1880) 77.

24. Strabo 2.1.9, translated by Horace Leonard Jones, *The Geography of Strabo* (New York 1917).

25. Strabo 2.1.9 and 15.1.56–57 = Megasthenes *FGrHist* 715 F27 (cf. also F28–30).

26. For the account of India which follows, compare Strabo 15.1.11–12, also based on Eratosthenes. The citations of Ctesias, Onesicritus, Nearchus, and Megasthenes are also in Strabo and undoubtedly were taken over from Eratosthenes.

27. According to Eratosthenes (Berger, *Eratosthenes*, 227–28), the west side was 13,000 stades, the east 16,000. Megasthenes said the north-south dimension was 22,300 stades at its narrowest. Eratosthenes gave the east-west dimension as 10,000 plus x, Megasthenes as 16,000 at its shortest. See the diagram and discussion in Bevan, "India in Literature," 400–402, and Berger, 230–32.

28. Note that Strabo follows the same plan: 15.1.11–12, the size and shape of India; 15.1.13, the rivers. Herodotus had treated the Nile in a similar position in his Egyptian *logos*, 2.10–34, but a closer parallel for the overall treatment of the Indian rivers is his account of the rivers of Scythia, 4.46–58.

29. However, the scheme of his sources, chiefly Megasthenes, may not have been clear either; Strabo wanders vaguely on the subject in 15.1.13–38.

30. Herodotus had argued from the size and number of its tributaries that the Danube was the mightiest river in the world (4.48).

31. This statement may be meant as a challenge to Herodotus' list of major tributaries of the Danube in 4.48.

32. The problem of use of hearsay was already present in Herodotus' ethnographic accounts: cf. 2.29.1 on the unreliability of information south of Elephantine (Aswan), and 2.123.1.

33. Eratosthenes' arguments against Dionysus in India can be found in Strabo 15.1.7–8. Arrian had kept an open mind on the story in *Anab.* 5.1.2.

34. *Anab.* 5.3.1–4; cf. Strabo 15.1.8–9.

35. *Ind.* 6.1: *ou pantē apistoi*. Strabo, after the same considerations, decided to accept what was "nearest to credibility" (15.1.10).

36. The amazing Silas was one of the standard wonders of India, reported long before Megasthenes by Hellanicus (*FGrHist* 4 F190) and Ctesias (688 F47). Strabo (15.1.38 = *FGrHist* 715 F10b) notes that the story was challenged by Democritus and Aristotle. This is just one example (the account of the gold-digging ants is another) where Megasthenes did not hesitate to record the stories told by his predecessors, no matter how incredible: cf. Truesdell S. Brown, "The Reliability of Megasthenes," *AJP* 76 (1955) 18–33.

37. Cf. *FGrHist* 139 F35, 133 F18.

38. See Pearson, *Histories*, 122. Meunier, "Sources," 17 ascribes it incorrectly to Eratosthenes.

39. These divisions are not quite the same as the Indian castes, since the major castes are four, whereas Megasthenes divides Indian society into seven classes.

40. Megasthenes, *FGrHist* 715 F4, 19, 20.

41. Strabo 15.1.58–66 = Megasthenes *FGrHist* 715 F33, Aristobulus 139 F41–42, Onesicritus 134 F17, Nearchus 133 F23.

42. See Reinhold Merkelbach, *Die Quellen des griechischen Alexanderromans* (Munich 1954) 50–53, 113–18. See now also the newly discovered Cynic-oriented dialogue between Alexander and the Brahmin Dandamis: Victor Martin, "Un Recueil de diatribes cyniques du Pap. Genev. inv. 271," *MusHelv* 16 (1959) 77–115; J. Duncan M. Derrett, "The History of 'Palladius on the Races of India and the Brahmans,'" *ClMed* 21 (1960) 64–135; Gunther Christian Hansen, "Alexander und die Brahmanen," *Klio* 43/45 (1965) 351–80. Derrett, "Palladius," 74–80, mistakenly attempts to make Arrian the author of the papyrus text, taking some support from the notice in Pseudo-Callisthenes 3.10 = Palladius (*FGrHist* 156 F175). See the refutation by Hansen, "Brahmanen," 364–66. For bibliography and an evaluation of the question see Schwarz, "Neue Perspektiven," 8–10.

43. *Anab.* 6.16.5.

44. On Nearchus, see below, n. 47.

45. Hdt. 3.102–105. The gold-digging ants also found their way into poetry: cf. Callimachus frag. 202, ed. Rudolfus Pfeiffer, *Callimachus* (Oxford 1953) with addenda, II, 118–19.

46. Clearly Arrian is uncomfortable with these ants but respects Nearchus enough to wish to mention them. His attitude toward the other animals is quite different.

47. On Nearchus' life and his book, see F. Jacoby, *FGrHist* II D, comm. to 133 (Berlin 1930); H. Berve and W. Capelle, *RE* s.v. Nearchos 3, XVI, 2 (1935) 2132–54; Pearson, *Histories*, 112–49; Otto Seel, *Antike Entdeckerfahrten* (Zurich 1961); Hermann Strasburger, "Alexanders Zug durch die gedrosische Wüste," *Hermes* 80 (1952) 456–93; Gerhard Wirth, "Nearchos der Flottenchef," *Acta Conventus XI 'Eirene,' 1971* (Wroclaw 1971) 615–39; and E. Badian, "Nearchus the Cretan," *YCS* 24 (1975) 147–70. Badian notes the difficulties in accepting that Nearchus was chiliarch of the hypaspists. In general, Badian challenges the reliability of Nearchus' account, concluding that it is an "impassioned personal and political Tendenzschrift" (169). He is certainly right in emphasizing Nearchus' personal motives but seems too sweeping in presenting Nearchus' career as a string of failures, and he does not appreciate the changes which Arrian might have introduced in the narrative. The fundamental work on the identification of the places described

by Nearchus is Wilhelm Tomaschek, "Topographische Erläuterung der Küstenfahrt Nearchus vom Indus bis zum Euphrat," *SB Wien* 121 (1890) Abh. 8.

48. *Ptolemaios und Alexander* (Leipzig 1934) 12.

49. He is only cited by four authors: Arrian; Strabo, who used him extensively; Philostratus, who probably never saw his book, despite the single citation (133 F12); and Pliny, who dictated to his secretary the distances between points along the Makran coast (133 F1h, 13−15).

50. Chantraine, in the introduction to his edition of the *Indike*, 11−12, writes, "Le style de l'*Indike* appartient proprement à Arrien; il n'est pas d'un géographe qui énumère des faits ni d'un officier qui rédige un rapport, mais d'un écrivain qui sait raconter."

51. Pearson, *Histories*, 112, 123, 149. Cf. above, n. 9.

52. Pearson, *Histories*, 120.

53. Cf. Jacoby, *FGrHist* II D, p. 445 and Pearson, *Histories*, 149.

54. Nearchus, *FGrHist* 133 F2 = *Anab.* 6.13.4−5 is the only explicit citation, but other passages probably dependent on Nearchus are noted by Pearson, *Histories*, and Strasburger, "Zug."

55. This roster of trierarchs reflects the same mentality which led Arrian to preserve so many lists of satraps, officers, and lesser officials in the *Anabasis*, and which may be found also in the *Events after Alexander* (e.g., S24, 6 = F10A).

56. In an attempt to increase the importance of this event Arrian assigns it an Athenian archon date, but he appears to be mistaken. See Jacoby's commentary and Pearson, *Histories*, 145.

57. We might compare the effect that Arrian expects from his own use of shouting and artillery against the Alans, *Ect.* 25−26.

58. After the journey along the coast of the fisheaters, Arrian places a general account of their habits (29.6−16), the whale story (30), and the adventure of the island of the sun (31).

59. The Greek is presented in parallel columns by Jacoby, *FGrHist* II B, pp. 697−98. On the evidence this scene gives for the relations between Nearchus and Onesicritus, see Badian, "Nearchus," 159−60.

60. In Greek, *ekperipleō* (in two forms), *estalē, ou gar, hormous.*

61. The passage is one of our best indications of the purpose of Nearchus' expedition: see Pearson, *Histories*, 141−42.

62. Strasburger, "Zug," 55−58; Pearson, *Histories*, 147−48. Badian, "Nearchus," 153−56, 160−68, demonstrates how the scenes with Alexander tend to flatter Nearchus.

63. With the major exception of Strabo 15.1.5 = 133 F3b.

64. See the translation and evaluation of this incident by Pearson, *Histories*, 131−35, and the further consideration by Badian, "Nearchus," 160−65, who believes that Nearchus' version can be checked—and condemned—by comparison with the other accounts. The description of their meeting in Diod.

17.106.4–7 is quite different, though it also attempts to heighten the drama of the reunion by having Nearchus return in the midst of a celebration in the theater. The notices in other authors are perfunctory (Plutarch *Alex*. 68.1, Curt. 10.1.10).

65. See *Anab*. 7.19.6, 7.25.2–5. Jacoby, *FGrHist* II D, p. 445, thinks it probable that Nearchus spoke of Alexander's last plans.

66. He concludes 133 F1 at the end of *Ind*. 42.

67. Note that Nearchus is cited at 7.20.9 in connection with the exploration of the Arabian coast.

68. Arabia had been annexed in A.D. 106. On trade from the Red Sea eastward in Arrian's day see n. 12 above.

69. See W. W. Tarn, "The Proposed New Date for Ipsus," *CR* 40 (1926) 13–15.

70. The final note on Hanno's attempt to circumnavigate Africa (43.11–13) is meant to be a further proof of the impossibility of the journey around Arabia. Hanno had to turn back because of the fierce heat, yet Africa in its northern parts is more fertile and well-watered than northern Arabia.

71. Strasburger, "Zug," argues that the account of the disasters in Gedrosia in *Anab*. 6.24ff. is from Nearchus. There are many objections to this theory, not least that such an account would have no place in the *periplus* which Nearchus' work seems to resemble. See also E. Badian, "Alexander the Great, 1948–67," *CW* 65 (1971–72) 37–56, 77–83, at 50.

72. However, it is not at all certain that Nearchus' book went into detail on these matters. See Pearson, *Histories*, 142. We know from Pliny (*NH* 6.107 = 133 F14) that Nearchus mentioned the river Sabis in Carmania, although it does not figure in Arrian (cf. *Ind*. 32.1–2). On the other hand, Pliny complains that Nearchus omitted some places and distances: *NH* 6.96 = 133 F13. See Jacoby, comm. to 134 F28, and H. Triedler, *RE* s.v. Xylineopolis, IX, 2 (1967) 2164–71.

73. See Jacoby, comm. to 133 F1 (II D, pp. 455–56).

74. Pearson, *Histories*, 143–44.

75. See Megasthenes 715 F27, 29 and 30 from Strabo, Pliny, and Plutarch.

CHAPTER 8

1. The fragments of Arrian's lost histories were collected and printed almost simultaneously by two outstanding scholars, by Felix Jacoby as no. 156 in *FGrHist* II B (Berlin 1929), with a separate volume of commentary (Berlin 1930), and by A. G. Roos, *Flavius Arrianus* II (Leipzig 1928) 197–290. Roos attempted to gather all the fragments, including the many anonymous notices he recognized in the *Suda* and elsewhere, and arrange them in the order in which they might have occurred in Arrian. Jacoby restricts himself to

named fragments of Arrian and includes references to other material in his commentary. Jacoby arranges all fragments not assigned to books according to the author by whom they are quoted. I here cite first the number from Roos, and then, if Arrian is named, the fragment (F) of Jacoby. Occasionally, reference is made to the material in Jacoby's commentary in *FGrHist* II B.

2. Photius, *Bibl.* cod. 58, 91, 92, 93. For the text see now the edition by R. Henry, I (Paris 1959) 51—52, and II (Paris 1960) 16—34..

3. On these excerpts, see Cohn, *RE* s.v. Constantinus 16, IV, 1 (1901), esp. 1037—39 and the earlier bibliography cited there; A. Dain, "L'Encyclopédisme de Constantin Porphyrogénète," *Lettres d'humanité* 12 (1953) 64—81, esp. 71—75; Gyula Moravcsik, *Byzantinoturcica*² (Berlin 1958) I, 359—61.

4. On the *Suda* see A. Adler, *RE* s.v. Suidas 1, IV A 1 (1931) 675—717, especially on the use of the Constantinian excerpts, cols. 700—705. See also A. G. Roos, *Studia Arrianea* (Leipzig 1912) 2—4.

5. For Eustathius see the discussion below of the *Bithyniaca*.

6. Stephanus of Byzantium uses Arrian's lost works twenty-eight times (*Parthica* nineteen, *Bithyniaca* nine) as sources for geographical names. He and an anonymous Byzantine grammarian (*peri syntaxeos*) who makes ten citations from the *Events* are especially valuable because they assign the quotations to the individual books within the works.

7. On Photius, see in general K. Ziegler, *RE* s.v. Photios 13, XX, 1 (1941) 667—737, esp. 684—727 on the *Bibliotheca*, and R. Henry's introduction to his edition. Antonio Nogara provides a recent and thorough study of the debated question of Photius' method, with copious bibliography: "Note sulle composizione e la struttura della Biblioteca de Fozio, Patriarca de Constantinopoli, I," *Aevum* 49 (1975) 213—42. See also Thomas Hägg, *Photios als Vermittler antiker Literatur* ("Acta Univ. Upsaliensis, Studia Graeca Upsaliensia," 8; Uppsala 1975), and "Photius at Work: Evidence from the Text of the *Bibliotheca*," *GRBS* 14 (1973) 213—22 (on his account of Philostratus' *Vita Apollonii*); Henri Tonnet, "Les notes marginales et leur transmission dans quelques manuscrits d'Arrien," *Revue d'histoire des textes* 3 (1973) 39—55; and Friedrich Lenz, "La tradizione indiretta dei discorsi di Aristide nella 'Bibliotheke' di Fozio," *StItal* 14 (1937) 203—25, 261—79.

8. For modern accounts of Parthia, see Malcolm A. R. Colledge, *The Parthians* (New York and Washington 1967); Richard N. Frye, *The Heritage of Persia* (London 1962) 178—206; Roman Ghirshman, *Iran, from the Earliest Times to the Islamic Conquest* (Harmondsworth 1954) 243—88; and Nelson Carel Debevoise, *A Political History of Parthia* (Chicago 1938).

9. On the impression made by the disaster at Carrhae, see Dieter Timpe, "Die Bedeutung der Schlacht von Carrhae," *MusHelv* 19 (1962) 104—29. Before this the Romans showed no particular fear, as is demonstrated by Josef

Dobias, "Les premiers rapports des Romains avec les Parthes et l'occupation de la Syrie, "*Archiv Orientalni* 3 (1931) 215−56.

10. Writers of *Parthica* are collected by Jacoby in *FGrHist* III C, nos. 779−82. See the succinct and useful comments of Arnaldo Momigliano, *Alien Wisdom* (Cambridge 1975) 139−41. Arrian is by far the best preserved of any author of *Parthica*.

11. The *Parthian Stations* of Isidore of Charax is a bare list of names of cities, with occasional landmarks, on the caravan route from Zeugma on the Euphrates to Kandahar. The text is in Karl Müller, *Geographi graeci minores* (Paris 1855) 244−54, *FGrHist* 781 F2, and, with map and commentary, in W. H. Schoff, *The Parthian Stations of Isidore of Charax* (Philadelphia 1914). A story from Isidore's *Periegesis of Parthia* is preserved in Athenaeus (*FGrHist* 781 F1).

12. On Lucian see, besides Jacoby, *FGrHist* 203−10, G. Avenarius, *Lukians Schrift zur Geschichtsschreibung* (Meisenheim/Glan 1956); and *Lukian, Wie man Geschichte schreiben soll*, ed. Helene Homeyer (Munich 1965). For Fronto, see *Epistulae M. Cornelii Frontonis*, ed. M. P. J. van den Hout (Leiden 1954) 125 (letter of Verus to Fronto) and 191−200 (*Principia Historiae*, a rhetorical comparison of the Parthian wars of Trajan and Verus); translation by C. R. Haines in the Loeb edition of Fronto (London 1920) II, 195−97, 199−219. Dio of Prusa, an older contemporary of Arrian from Bithynia, wrote a book on the Getai, *Getica*, later used by Jordanes, the sixth-century historian (*FGrHist* 707). Dio (*Or.* 36.1) speaks of wishing to visit the Getai while in exile at Olbia on the Black Sea (ca. 82−96). The fragments in Jordanes refer only to earlier times, but Dio may have brought his history down as far as the Dacian wars of Trajan. On the other hand, we know that the *Getica* of a certain Crito, who was on Trajan's Dacian campaign, described the war (*FGrHist* 200). This history would have furnished a recent model for Arrian's *Parthica*.

13. In this design he appears to have been imitated almost a century later by Asinius Quadratus in his nine books of *Parthica* (*FGrHist* 97).

14. The problem of genre is especially important in considering lost works, because our attempts at reconstruction are dependent in large part on our conception of the literary form of the work. It is misleading to call the *Parthica* "narrative ethnography," as Jacoby did in his early classification in "Über die Entwicklung der griechischen Historiographie und den Plan einer neuen Sammlung der griechischen Historikerfragmente," *Klio* 9 (1909) 80−123 at 107 = *Abhandlungen zur griechischen Geschichtschreibung* (Leiden 1956) 16−64 at 47. In *FGrHist* II B, comm., 566, Jacoby places it somewhat more accurately with the "type of ethnography already beginning in the oldest *Persica* and *Sicelica*, in which pre-history and description of land and peoples forms only an introduction to political history, which here is mostly military

history." However, the fragments give no indication that Arrian attempted to write a political history of Parthia.

15. We may compare the account of the people of Britain and the Roman attempts to pacify the island in Tacitus *Agricola* 10−17, which serves as prelude to the narrative of Agricola's conquest of the island (*Agr.* 18−38). Cf. Sir Ian Richmond and R. M. Ogilvie, *Cornelii Taciti De Vita Agricolae* (Oxford 1967) 15, and Ronald Syme, *Tacitus* (Oxford 1958) I, 121−22.

16. See Jacoby, *FGrHist* II B, comm., 566−67; Roos, *Studia*, 1−64.

17. Roos, *Studia*, 4−10; Jacoby, *FGrHist* II B, comm., 567−71.

18. Cf. Frye, *Persia*, 180.

19. See the parallels cited by Roos to P1 (p. 226, lines 12ff.), and the traditions of intercontinental warfare recalled by Herodotus, 7.20.

20. Agathocles in Syncellus' parallel version.

21. On this claim see W. W. Tarn, "Queen Ptolemais and Apama," *CQ* 23 (1929) 138−141 at 140.

22. Frye, *Persia*, 181.

23. Józef Wolski, "Arsace II," *Eos* 41 (1946) 160, castigates the story as invention, but its potential veracity is defended by Frye, *Persia*, 181; Ghirshman, *Iran*, 243; Colledge, *Parthians*, 26; and Debevoise, *Parthia*, 9. Wolski makes a firm rejoinder in "Untersuchungen zur frühen parthischen Geschichte," *Klio* 58 (1976) 439−57. It is doubtful whether other fragments are correctly ascribed to Book I by Roos (P18−21): see Jacoby *FGrHist* II B, comm., 567−68.

24. On this war see Debevoise, *Parthia*, 213−47; R. P. Longden, "Notes on the Parthian Campaigns of Trajan," *JRS* 21 (1931) 1−35 and *CAH* XI (1936) 239−50; Julien Guey, *Essai sur la guerre parthique de Trajan (114−117)* ("Bibliothèque d'Istros," 2; Bucharest 1937); F. A. Lepper, *Trajan's Parthian War* (London 1948); Marie Louise Chaumont, "L'Arménie entre Rome et l'Iran," in *ANRW*, II, 9, 1 (1976) 71−194, esp. 130−43; and Maria Gabriella Angeli Bertinelli, "I Romani oltre l'Eufrate nel II secolo d.C.," ibid., 3−45, esp. 5−23.

25. On these coins see Paul L. Strack, *Untersuchungen zur römische Reichsprägung des zweiten Jahrhunderts* (Stuttgart 1931) I, 224−25.

26. See Lepper, *Parthian War*, 128.

27. See especially Guey, *Guerre parthique*, 17−35, and Lepper, *Parthian War*, 156−204.

28. Compare the words here, "There seems to be no question," with the identical phrase in *Anab.* 7.22.5, "There seems to be no question that Seleucus was the greatest king of those coming to power after Alexander."

29. One is reminded of the virtues ascribed to Agricola by Tacitus (cf. Richmond and Ogilvie, *Vita Agricolae*, 20). The list of the virtues proper to a general was traditional.

30. See on this subject the works cited in chapter 5, n. 14. On the Livy passage see also Hans Rudolf Breitenbach, "Der Alexanderexkurs bei Livius," *MusHelv* 26 (1969) 146—57. In the time of Trajan, it should be remembered, Dio Chrysostom wrote *On the Virtues of Alexander* in eight books, now lost, and Plutarch wrote the parallel lives of Caesar and Alexander as well as a pair of speeches, *On the Fortune or Virtue of Alexander*.

31. Trajan's generosity to the oracle of Apollo at Didyma may have reflected an imitation of Alexander: see C. P. Jones, "An Oracle given to Trajan," *Chiron* 5 (1975) 406. Tacitus may possibly have been thinking of Trajan in comparing Germanicus with Alexander: see Syme, *Tacitus* II, 770—71. Cf. also Gerhard Wirth, "Alexander und Rom," in *Alexandre le Grand: image et réalité* ("Entretiens Hardt," 22; Geneva 1975) 181—221 at 197—200.

32. A Heracles type appears in 100 A.D. and continues with variations throughout Trajan's reign: see Harold Mattingly, *Coins of the Roman Empire in the British Museum* (London 1936) III, lxvii—lxviii; Strack, *Untersuchungen*, 95—104. The Heracles portrayed is usually Heracles Gaditanus, in whose temple at Gades there was a statue of Alexander—the very one which had brought Julius Caesar to tears in 68 B.C. See Suetonius *Divus Julius* 7 and Jean Gagé, "Hercule-Melqart, Alexandre et les Romains à Gadès," *REA* 42 (1940) 425—38. In general on Trajan and Heracles see G. W. Bowersock, "Greek Intellectuals and the Imperial Cult in the Second Century A.D.," in *Le Culte des souverains dans l'empire romain* ("Entretiens Hardt," 19; Geneva 1973) 179—212 at 193—94.

33. See Roos, *Studia*, 39; Karl Hartmann, "Über das Verhältnis des Cassius Dio zur Parthergeschichte des Flavius Arrianus," *Philologus* 74 (1917) 73—91; Jacoby *FGrHist* II B, comm., 567; and Gerhard Wirth, "Arrian und Traian—Versuch einer Gegenwartsdeutung," *Studii Clasice* 16 (1974) 169—209, esp. 202—7. Fergus Millar, *A Study of Cassius Dio* (Oxford 1964), does not consider the question.

34. *Studia*, 54.

35. Wirth, "Arrian," 169—209, gives a rather different assessment of the Alexander-Trajan parallel in the *Parthica*.

36. For a survey of the vassal kingdoms in Parthia, see Frye, *Persia*, 187—90; and Geo Widengren, "Iran, der grosse Gegner Roms: Königswalt, Feudalismus, Militärwesen," in *ANRW* II, 9, 1, 291—306, esp. 263ff.

37. Cf. the references to the tombs of Sardanapalus and Cyrus in *Anab.* 2.5.3 and 6.29.4.

38. Arrian's presence with the Roman army on the Parthian expedition has in the past been variously affirmed—Henri Doulcet, *Quid Xenophonti debuerit Flavius Arrianus* (Paris 1882) 9; Alfred von Domaszewski, "Die Phalangen Alexanders und Caesars Legionen," *SBHeid* 16 (1925/26) Heft 1, p. 5 (as an equestrian officer); Gerhard Wirth, "Anmerkungen zur Arrian-

biographie," *Historia* 13 (1964) 228—and denied—Jacoby, *FGrHist* II B, comm., 567 and 575; Lepper, *Parthian War*, 2. Caution is in order, but there is no chronological difficulty, despite Syme's hesitancy: "Too old (it would appear) to serve as a *laticlavius* at that time, too young to command a legion" (*Historia* 14 [1965] 354 = *Danubian Papers* [Bucharest 1971] 236).

39. E.g., Schwartz, *RE* s.v. Arrianus, 1236, and Jacoby, *FGrHist* II B, comm., 567.

40. See the treatment of this question in connection with the *Ectaxis* in chapter 3.

41. Lepper, *Parthian War*, 7 and 128, notes this fragment but does not attempt to explain what exactly Trajan wanted to do at the Caucasian Gates. Wirth, "Arrian," 189, also sees P6 as evidence that Arrian was given a command by Trajan in this area.

42. Wirth, "Arrian," 189 n. 79, sees a number of other fragments from the *Parthica* as evidence of autopsy.

43. See also appendix 5.

44. Trajan was honored as a victor by Hadrian, who permitted him a posthumous triumph, regularly celebrated *ludi Parthici*, and continued to use *Parthicus*, the name the emperor had been voted in 116, in Trajan's official nomenclature: see Guey, *Guerre Parthique*, 144.

45. The modern use of *Successors* or *History of the Successors* is concise but misleading, since Arrian's work covers so little of the period of the Diadochi.

46. Ulrich Koehler, "Über die Diadochengeschichte Arrians," *SBBerl* 1890, 557−88; Ricardus Reitzenstein, "Arriani *ton met' Alexandron* libri septimi fragmenta," *Breslauer philologische Abhandlungen* 3, 3 (1888); Roos, *Studia*, 65−75; and the editions of Roos and Jacoby.

47. The extant sources for this period are Curt. 10.6−10 (restricted to the first division of power at Babylon), Diod. 18.1−39, Justin 13.1−8, and Plutarch *Eumenes*. For modern accounts, see W. W. Tarn, *CAH* VI (1927) 461−504; Julius Beloch, *Griechische Geschichte*² (Berlin and Leipzig 1927) IV, pt. 2, 623−39; M. J. Fontana, "Le Lotte per la successione di Alessandro Magno," *Atti della Accademia di scienze lettere e arti di Palermo*, ser. 4, 18, 2 (1957−58); the review of Fontana by E. Badian, *Gnomon* 34 (1962) 381−87 = *Studies in Greek and Roman History* (Oxford 1964) 262−70; Edouard Will, *Histoire politique du monde hellénistique (323−30 av. J.-C.)* Pt. I ("Annales d'Est," memoire no. 30, 1966) 19−35; and R. M. Errington, "From Babylon to Triparadeisos: 323−320 B.C.," *JHS* 90 (1970) 49−77. Unfortunately, Pierre Briant, *Antigone le Borgne: les débuts de sa carrière et les problèmes de l'assemblée macédonienne* ("Annales littéraires de l'Université de Besançon," 152; Paris 1973), became available too late for me to use for this section. Perdiccas' death and Triparadisus can now be dated in 320, not 321: see Errington, 75−77, following Eugenio Manni, "Tre note di

cronologia ellenistica," *Rendiconti dell'Accademia nazionale dei Lincei*, ser. 8, 4 (1949) 53–61. I use these dates, but the traditional dating makes no significant change in the interpretation of Arrian's history.

48. *Editio princeps* by V. Bartoletti, "Frammenti di storia di Diadochi (Arriano?)," *PSI* XII, 2 (1951) 158–61, no. 1284, identified as Arrian by Kurt Latte, "Ein neues Arrianfragment," *NachGöttingen* 1950, 23–27 = *Kleine Schriften* (Munich 1968) 595–99; see also Gerhard Wirth, "Zur grossen Schlacht des Eumenes 322 (*PSI* 1284)," *Klio* 46 (1965) 283–88, and A. B. Bosworth, "Eumenes, Neoptolemus, and *PSI* XII 1284," *GRBS* 19 (1978) 227–37. The text is printed by Wirth in the second edition of Roos II, 323–24. Bartoletti argued that the fragment referred to the battle of Eumenes against Craterus, but Bosworth has demonstrated that the earlier battle with Neoptolemus must be meant.

49. Plutarch *Eumenes* 5.5. Simple notices of the battle are found in Diod. 18.29.5, Justin 13.8.4–5, and Photius' summary of Arrian, S1, 27.

50. See the comparative table in Jacoby, *FGrHist* II B, comm., 554–55.

51. On Diodorus' use of Hieronymus see E. Schwartz, *RE* s.v. Diodorus 38, V, 1 (1905) 685 = *Griechische Geschichtschreiber* (Leipzig 1959) 68; Jacoby, comm. to *FGrHist* 154, II B, pp. 544–45.

52. For a trenchant analysis of Ptolemy's purposes and bias in writing his narrative, see R. M. Errington, "Bias in Ptolemy's History of Alexander," *CQ*, n.s. 19 (1969) 233–42. Errington notes that it was important for Ptolemy to establish the "correct" view of Alexander and his relation to Perdiccas in the years immediately after 323.

53. "Ptolemy's History," 241. The prevailing view of the date of composition of Ptolemy's narrative was first attacked by E. Badian, in his review of Pearson's *Lost Histories*, *Gnomon* 33 (1961) 666 = *Studies*, 258. Cf. the discussion of Ptolemy's history in chapter 5.

54. Note that Photius in his summary of the *Anabasis* narrates the mutilation of Bessus and Alexander's capture of Pasargadai out of order (*Bibl.* cod. 93, 67b 36–37, 39).

55. See besides Photius' summary S14, S17 = F179, S21 = F124, S24–25 = F10, S26 = F177b, S31 = F117, and *PSI* XII, 1284.

56. The contrast with Alexander was present, but hardly explicit. *Suda* s.v. Alexandros, which Koehler, "Diadochengeschichte," 585, relates to this because of the similarity of diction, is taken from *Anab.* 3.10.2, not *Events*.

57. See Roos, *Studia*, 71; Jacoby, comm. to 156 F178. Neither of the two passages united by the *Suda* seems to be related to Leonnatus' death in the Lamian War (cf. S1 = F1, 9).

58. I am very doubtful that the encomium of Demosthenes preserved by the *Suda* (S23) is from Arrian.

59. Ptolemy's history may also have stopped at the same point, and for much the same reason, as argued above.

60. Despite Roos II, xxix n. 1, the correct form of the title is probably *Bithyniaca* and not *Bithynica*. Eustathius, who used the work most frequently, regularly calls it *Bithyniaca*. Jacoby uses throughout *Bithyniaca*, Roos *Bithynica*.

61. For the place of local history in Greek historiography see Jacoby, "Entwicklung"; Lionel Pearson, *Early Ionian Historians* (Oxford 1939). See also the bibliography by W. Spoerri in *Der kleine Pauly* 3 (1969) s.v. Lokalchronik, Lokalgeschichte, 715—17. Histories of Greek cities are collected by Jacoby in *FGrHist* III B. Histories of Bithynia are found in III C, with histories of non-Greek lands and peoples, but because of the Greek settlements there, are more closely akin to the histories of Greek states than to the historical ethnography found in *Persica* or *Aegyptiaca*.

62. On the revival of local history see Walter Spoerri in *Lexikon der alten Welt* (Zürich and Stuttgart 1965) s.v. Geschichtsschreibung, griechische, cols. 1070—71. On Greek attitudes to their past, see E. L. Bowie, "Greeks and Their Past in the Second Sophistic," *Past and Present* 46 (1970) 3—41. Bowie does not realize, however, in his treatment of local history (19—22) and his comment on Arrian's *Bithyniaca* (27), that the fact that local histories terminated with the advent of Roman rule is not evidence of a rejection of the Roman present but simply a characteristic of the genre: all local histories, and ethnographies as well, end with the subjection of the state to another power.

63. Contrast the several known histories of Heraclea, *FGrHist* 430—34, as well as others on Byzantium, Ilium (Troy), Cyzicus, and Lampsacus.

64. Greek historiography always presumed an independent state or states as the object of its interest. The history of a city or country ceased with its subjection to another power—one reason for our ignorance of Greece under Roman domination.

65. Strabo 13.1.45. On Demetrius see E. Schwartz in *RE* s.v. Demetrios 78, IV, 2 (1901) 2807—13 = *Griechische Geschichtschreiber* (Leipzig 1959) 106—14; Rudolf Pfeiffer, *History of Classical Scholarship from the Beginnings to the End of the Hellenistic Age* (Oxford 1968) 249—51.

66. Still less that it was Arrian's *Lebenswerk*, for which the *Anabasis* and other books were practice exercises, as argued by E. Schwartz, *RE* s.v. Arrianus, 1236. See the corrective remarks by Jacoby, *FGrHist*, comm. to 156, II B, p. 552. The date of composition of the *Bithyniaca* is not certain, since the only outside evidence, the notice in Photius, is variously interpreted. See appendix 5.

67. Other stories of this type taken from local histories may be found in Parthenius and in Plutarch's *Brave Deeds of Women*, nos. 7 and 18 (*Mor.* 246D—247A, 255A—E). See Philip A. Stadter, *Plutarch's Historical Methods* (Cambridge, Mass. 1965) 57—58, 97—101.

68. The fragments of Demosthenes are in *FGrHist* 699 and Iohannes U.

Powell, ed., *Collectanea Alexandrina* (Oxford 1925) 25–27.

69. The first part of B36 (= F20b) contains the statement "he marched to Chrysopolis, then during the night crossed the Bosporus," which apparently forms part of a historical narrative, but the subject is not known. Arrian reported that Libyssa, the city in Bithynia where Hannibal died, was called *ta Boutiou* (B65 = F28), but this may have been in a gazetteer, not a historical narrative. The passage relating that Pharnabazus castrated Chalcedonian boys and sent them to Darius (B37 = F79) is more possibly from a historical narrative, though it may belong to an ethnographical section, reporting the custom among the Chalcedonians of treating the twenty-first of each month as unlucky.

70. Eustathius has no less than sixty-seven of the eighty-two citations of the *Bithyniaca*. Stephanus of Byzantium is next with nine, and the rest have one each.

71. Grammatical points: B20b = F77b, B23 = F22, B24 = F23, B31 note = F91, B41 = F101, B67 = F119b, B70 = F89a, B72 = F99.

72. Marchinus van der Valk, *Eustathii Commentarii ad Homeri Iliadem pertinentes* (Leiden 1971) I, L.

73. Verbatim citations: B9 = F82, B14 = F103, B20 = F77b, B21 = F83, B22 = F97, B28 = F173, B31 note = F91, B33 = F67, B34 = F96, B36 = F20, B38 = F81, B40 = F87, B43 = F76a, B46 = F63, B47 = F75?, B52 = F73, B54 = F72, B55 = F71, B57 = F65, B70 = F89a.

74. B29 = F58 (Europa carried off by Tauros, king of Crete), B31 = F64 (Cadmus and Harmonia), B33 = F107 (Iasion was an enthusiast of Demeter, not her lover), B35 = F92 (Briareus as a king ruling the sea, *thalattokrator*).

75. See B5 = F26, B7 = F17, B11 = F59, B12 = F110, B13 = F61a, B16 = F68bis, B18 = F27, B20 = F77, B21 = F83, B30 = F86, B32 = F95, B33^2 = F67, B35^1 = F92, B37^1 = F78, B38 = F81, B40 = F87, B47 = F75, B49 = F84, B51 = F74, B55 = F71, B56 = F68, B57 = F65, B58 = F70, B59 = F66. Note the criticism of those deriving the name of the Nile from Neilasios (B61 = F57). In B39^1 = F61c we may assume that Prieneus is the eponym of Priene. At B10 (= F106) the name of the dance *sikinnis* is derived from an otherwise unknown homonymous nymph.

76. Other foundation notices are listed in n. 75 above. Note that as often in local historians, the historical foundation is antedated by a mythological one: thus Astacus (later moved and refounded by Nicomedes I as Nicomedia) was founded according to Arrian by Astacus the son of Poseidon, long before its colonization by Megarians ca. 712 B.C. (B5 = F26). Cf. also the story of the foundation of Chalcedon (B37^1 = F78). The story of Crocodice is similar to others which have become more distinctly mythological, such as that of Nisus and Scylla, as told by Ovid *Met.* 8.1.151.

77. Cf. B20 = F77, B21 = F83, B31 = F64.

78. Cf. B11 = F59, B13^1 = F61a, B18 = F27, B21 = F83.

79. Religion: B3 = F16, B9 = F82, B10 = F106, B23 = F22, B24 = F23, B33¹ = F107, B37² = F79, B37³ = F80. Custom: B25 = F100, B27 = F108, B66 = F104.

80. Note the patriotic bias of B10 = F106, B22¹ = F97, B26 = F94, and B42 = F88.

81. Mount Olympus in Mysia was heavily wooded and furnished a haven for brigands: cf. Strabo 12.574. The proper form of the name is Tillorobus, not Tilliborus, as we learn from inscriptions from Termessus: see M. L. Radermacher, "Nochmals der Räuber Τιλλόροβος," *Anzeiger Akademie Wien*, Ph.-hist. Kl. 73 (1936) 8; and Louis Robert, *Études Anatoliennes* (Paris 1937) 98 n. 3. F. Zimmermann, "Ein Bruchstück aus Arrians Τιλλιβόρου βίος," *Archiv für Papyrusforschung* 11 (1935) 165−75, attempted to assign *POxy* 416 to Arrian's *Tillorobus*, but the style seems quite different from Arrian's and the identification has not been accepted.

CHAPTER 9

1. See, e.g., E. L. Bowie, "Greeks and Their Past in the Second Sophistic," *Past and Present* 46 (1970) 3−41, esp. 24−27 (reprinted, with some additional material in the footnotes, in *Studies in Ancient Society*, ed. M. I. Finley [London and Boston 1974] 166−209). Something of the same attitude is expressed by B. P. Reardon, *Courants littéraires grecs des IIᵉ et IIIᵉ siècles après J.-C.* (Paris 1971) 213.

2. See George Kennedy, "The Sophists as Declaimers," in *Approaches to the Second Sophistic*, ed. G. W. Bowersock (University Park, Pa. 1974) 17−22, esp. 19.

INDEX

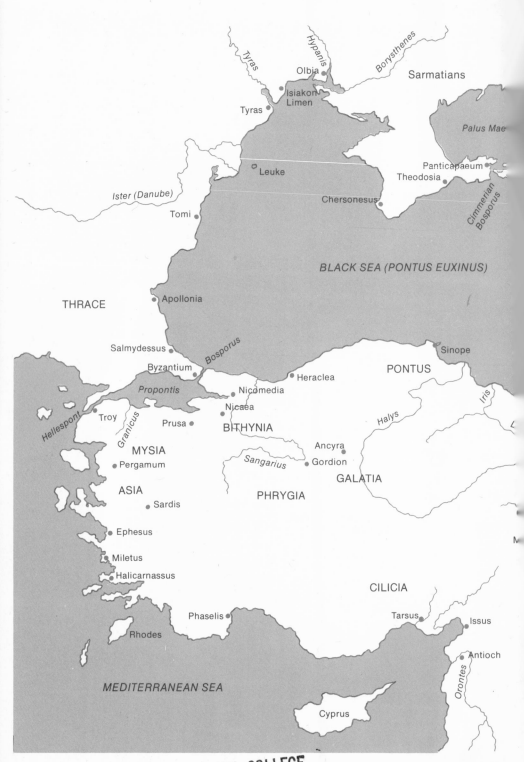